DARKER WITH THE DAWN

NICK CAVE'S
SONGS OF LOVE AND DEATH

ADAM STEINER

ROWMAN & LITTLEFIELD
Lanham • Boulder • New York • London

Published by Rowman & Littlefield
An imprint of The Rowman & Littlefield Publishing Group, Inc.
4501 Forbes Boulevard, Suite 200, Lanham, Maryland 20706
www.rowman.com

86-90 Paul Street, London EC2A 4NE

Cover art: "The Typist" by Jonny Nicholds. Find him on Instagram @Jonnynicholdsart

British Library Cataloguing in Publication Information Available

Library of Congress Cataloging-in-Publication Data

Names: Steiner, Adam, 1985- author.
Title: Darker with the dawn : Nick Cave's songs of love and death / Adam Steiner.
Description: Lanham : Rowman & Littlefield, 2023. | Includes bibliographical
  references.
Identifiers: LCCN 2023024722 (print) | LCCN 2023024723 (ebook) | ISBN
  9781538160350 (cloth) | ISBN 9781538160367 (ebook)
Subjects: LCSH: Cave, Nick, 1957- —Criticism and interpretation. | Rock music—
  Australia—History and criticism.
Classification: LCC ML420.C39 S84 2023 (print) | LCC ML420.C39 (ebook) |
  DDC 782.42166092—dc23/eng/20230606
LC record available at https://lccn.loc.gov/2023024722
LC ebook record available at https://lccn.loc.gov/2023024723

For A. C.

CONTENTS

Prelude (To a New Day)   xi

BOOK I: DUSK

1   Let the Light In   3

2   Rock and Roll Savior   13

3   Is This Desire . . .   27

4   Bad Blood   55

5   Laughter in the Dark   81

BOOK II: MIDNIGHT

6   One Eye on Death   111

7   Broken Tongues   131

8   A Tear in Time (Cosmic Hex Junk Franchise)   153

9   Here Cometh the Man   167

CONTENTS

BOOK III: DAWN

10	Rock and Roll Suicide	179
11	Prayers on Fire	197
12	In Bloom	219
13	Fire in the Light	231

Epilogue	249
Acknowledgments	251
Notes	253
Bibliography	317
Index	323
About the Author	327

The lights blink ON inside a wall of jittery TVs stacked the height and width of a man laid out to die we see a weeping wall channel-hopping through a series of images clashing and crashing together a final prayer to the dead white king of rock and roll it blends nostalgic images of a fake childhood alongside emerging wonders of Jonny Cash, Elvis become Nick the Stripper strung up in a loincloth like Saint Sebastian struck by flaming darts of pleasure, taking kamikaze stage dives, shirtless and sweating a fierce mass of limbs writhing on the floor, "give me another cigarette or I'll kill you," a mouth bigger than your head yells FUCK threatening to swallow the camera whole, behind a spidery crow's nest of black hair and crushed white shirt nods-off mid-sentence glowering eyes fix the corner of the room into sharp stare, wearing all-black everything cut-through with a slash of scarlet rage in snow-capped Berlin, looking for another fix in the new frontier of East meets West via the antipodean fever dream of old-world utopia, propping up the plastic bar tables in São Paulo hidden behind a row of bottles and cigarette smoke while the panoramic Jesus reaches its arms around the horizon of Rio de Janeiro wedding bells chime in the Year of our Lord 2000 anno Domini—we see a man as god-secondhand guru-singer-for-hire-shit slinger-electrified saint boxed in to a moving portrait framed behind cold glass and feverish wires, a rush of images, sifting static in and out of color they sit like grains of sand in each corner of the eye, a tape loop stretched back into its scream chained to a past that never went away, as an accelerated ticker counts up the days within a life, bringing us to the present, we discover the doomed survivor who has outlived his own prophecy of self-destruction, a man wandering lost in his own desert painted into domestic scenes then snarling along the seafront on all fours, behind us flickering lights zip past, streetlights merge with stars howling down the gleaming reflection of a reflection slid across the humming metallic body alive the purr of its engine, like seeing yourself staring upward from the depths of the ocean floor, the drowned man, an echo of the real; they are all pushed into the distance by the shifting lens and the motion of the imaginary road, there goes shine met with shining, lost refracting into itself each drop of water still holds the reflection of a moment as they pass each other by as the car winds out of the town that left memory behind the sea slips away like a soundstage or a background reel wound back and forth, day into night, fast rewind of the tides, waves of tomorrow, eyes flick up like a hungry animal, staring forward into the rearview mirror where the back seat of a car becomes the interview space for stray celebrities, cast adrift inside the body of a shipwreck becomes a rolling rock of salvation, pushing ahead of control into transition, urged on by a burning the need to keep moving toward creative reinvention, shaking chains of history towed behind him in his wake, he cannot help occasionally looking back trying to outrun the world living in the now of bright headlights that only show the first few feet of the road ahead running endlessly beyond reaching from the present to the future through the past surrendered into dusk and the inevitable turning of the day folded back into night, the rise and fade of the Morning Star eclipsed by the brilliant all-seeing fury of the sun

PRELUDE (TO A NEW DAY)

Throughout the music of Nick Cave and The Bad Seeds there is a common thread moving from love, sex, murder, and death to further questions of faith and the nature of God, good versus evil, and more recently, grief and loss.

Nick Cave and The Bad Seeds' music has spiraled out from my first listen to 2013's *Push the Sky Away*, working my way through the back catalog, jumping from *Lyre of Orpheus/Abattoir Blues*, released almost a decade earlier in 2004, to *Your Funeral . . . My Trial* in 1986. Across the eras it would seem like the music of a different person, someone else, but also continued a common thread of rock and roll revolution. Cave's most recent records, spanning *Push the Sky Away, Skeleton Tree*, and *Ghosteen*, mark a new era in the sound of The Bad Seeds and a major shift in Cave's songwriting. Alongside Warren Ellis, Cave would embrace jagged electronica textures and ambient synths, fractured narratives, all informed by a new way of seeing the world. For me the artistic shift has a parallel in David Bowie's creative reinvention, from *Low* in 1977 leaping forward to his final album *Blackstar* in 2016.

Cave and Ellis would make the 2021 album *Carnage*, a collection of songs that are at once beautiful and brutal, managing to express the twin internal tensions that spans The Bad Seeds' discography, reaching forward and backward across time. Cave said to his friend, journalist Sean O'Hagan, that he disliked old quotes being thrown back at him; this book draws upon such material to go beyond my personal relationship with the songs to set them in context alongside Cave's many influences, themes, and inspirations. An artist friend said the book was like an incunabulum, literally translated as swaddling clothes or cradle, referring to the gathered-together pages of an artist's progression from their earliest development—a living archive—which is never completed as the artist continues to evolve and our experience of their work changes along with them.

Cave notes, "People say I can't write like I did back then," but it is perhaps better to see each album for what it is, with no two Bad Seeds records sounding quite the same, rather than looking to recapture the past. Cave refers to the exciting *danger* of trying to work out what his new music will be rather than trying to revisit and replicate what has gone before, a hard thing to achieve within a forty-year musical career.

Cave remains an artist working across multiple forms, often blurring the lines between songs, scripts, novels, poetry, soundtrack, and most recently sculpture. Living through his rich song world, his music becomes an intertextual dance between creative legacy and the *imminent* present. Cave defined the Bad Seeds' continued spirit of reinvention and revolution as "a solemn duty to turn against what has gone before."

As the start of Jane and Iain Pollard's fictional meta-documentary *20,000 Days on Earth*, Cave would declare: "At the end of the 20th century, I ceased to be a human being." Filmed through 2012 and 2013, it would only be released in 2014, it presents a surreal day-in-the-life road movie with Cave's actions scripted shot-for-shot alongside real, improvised discussions between Cave and people from across his life. Despite admitting to the author of *Boy on Fire* Mark Mordue in 2017, 'I've always been uncomfortable with the way I am—I'm still learning to be comfortable with certain aspects of what it's like to live and be a human being," like any of us Cave continues grow as a person—at once the same, but different—older, wiser and steeped in the experiences of the past, but still ever changing.

When the unquiet hours depart
And far away their tumults cease,
Within the twilight of the heart
We bathe in peace, are stilled with peace.

—*THE HOUR OF TWILIGHT*, GEORGE WILLIAM RUSSELL

BOOK I
DUSK

LET THE LIGHT IN

> Where you come from is gone, where you thought you were
> going to was never there, and where you are is no good unless
> you can get away from it. Where is there a place for you to
> be? No place. . . . Nothing outside you can give you any
> place. . . . In yourself right now is all the place you've got.
> —FLANNERY O'CONNOR

Merging into view like a faded memory, we see Nick Cave planted to the spot, standing tall and dark in the corner of a room. He holds open a Georgian window shutter flooding the room with sunlight to illuminate the naked body of his wife, Susie Cave. A model and creator of the Vampire's Wife fashion brand, here she serves as willing muse, bleached brilliant white, like a statue come to life, skipping across the floor her hands and jet-black hair cover her face, feet barely touching the ground as she cuts across her husband's gaze.

The play of space and light in the cover image for Nick Cave and The Bad Seeds' 2013 album *Push the Sky Away* would become the metaphor for the record's creative rebirth, expressing its themes of shadow play and murmurations of deep feeling beneath the monochrome surface. The shutter is transformed into a door to the sun, both open and closing, it hints at both escape and a return. The ambiguous setting of the scene manages to reflect the album's elegiac treatment of love and lust, death and aging. Cave was at pains to point out that the picture wasn't his idea; and he was more reluctant to use it for the album cover than his wife was. He explained that he walked in on a photoshoot for a French magazine when photographer Dominique Issermann asked him for more light. Issermann captures a spontaneous glimmer of intimacy between husband and wife passing through each other's lives. In Jane and Iain Pollard's fictional meta-documentary *20,000 Days on Earth*, filmed during the album's recording but released the year after in 2014, Cave reflects upon the ways in which Susie appears as a voice drifting in and out of the songs, her words haunting his.

After years of wandering, Melbourne-London-Berlin-São Paulo-London (again), *Push the Sky Away* would become Cave's Brighton album. Drawing on the view from high windows onto the seafront of the coastal town trapped between the jaws of sea and sky, it became a missive from the edge of the world. An established figure in rock music, assured in his creative powers, Cave would bristle against the public image of him as "hell-raiser cleans up, and now lives a comfortable life in a seaside town type of thing."[1] The surface calm of wealth, security, and success that Cave was earlier criticized on the laconically haunting "Easy Money" (2004) concealed a deeper discomfort, fearing himself absorbed into the classic rock establishment where everything new is held against a dying image of the past. Cave's lyric from "Jubilee Street" refers to himself as "out of place and time / and out of my mind" looking out from his comfortable family home ruminating upon love, the slow creep of middle age, and morality, he felt the changing shape of the world shifting beneath his feet.[2] We see Cave as a creative force open to change, flux, and artistic evolution, not to repeat himself or remain stuck in the past as the many incarnations of The Bad Seeds. Cave is looking out to the far side of the morning, uncertain of what tomorrow will bring.

Push the Sky Away would signal a creative rebirth for Cave, where the album's sonic signature often veers between ambient restraint and cataclysmic shows of force, a style that managed to celebrate the intensity and dynamism of The Bad Seeds as a band unit while subtly shifting their sound toward broader experimentation. In a recent statement about the album, Cave said, "The record opened up a whole different approach to the way we created our music. It was the beginning of a way of writing—a kind of controlled improvisation. Because of this shift, the record was to some extent divisive—but it was the necessary reinvention that the Bad Seeds desperately needed."[3] In spite of the album's change of direction, key tracks such "Jubilee Street," "Higgs Boson Blues," and "Push the Sky Away" would become sleeper "hits" merged into a popular consciousness as anthems of rejuvenation and resilience. Performed by The Bad Seeds across a number of festivals in the summer of 2013, they remain a staple of the band's live sets ten years later, bringing them legions of new fans.

In keeping with Cave's new creative dawn, The Bad Seeds would undergo significant lineup changes. Some traditionalist Bad Seeds fans would lament the shift from "old Nick Cave" and the double losses of founder member Mick Harvey, who quit in 2009 citing "a variety of personal and professional reasons," and the blinkered anti–rock and roll guitarist Blixa Bargeld—Cave's own inverted Robert Fripp—who had already quit the band in 2003.[4] After one too many arguments and incidents of storming off, personality had outgrown musical input. Cave would note that Blixa had stuck to his own rules in order to avoid becoming another burnt out rock star cliché: (1) don't become a rock star, (2) realize there is another life outside of this, and (3) don't burn.

Cave was well aware of previous tensions between Harvey and Ellis, contrasting approaches facing off between exactitude and instinct. The new album would also herald the arrival of fresh blood, George Vjestica adding guitar and former Magazine and Bad Seeds founder member Barry Adamson returning for some bass tracks, organ parts, and touring duties. Alongside stalwarts of (two) drummers Jim Sclavunos and Thomas Wydler, the ever-notable Martyn Casey on bass and would prove to be the swan song for the late Conway Savage, keyboard and electric piano player since 1992, who would die in 2018. Cave would acknowledge the rare abilities of The Bad Seeds from that era: "They are unlike any other band on earth for pure, instinctive inventiveness." Much of this band lineup remains with Cave to the present day.

For Mick Harvey, The Bad Seeds, like The Birthday Party before it, was more about attitude than fitting into any genre or sonic signature. Admitting that the band had tunes, he also described their self-destructive mission to become "appealing and unsustainable." In particular he found the contemporary Bad Seeds' live approach lacking: "It's entertainment, and I've never been about the entertainment."[5] The band's original scorched-earth policy freed them up to become something markedly different from what had gone before; both bands were known for pushing the boundaries beyond straight rock and post-punk's already broad horizons, creating songs that consciously attacked the idea of music as leisure activity, simply to be enjoyed or consumed. For him that essential spirit was more or less lost by the time of Grinderman, which he saw as a distraction and damaging to The Bad Seeds' brand, where for Cave it became an emancipatory clean slate to clear his head musically. Grinderman, a four-man band scraping elements of garage rock and Gonzoid experimentation, was comprised of Nick Cave, Warren Ellis, Martyn P. Casey and Jim Sclavunos, offering a stern rhythm section with vocal and musical freakouts from Cave and Ellis. Formed in 2006 as a splinter group from The Bad Seeds, and harking back to the wild years of the Birthday Party, it became a clean break for Cave to reengage with a primal edge that some said had been lost to wild-sea balladeering.

Cave was initially disparaging about Harvey's departure—a founding member of the band, characterized as someone who used to lay down guitars everywhere, miring the band in a more standard rock format. While Cave's singer-songwriter piano would often provide the backbone of many Bad Seeds tracks, biographer Mark Mordue noted that Harvey was often the glue that held the band together through the worst of times. More than a simple guitarist wearing his Lou Reed rhythms on his sleeve, he was a multi-instrumentalist who finished drum tracks, added organ and piano parts, even building up the loops that drive forward what is arguably The Bad Seeds' and Cave's most important song "The Mercy Seat."[6]

It would also be unfair not to admit the sonic intimacy of earlier Bad Seeds albums. The use of organs and Wurlitzers adds a melancholy warmth to "Sad Waters" and "Your Funeral My Trial," alongside Harvey's relentless Velvet Underground rhythm guitar on "Straight to

You," sweet but never sickly—a gentle warmth whistles through, lifting the song beyond the main guitar riff. Elsewhere Conway Savage's Rhodes electric piano adds haunting depth to the beautiful but otherwise straightforward "Loom of the Land."

Following the more free-range recording processes of the Grinderman project and *DIG!LAZARUSDIG!!* Warren Ellis stepped to the fore in Harvey's stead as a multi-instrumentalist and informal rearranger of songs, bringing a new ear and sonic approach to what The Bad Seeds could become. Ellis and Cave first met around the time of *Your Funeral . . . My Trial* (1986), finding himself living with a mutual dealer friend who used to sell heroin to Nico and Johnny Thunders. He would later appear as a session player in 1994's *Let Love In*; after offering the suggestion of chord change and half expecting to be fired, Ellis was invited back the next day, and their working relationship continued. Cave later said he did not remember Ellis from these sessions when he asked him to join The Bad Seeds officially in 1997.[7]

Where for much of his time with the band Ellis had been more of a spectator to increasing friction between the big personalities of Cave, Blixa Bargeld, and Mick Harvey, who gradually found less space for themselves on each record, putting strain on decades-long relationships. Cave would explain the sudden change: "For a practical reason: our fucking guitarist, Mick Harvey, has quit the Bad Seeds. Without him we always had a tendency to fill in the blanks. Mick always added a storm of guitars everywhere. . . . We wanted to replace him but when we listened to the first recordings, all this space in between the instruments impressed us. It was too beautiful to be stained by guitars."[8]

The album would also bear the hallmarks of Ellis' love for Alice Coltrane's Eastern-tinged use of drones.[9] Building songs by layers as if painting with sound, Ellis made a point of embracing the pregnant pause instead of trying urgently to fill the silence. He sought to enrich each song's atmosphere in a haze of electronic ticks, punctuated by loops of delayed guitar noise. Ellis would sample band performances then feed these into the record, becoming tidal sounds that beat back against themselves adding new dimension to the songs.

Recorded in 2012 at La Fabrique, a recording studio based in a nineteenth-century mansion in the south of France and in Brighton.[10] A suitably louche and free-flowing recording process, not the doom and angst of the band's most liberated period of excess- and tension-fueled recording session, exacerbated by Cave's heroin addiction: "When we played a song, we never knew where we were going, or long it'd last. . . . Even I didn't have a flight plan. It's a way to maintain the beauty and danger."[11]

Cave would note: "The more records you make the less roads it seems you have left to go down, which makes it really challenging to move forward." Cave was keen to stretch The Bad Seeds' musical form, identifying the need for an interlocutor like Ellis to help break The Bad Seeds' musical mold, later citing Richard Russell's production work with Gil Scott-Heron on *I'm New Here* (2010) and Kanye West's *Yeezus* (2013).[12] Trying to describe the duo's new approach Cave said, "If I were to use that threadbare metaphor of albums being like children, then *Push the Sky Away* is the ghost-baby in the incubator and Warren's loops are its tiny, trembling heartbeat."[13]

The altered formation of the band yielded more space for The Bad Seeds to maneuver: "to let a little bit of air and a little bit of light in." Without the demands of standardized "rock" chord progressions, the new songs allowed for pregnant pauses and elements of electronic interference to dirty up the sound as well as building toward elevating harmonies. Cave would heap praise upon the dynamism of the band as well as note the transitional state of the recording process: "I enter the studio with a handful of ideas, unformed and pupal; it's the Bad Seeds that transform them into things of wonder."[14] In keeping with this spirit the album is enriched by moments of pure serendipity, as Cave remembered: "We just added the choir, the kids from the local school. None of the kids spoke English, it was beautiful." Directed to sing phonetically, the organic choral backing helped to make "Push the Sky Away" a rare anthemic track for The Bad Seeds.

Warren Ellis' background as a self-taught violinist encouraged a more instinctive approach to writing and recording music, borne out by his work in the trio band Dirty Three.[15] Ellis claims to struggle with basic questions around his chosen instrument: "Tuning. And timing. And technique. So, everything really." But elsewhere he would acknowledge that seeming limitations such as Billie Holiday's limited vocal range can also become a signature strength, mentioning the anecdote that "she only had 12 notes, but it was what she did with those 12 notes that mattered." This lack of pretension, replaced with sincerity, marks Ellis as a truly artistic foil.[16] Ellis applies a strongly improvisational, free-flowing method to piece songs together, echoing the radical authenticity of Jack Kerouac's mantra: "first thought, best thought." Ellis preferred the urgent spontaneity of first-time takes, of which Cave noticed, "the more you learn the song, you lose some of that energy."

Ellis would cite this immediacy as a way to capture the joyful happenstance of realizing an idea without a fixed style or sound in mind: "In the studio, with the band, they're the things that always surprise you, the accidents. The things that you thought were going to work, they don't ever get through."[17] This allowed him and Cave the confidence to reject their preconceived notions of what a song could be. Accordingly *Push the Sky Away* and the two Bad Seeds records that directly followed it pursued increasingly expressive, textural ambient sounds and surprise deviations rather than a singular dominant melody or tune, nontraditional structures and wordless choral harmonies. Cave's lyrics would become denser and informed by fractured poetic forms and surreal imagery, somehow reflecting a more broken world.

Push the Sky Away would be the first record on which Ellis had written so many Bad Seeds songs alongside Cave, the logical progression from their soundtrack work together begun with *The Proposition* in 2005. Cave encouraged Ellis to take the music as far as he could. The use of a mandolin, for example, was a new texture alongside other "unidentified instruments" suggesting an intensely experimental process, harking back to The Bad Seeds gutting pianos and smashing pieces of metal in the studio, setting raw sound against proficient musicianship, for the two approaches to become united into an expansive band aesthetic. Equally Cave and Ellis took steps away from their respective instruments of piano and violin, yielding fresh results: "a scary sound because we didn't recognise it."[18]

Cave and Ellis seemed to be working in conscious defiance of the neo-blues meets postpunk swagger of The Bad Seeds' early records: "On this album it's not always apparent what instruments the band is playing: they may be traditional musical instruments but other sounds are clearly generated by objects unrelated to musical instruments." However, Cave would attest that The Bad Seeds had always been a constant engine of reinvention, such that *Push the Sky Away* stands as testament to the band straddling their own musical heritage.[19] Hugo Race, sometimes guitarist on several 1980s Bad Seeds records, remembered working on the band's debut album: "[The band's] brief was to come up with a new take on everything; Nick was really looking for originality and authenticity." By 2013, Barry Adamson, a Bad Seeds veteran returned to the fold, would be surprised by the continued (r)evolution of the band that now seemed to have come full circle toward a new beginning: "It was like it had normalized. Nick was using convention and turning it on its head."[20]

Push the Sky Away would become known as an album of penetrating brilliance that cuts forward and back across The Bad Seeds' legacy to occupy a place of endings as entrances. From the anthemic to the experimental, the songs' elegiac treatment of love and lust, death and aging persist within a rich and expansive vision; like the hazy chemistry of a photograph slowly emerging into view, they are fleet moments that will later fade into fragmented pixels, black holes in the memory.

With the album cover shot in the same bedroom where Cave wakes at the start of *20,000 Days on Earth*, the album itself almost follows the same twenty-four-hour cycle moving from dawn to dusk, becoming the imagined soundtrack to the film.[21] The album ends with the song "Push the Sky Away," its encroaching horizon a permanently shifting vista that is suddenly poised upon the stillness of an infinite moment. The shutter, once full of light, now becomes a door closing upon the end of day but also left ajar to the return of the fading sun.

In stark contrast to the scenes of devastation in Cave's earlier music, *Push the Sky Away* presents an album flush with possibilities, offering both escape and the possibility of return where each day becomes an invitation to begin again. Marking the end of one era and the beginning of a new one, Cave said the album "set the blueprint for a decade of creativity." Though it would initially stand as the confirmation of Cave's settled family life in Brighton, the album would later be reimagined through the album's title track, Cave finding affirmation in the face of mortal defeat, where to hold back the horizon is to resist the dying of the light.

ROCK AND ROLL SAVIOR

A raging storm draws a thick curtain of black rain down upon the crooked and cracked land. Sweeping in across the horizon, water keeps on falling, the darkness only cracked by crooked spears of lightning and thunderous handclaps. A howling wind whips all along the skyline, bound inside the cyclone of a storm shot through with raindrop bullets, stretching time like a melting clock, beating into the merciless earth.[1]

In the stifled heartbeat of a repeating bass riff we hear a great rumbling terror move forward in its stuttering approach, every hiccupping second-third note breaking its terrible stride.[2] The rivers have broken their banks, still waters are gathered to a rage, now nothing is here but the endless tide of the flood.[3] Only Cave's voice breaks through the haze to guide our eye, in both excitement and warning, to "looky, looky yonder" at the skyline folding day into night.[4]

A sea of cloud bears down, smothering the land in leaden gloom, the electrified air swallowing up every last breath. The shadow of a great sweeping hand passes over the hearts of newborn twins, one stillborn, the other fighting for life, between them the wonder and the wrath of God as a moon-crowing chorus cries out the name of the forsaken place "Tupelo."

The seemingly endless rain opens The Bad Seeds' second album *The First-born Is Dead* (1985) and falls throughout the song, as it does throughout so many of Nick Cave's songs. On "Tupelo" Cave invites the listener to bear witness to cataclysmic death and destruction wreaked by a natural disaster. We are dragged back to the southern town in deepest Mississippi, the birthplace of Elvis Aaron Presley in 1935—the new Jesus—brought into the world to fulfill his destiny as the future king of rock and roll,[5] alongside his dead twin Jesse Garon Presley. Simultaneously his destiny reaches into the near future when a series of twelve tornadoes strike Tupelo on April 5, 1936, along with two days of flash floods that almost wiped out the town—all of which one-year-old Elvis survived. Cave collapses time where death, chaos, and creation are compressed into a singular frenzied moment.

Witnesses described the deluge as turning streets into rivers, telegraph poles are ripped out of the earth like sticks of corn from the fields, there are fires, and a rolling blackout descends on the town. The winds were so powerful that pine needles flew through the air and were embedded in trees like darting arrows. The simple clapboard house that Elvis' father built for his family shook with the earth but remained standing, while others fell flat like they were built out of playing cards. The Gum Pond area of the town was all but destroyed, with several people hurled up into the air and dashed back down to earth so violently that their *broken* bodies were never recovered whole.

Cave compounds these events into his song, stretching the facts into myth as the flood of Tupelo carries with it echoes of the Great Mississippi Flood of 1927—where the levees broke in 145 different places along the river, its nearest bend one hundred miles away from Tupelo.[6] More than 200,000 residents of the Mississippi Delta area were displaced and effectively exiled from their former home. Tens of thousands never returned, partly because there was nothing to go back to, but also due to the hostile racial climate of the time as displaced African Americans needing relief were treated as unwanted immigrants in a foreign land. On the 1930 track "High Water Everywhere Part 1" Charley Patton sings of the refugee camps that flood victims were hustled into. Seeing the occupation of the moral high ground, he sings that it is not safe to leave for fear of being "barred," meaning to be fenced in and put to work in camps.[7]

The Bad Seeds' "Tupelo" draws upon the more traditional blues song of John Lee Hooker's "Tupelo,"[8] recorded in 1959/1960, more than twenty years after the natural disaster had taken place. The song recounts the loss and devastation wreaked upon the small town, alongside nearby Gainesville. Hooker's "Tupelo" keeps the story of the catastrophe alive and is delivered in memoriam to those who were no longer alive to tell it.

With the line "What a mighty time" Hooker evokes the sheer force of the Tupelo storm and tragic loss of human life that he had seen become a footnote to history. It also stands as a veiled reference to the shock and awe of (un)earthly powers to give and take away life within a single stroke. In the face of the tragedy Hooker discovers the cruel irony of faith; where God is either acting with terrible force or simply looking away, faith is no guarantee of salvation.

> Could hear many people cryin' "Lord, have mercy
> 'Cause you're the only one that we can turn to."

The dampened bass throb of The Bad Seeds' "Tupelo" echoes Hooker's steady, loping rhythm where his feet tap along as the song's metronomic heartbeat, his voice lending a gentle hum above. Mick Harvey's bassline chases the internal tension of Hooker's sound with the hammered-on and pulled-off guitar notes that grow denser as his left hand reaches out to the notes around it, a quietly desperate and frantic motion masquerading as surface calm. The juggernaut bass intensifies, the children of Tupelo hear the rhythm of their own blood against the sheet squall of the rain, their senses grown deaf to all thought and feeling beyond abject terror. The Bad Seeds' "Tupelo" is less a cover version than a complete reimagining of Hooker's original. Written by Cave alongside Barry Adamson and Mick Harvey, the band brought Sturm und Drang to the blues standard, making the song gravitate around the birth of Elvis. It becomes their mission to short-circuit the haunting ambience of Hooker's elegy.

Live performances of "Tupelo" continue to expand into an unwieldy monster of sonic force overwhelming its creators. Cave's tumbling words march the song forward, a deranged antenna struck by manic revelation. He dredges up the blues spirit amid a rising tide of bristling guitars and ominous smashing cymbals, only for The Bad Seeds to bring the whole edifice crashing down around them in great swells of tension and release. Amid this autodestruction the chorus spills into chaos as Warren Ellis holds his violin above his head toward the heavens like a lightning rod inviting a riotous squall of feedback.

"Tupelo" marks Elvis' birth as musical messiah, announcing the second coming of the blues—crashing into the creation tale of Jesus Christ—both delivered as mankind's savior only to be delivered and crucified as its sacrificial lamb.[9] This is the starting point of rock and roll as a major cultural force, the breaking point at which populist music is electrified into the band format. Transcending grassroots jazz, rockabilly, and skiffle, it seemed to sweep away everything that had come before it. On the other hand, The Bad Seeds' music becomes a dark funereal celebration for traditional rock and roll in the mid-1980s, just after The Birthday Party rode the wave of postpunk revolution. In all this confusion Cave managed to conjure forth the future while dredging up the bones of the past to create a terrific new present beyond the original innovators such as John Lee Hooker, with "Tupelo" straddling history as it blurred time.

Elvis' "lust for status" would arrive as a transformative power to remake the world. Greil Marcus nails this down: "The singer was to enter this world, suffer it, make that world real, and thus redeem it."[10] In the final damning line of "Tupelo" Cave's apocalyptic lyrics seem to invoke the death of the town drowning in rain as tears, sunk under the weight of its own Bible Belt redemption: "you will reap what you sow." The destruction visited upon Tupelo becomes the town's collective "shame," suggesting that Tupelo and Presley's fates are intertwined as a vision of somehow divine punishment drawing upon Hooker's song with the image of people gathered to harvest but instead confronted with imminent doom as their crops are washed away.[11] After Tupelo is sacrificed in his name, Elvis must carry its burden as he strides beyond his birthplace to meet with destiny—so big he became small. He is later consumed by the emergent music industry.[12]

"Tupelo" contains the lyric "the firstborn is dead," referring to the symbolism of twin brothers, divided across life and death. It becomes the album's title track, framing the songs that follow. There is also some inspiration from the Hebrew translation of the Bible where Jacob "moves on his brother's heel," raising the stark and primal image of a grasping hand of a child who tries to equal or usurp his own brother (Esau) so that he might live or simply to be the firstborn favored son.[13] In "Tupelo" Elvis' weaker twin becomes a sacrifice, accidentally martyred to deliver his brother who flourishes in his stead, solely drawing upon all of his mother's love and strength.[14] In Cave's first novel, *And the Ass Saw the Angel*,[15] the book's mute protagonist Euchrid Eucrow grasps his brother's heels and slides out after him from the womb. "With all the glory of an uninvited guest," the second son tries to best the first. Cave regurgitates from "Tupelo" the image of Euchrid's stillborn twin buried in a shoebox, with the added embellishment that it is tied with red ribbon a vivid streak of the umbilical cord's mingled red, purple, and blue, blood into bruise.[16]

In the many shoeboxes of Eucrow we find gathered toenail clippings, hair, and cicada shells in a grisly collection of body matter,[17] like the locks of women's hair nailed as scalps to the walls of Cave's one-man box room in Berlin. These gathered remnants echo the significance of religious relics; as gory as they are increasingly absurd, the process of physical shedding exposes the precarity of the body, particularly when compared to the unbearable weight of the ephemeral soul, stripped of life into stillness. In "Tupelo" the shoebox as a flimsy cardboard coffin expresses both the fragility of the newborn corpse and the tragedy of the insubstantial pauper's grave.[18]

The biblical power of "Tupelo" draws in part upon Presley's own religious background, which deeply informed both his and Cave's earliest music. Greil Marcus noted: "Even if Elvis' South was filled with puritans, it was also filled with natural-born hedonists, and the same people were both." Cave for his part could carry this duality with him. Presley was born into the stringent Calvinist sect of Christianity, but in the South, this manifested as powerful preachers, carrying the force of God in heart, voice, and body, to become the "faith of grace, apocalypse, and emotion." There is a combined effect of sermon and gospel music performed upon the congregation-as-audience that Elvis would grow up among: "The preacher rolled fire down the pulpit, men and women rocked in their seats, bloodying their fingernails, scratching and clawing in a lust for absolute sanctification. . . . It was a faith meant to transcend the grimy world that had called it up."[19]

Cave's lyrics are chanted in the idiom of twisted and broken speech, free-flowing like the driving rain, comparing it to the performative power of hoodoo, a syncretic set of practices in the rural US that arose in parallel to the voodoo traditions of the Caribbean and Africa. Hoodoo is less about outright worship than it is about channeling and summoning power. This is in contrast to more symbolic Christian acts of worship: the blood and body of Christ and the saying of Mass using spiritualized metaphor to express communion with God and the legacy of Jesus. Hoodoo exists as a more physical form of magic, whereas organized religion often becomes a war against the body, seeking control over the soul. However, hoodoo rituals such as the "ring shout"—during which practitioners build up spiritual energy as they "shout" while running counter clockwise in a dancing circle—are comparable to the fevered Christian parishioners cycling about the pyre of their own burning feelings.

In spite of his spiritual upbringing, Elvis' sensual physicality would show him losing partial control of his body as a deep expression of his own physical grammar. A stage presence given to the unconscious appearance of shaking and rolling his eyes cut with hip thrusts and a gyrating pelvis on broken legs, leaning over the edge of the stage so the girls in the crowd felt themselves almost close enough to touch the hem of his garment—or to lick the sweat from his heel—each time reaching out closer to their god. Michael Ventura noted: "You could hear the moves, infer the moves, in his singing. No white man and few black artists had sung so completely with the liberation of the whole body."[20] We witness the human form electrified by the soul; ekphrastic statuesque dancing turns into bleeding, burning, howling poetry. Such performances became revolutionary celebrations of the body—overturning

Christian dogma of shame, meekness, and concealment: "The Voodoo rite of possession by the god became the standard of American performance in rock'n'roll." The performer is moved not by religious fervor but "by the spirit they felt in the music," in communion with the audience. As he professed one love, outlasting all others, and presented many deaths as the shadow of recurring emotional pain and spiritual doubt, Cave would borrow from Elvis' lexicon of testifying-become-signifying. The earliest Bad Seeds performances were a feat of physical endurance, balancing a sustained heroin addiction with a musical career such that the two seemed to become codependent, struggling through in the hope that, unlike Elvis, he would never to have to work a normal, doldrum-day-dead-end job his entire life.[21]

The Firstborn Is Dead whether by accident or design becomes a "Deep South concept album,"[22] that in its most theatrical moments draws upon the heritage of classic Americana in all its span but still manages to subvert it to become something other, bending cultural history askew. By 1983 Cave had more or less relocated the band to Berlin, the last outpost of the "other" West in Europe—the entire enterprise became a work of will, imagination, and abiding love for the records of past America's now distant time and place. Mick Harvey sees the album as a fragmented pastiche, an attempt to draw upon blues lineage but also to rise above it, becoming a postmodern tribute to authenticity itself.[23] A transitional record bookended by "Tupelo" and "Blind Lemon Jefferson," *The Firstborn Is Dead* combines Cave and The Bad Seeds' earliest musical influences with the perspective of the band they would become, dissecting the connective tissue from which they would continue to evolve, seeing their sound deepen and broaden with each new album.

Tennessee Williams said that "the South" was a construct of the popular imagination; there was no such place beyond the art that helped create it, mythic truths that would later transcend it.[24] The power of the blues draws upon the nascent energy of the land and its history, reified in the Southern Gothic tradition that haunted the shadow narrative of Elvis Presley. In isolation Tupelo is hardly an auspicious place, but it expresses the musical culture he grew up in.[25] Born on the wrong side

of the tracks, Presley was raised in the poorest part of town alongside the black community. In an era of Jim Crow laws, which even after the Emancipation Proclamation of 1865 had brought about the abolition of slavery, enforced a psychic barrier of difference and alien territory between white and black neighborhoods, ghettoized by physical and mental barriers.[26] The situation of his humble background exposed Presley to both gospel and blues music, and the roots of these musics in "spirituals"[27] that would likely have been sung by the enslaved ancestors of his neighbors only a generation before.[28]

Gospel drew uniquely upon the religious vernacular, the songs rooted in Christian narratives of deliverance and salvation, the struggle in a world of sin that found real-life counterparts for biblical characters.[29] In his first book of autobiography,[30] former slave and later abolitionist orator Frederick Douglass claimed the spirituals as folk songs and that they were the true testament against slavery: "They were tones loud, long, and deep; they breathed the prayer and complaint of souls boiling over with the bitterest anguish . . . a prayer to God for deliverance from chains." Douglass' description seems to prefigure the spirit that blues music would become: "The songs of the slave represent the sorrows of his heart; and he is relieved by them, only as an aching heart is relieved by its tears." In order not to drown in their pain, the singer must rise above it.

The push and pull of deliverance and self-abnegation were offered too in Cave's music, alongside the glorious troubles of the blues singing tribute to "the joys and the pain of the world of flesh." From the more comfortable white perspective he was able to cross over into the more metaphysical realm of spiritual deliverance from evil and wrestle with the rules and societal strictures of biblical moral codes. With so much of his music Cave reached for tenderness and insight while throwing the kitchen sink of biblical narrative along with it.

Southern spirituals and gospel would transmute into the blues, thought to have originated in Mississippi or Alabama sometime after 1860, marking a divide that reflected the two sides of the black experience like a flipped coin. The "pre-freedom longing for escape" was an expression of pain, suffering, and hope of people "living in bodies that did not belong to them," cast between heaven and earth with the blues expressing "the post-freedom realities of day-to-day life,"[31] realizing a new baptism of fire. If slavery is punishment without crime, then life beyond the plantation becomes remaining time served in a hostile and unwelcoming world.

The blues sparked rock and roll's native sensuality to become an "affective freedom" of real needs, loves, and desires that were "denied them in slavery and dismissed in freedom." The blues was a language that transcended situation, with universal sentiments that could not be denied by the hardest of hearts. Numerous examples feature in Cave's discography. "The Witness Song" from *The Good Son* (1990) draws upon the gospel song "Who Will be a Witness?" Elsewhere, The Bad Seeds' chilling cover of "Hey Joe" stands apart from the original blues and Jimi Hendrix's more famous choppy and fluid guitar. Cave and his band hammer the song home into an eerie drone, more dread-dirge than psychedelic dream. Cave's "City of Refuge" was based upon a blues standard that carries echoes of the history of fleeing slaves.[32] The Bad Seeds' wild-with-fear version has him running blind in a sandstorm, knowing that wherever you go, you take your problems with you. Howlin' Wolf reframes the scenario on his 1966 performance of "Down in the Bottom": "When you see me runnin' / you know my life is at stake." The song tells the story of a young lover escaping from his partner's "old man," perhaps to avoid a shotgun wedding, but it is the narrative of running, from the law or social authority, that Cave made the returning race in his songs. Perhaps when Howlin' Wolf sings it, he's carrying the echo of his ancestors' inherited trauma running from slave masters, a lynch mob, away from America.[33]

Fundamentally the blues are about "survival [or not] on the meanest, most gut level of human existence." This "meanness" has double meaning, reading as literal cruelty or lack of kindness, being done to, or by, the singer—raw and real. This hard-bitten (and hard-won) knowledge that could come across as sour, bitter, and angry, alongside the expression of deeper passions, the blues was sometimes considered in deviant opposition to gospel and spirituals.[34] These evocations of struggle fed into Cave's listening experience, softening and hardening his musical and emotional ear.[35]

Perhaps the great synthesizing agent of black musics that traversed the late nineteenth and early twentieth century was New Orleans cornet player Buddy Bolden. In his jazz playing he introduced the spirit of the blues to the European horn, channeled spirituals, gospel, and the blues, layering sadness upon sadness. Trombonist Bill Matthews remembered, "that boy could make the women jump out the window. On those old slow, low-down blues, he had a moan in his cornet that went all through you, just like you were in church or something." His sin was to try to combine "the devil's music and hymns at the same time"; for this he went mad "playing too hard and too often drunk too wild too crazy."

Cave mentions Michael Ondaatje's neofictional account of the short life of Buddy Bolden, *Coming Through Slaughter*, as a favorite book. Ondaatje merges spare facts and plenty of imagination to create a greater kind of truth that outstrips the legend of Bolden, more than any straight biography ever could. His vivid storytelling would foreshadow much of Cave's freewheeling style, crisscrossing fact and fiction into unique songcraft. Bolden reaches a sad end in a lunatic asylum after going berserk playing during a parade. He collapses with blood pouring from his mouth, choking upon the voice of the song caught in his throat. No recordings of his music are thought to survive, but the inspiration of his songs was handed-down down between musicians. Archivists would record Bolden's former players, now aged oracles, whistling tunes through the mouthpiece of their instrument—making sense of Bolden the man overcome by the myth that has outlasted him.

On "Tupelo" Cave draws deeper inspiration from the dark arts of the blues running full tilt toward dramatic religious liturgy, wearing masks of both tragedy and comedy, frowning and grinning at the same time. Throughout his career Cave has played with this tension, bouncing between heaven and hell on earth as cultural touchstones rather than poles of outright revelation or damnation. In his songs we see alienated people searching for escape or redemption, roving outcasts looking to be reborn. These sharp-ended story arcs follow the Southern Gothic tradition, at its essence a series of stark turns. Beneath the sanctity of family and community under the banner of Christian virtue people struggle to carve out their own private life, and often crack under this relentless pressure. Cave nods to this leap in "Tupelo" and later revisits it on "Sundays Slave" (1988), where the ecstatic escapism of Saturday is soon met with the great comedown of Sunday morning church going, to wipe clean the sin of the week until the next sabbath, eluding damnation once again.

This bleeds into the mythologizing of Robert Johnson and his early death in 1938 at age twenty-seven and the legend that he sold his soul to the devil at the crossroads, standing as one of stations of the cross where sin meets the possibility of salvation.[36] Johnson makes his choice (or is chosen) to become a great guitar player, never looking back to see what might have been lost in the exchange. He would be murdered at the hands of a jealous husband, or so the legend goes.[37] Johnson's confrontation with the blues becomes a kind of inner struggle, urgent and overwhelming. He sounds more like an addict than a prophet when he sings:

> *The blues, is a low-down achin' heart disease*
> *Like consumption, killing me by degrees.*

In the ghostly songs that emerged in his wake, Johnson becomes both doom-bringer and emotional emancipator, his devotion to music claiming him as a martyred saint. His and Cave's paths would cross again on the lyrical and thematic visitation of 2013's "Higgs Boson Blues," where Cave cannot decide whether Johnson or the devil came off with the better part of the deal of revelation renewed.

Cave would end *The Firstborn Is Dead* with "Blind Lemon Jefferson"— a contemporary of Johnson and Leadbelly—one many young black men crowned and condemned as the nascent king of the blues who would die young, aged thirty-six.[38] Cave explained that he did not have much interest in the musician himself, more what he represented: the notion of paying your dues, as presented in the trials and tribulations of blues music.

Cave has Jefferson standing at the station, beneath the cross of the outstretched sycamore tree.[39] Blixa Bargeld's scratching guitars and Adamson's wobbling bass cast a dizzy, dull fog over Cave's lyrical blotches of rain. Cave hints at the tap-tap of Jefferson's white cane becoming the knock, knock, hop, and bopping rhythm of two crows skulking and shuffling more like vultures, watchers after the wake, waiting to pick his bones. The song fades out as a big slow train coming to rest at the final stop of "Train Long Suffering," the harmonica finding its breathless last gasps, while the restless spirit of Jefferson's blues keeps on rolling.[40]

Like John Milton before him, Jefferson is presented as the blind seer, an oracle who through his own dark tunnel of the imagination discovers a vision into the future where his music and that of his peers would become a dominant cultural influence in the rock and roll of the mid-twentieth century.[41] Feeling himself cheated out of royalties (being offered a shiny new car in lieu of payment was a custom of the time), Jefferson dies in relative poverty. His song "See That My Grave Is Kept Clean" recalls being haunted by two white horses as he asks for a place to endure in his memory. The title lyric would be inscribed on his headstone.[42]

A timeless Bad Seeds track, "Tupelo" looms tall as the self-made myth that confirms Cave as both postpunk heretic and rock and roll redeemer. Offering a conjoined vision of past and present, it declares the band's future mission to save the contemporary music scene of the mid-1980s from itself by resurrecting the vitality of rock in a new language. "Tupelo" marks the moment The Bad Seeds became a band apart from the mainstream, continuing to pay warped tribute to the blues bound over to legend, tradition, and creative renewal—as they trashed, junked, and scrapped sound to remake the music of the past in their own image.

IS THIS DESIRE . . .

In the songs of Nick Cave love is a double-edged sword. In his 1996 lecture "The Secret Life of the Love Song" Cave states that no matter how they are written, every love song is a letter to God. He acknowledges love as a transcendent state, another weightless step toward spiritual connection, bridging the gap between life on earth and a nascent belief in something beyond ourselves. Elsewhere, love is the trigger for heinous acts of violent revenge, spurred on by an aching feeling so close to bereavement, which follows after being jilted, spurned, or otherwise betrayed by the object of his affections. Love carries the potential to wreak havoc upon all who come near its wayward forces, marking the dance of mutual connection as another leap of faith.

Ever since the more romantic edge of Cave's 1990s songwriting he has been associated with songs of love; the soft hand that counterbalances the brutal blows of murder ballads and the sleazy sensuality in his songs of lustful obsession. For Cave "God is love," where the power of "the word made flesh" is elevated through 'love' into a mystical earthly force as to become "the flesh made word." Beyond physical desire and raw sensuality, it is the rare transcendental qualities the beloved embody that we are drawn to; consider Christina Rossetti's famous line: "How do I love thee? Let me count the ways." The person standing before you is raised up toward a living metaphor.[1]

Cave suggests that the right love bears an openness that turns us away from indifference toward a sense of completeness, just as others might claim to "discover" religion, as though it had always been inside of them.[2] The biblical scholar Roland Boer notes that in his love songs Cave "elides God and woman so that the two are often indistinguishable." On "Brompton Oratory" Cave is brought to his knees by broken love in a way that neither God nor the devil could ever achieve, casting love as a holy transcendent power, yet still bound to earth.[3]

Also from *The Boatman's Call*, "(Are You) the One That I've Been Waiting For?" finds Cave calling upon love's sudden fatalism, arriving out of nowhere, carrying the weight of the inevitable.[4] Here Cave's blood is fired up by the electrified soul; everything has brought him toward this crucial moment, falling into a magical state of heightened existence. Years after the song was written Cave alluded to a continued spiritual element that inspired his words: "I think as an artist, particularly, it's a necessary part of what I do, that there is some divine element going on within my songs."[5] On "Darker with the Day" Cave is preoccupied by a deeper yearning that he cannot fully articulate, a pervasive mood of inchoate loss. In his lecture on the love song, he had discussed the Portuguese word *saudade*, a feeling of longing, melancholy, or nostalgia often expressed through songs and poetry, which met his own searching disposition toward the unfinished endlessness of love.[6]

Beyond the spiritual element of relationships Cave often shifts gears into the extremes of physical attraction—the grounding force of lust and desire driven into sex. He strides in and out of high-flying romance to carnal excess—the spark that leaps between emotion and flesh—just as easily turning from sensation to an emotional car crash. In "Hard on for Love" Cave attempts to repeatedly shock with the cut-and-thrust of its chanted title and diminishing returns of sexual puns, his mouth crammed full of biblical references and the metaphysical dead lift of blood into milk as conjoined ejaculations of life and death. "Hiding All Away" (2004) is even more overt, expressing sexual need as a show of brute force, the knowingly crude image of the hand shoved under a dress—passion confronted with the reality of physical threat. "Deanna" is one of Cave's songs that best explores the confusion where depth of feeling becomes loss of control: the young lover is overwhelmed with desire to defrock as both innocent and lethal. The male gaze of Leonard Cohen's "Last Year's Man" admits to the lover as both tender and the bad man whose deviance is attractive: "Some women wait for Jesus / Handsome women wait for Cain" (1971).[7]

"Deanna" paints the young love affair as an elegiac adventure where a series of minor crimes are blown up to feel like the forbidden romance of the century. Cave tells the story of a girl he knew back in Melbourne. Together they would break into people's homes and steal random objects and petty cash. They would also lie in their beds and take small sips from the liquor cabinet; playing house, like visiting ghosts in other people's lives. Cave riffs on the image of "Ku-Klux-Klan furniture," discovering a house full of furniture draped in white sheets, as if asleep waiting for its owner's return with eyeless stares. The girl builds a kind of burrow under a bridge to stash the loot, fulfilling a kleptomaniac habit—it's not (just) about the money but the adventure.

Through the song's raucous jam Cave expresses the split sides to their relationship, like a tarot card flipped between the Thief and the Lovers[8]—he sings of ejaculating death's head skulls on her pretty dress, the taint of sex and mortality, an echo of the death's head moth motif from Thomas Harris' *The Silence of the Lambs*. Through the romp of "Deanna" Cave paints himself as the Devil, declares that he is "down here"—suggesting cunnilingus in hell—not for her money or simply to make her come but to stake a claim upon her immortal soul.[9] "Deanna" displays a rare poppier stomp we would not hear again until 2004's "Get Ready for Love," both songs burning with a groove inherited from Iggy and The Stooges' "Search and Destroy." The song's title is chanted "Oh, De-Anna" across split syllables, breaking the back of the hook that bounces along an R&B-inspired spine-shuffling crunch through the *Tender Prey* album (1988).

Cave's lyrics stride across clichéd images of a fired gun and sex; penetration met with ejaculation. The abject body horror in the "issue" of blood or semen is a continued trope in his songs as the overlapping stain of sin and pain in love. In this "Deanna" also alludes to the extreme on-the-run scenario of the Terrence Malick film *Badlands* (1973), where a teenage girl and her slightly older lover, the sociopathic outsider Kit, come together, embarking on a season of violent madness against no one in particular but against the rest of the world.[10] Just like Cave and "Deanna" the couple indulge in fantasies of hitting the road in a Cadillac where "death rides in the backseat." The car as symbolic vessel of freedom and escape from small-town life, they race toward an inevitable confrontation with their own deaths, a situation they cannot outrun. Like Cohen, Cave poses the question as a challenge: faced with the *amor fou* of sex conjoined with madness and the possibility of violence—how many women wouldn't want to be so singularly adored and wildly desired?

In a 1988 interview Cave would explain that he and the mystery girl did once find a gun and that her story ended badly: "One day she was caught by this guy who was in this religious-instruction teacher's house. The wife of this teacher thrashed her and the guy did something to her, but I really don't know what it was." Clearly the two drifted apart.[11] Still with some regret Cave talked about the song's autobiographical strain years later: "My song 'Deanna' was seen as a particularly brutal act of betrayal, and thirty years on I still haven't been fully forgiven."[12] where Deanna Bond, the subject of the song, called it "the bane of my existence"

Cave's love songs are often illuminated in terms of high romanticism, where love becomes an all-consuming emotion that turns back on itself toward destructive tendencies on an apocalyptic scale. In the making and breaking of love the universe is pushed out of sync, as if by force of feeling, with Cave caught up in its flow. "Straight to You" (1992) asks the lengths to which the lover would go to be beside their loved one, racing through the streets, fighting their way against collapsing ivory towers, arrows of love tinged with cruel barbs, and swallows with sharpened beaks threatening to dive.[13] The song carries a biblical tone of the private day of judgment upon the waxing and waning of love broken against the world, where rising up into our greatest happiness can also seem to foreshadow its undoing.

"Straight to You" frames a heroic tone within a jangly guitar sound and heaving chorus, masking disaster inside a mainstream indie sound of the early 1990s, divided between melodrama and majesty. Given The Bad Seeds' tenacious abilities it sits oddly among the buccaneering spirit of *Henry's Dream*. But for all its sweeping gloss the song's lyrics steadily echo the horrific scenes of a world gone mad unfurling across the title track's nightmare dreamscape.[14] In *The Boatman's Call* (1997) we find Cave devastated by relationship breakdown and forced to rebuild his life, as if learning to love again. In 2001's "Darker with the Day" Cave wanders the streets missing his wife, he lays out these anxieties gazing into the abyss of every crack in the pavement, becoming a chasm of yearning and self-doubt. Each day without her becomes a further step into negative space. This continues a through line from 1990's "The Ship Song," "Into My Arms," and later "I Need You" in 2016, where Cave seeks connection and security anchored in a shared and enduring love when he is most reminded of its absence.

In 1990 Cave once admitted, "I used to fall in love at the drop of a hat," "Straight to You" has the song's narrator captive to love. With the next Bad Seeds album *Let Love In* (1994), Cave expands on this emotional bondage. The title track kicks off with flourishing piano and Western twangs of guitar. Love hits in a series of waves, each greater than the last, with Cave struggling to let go and give himself over to the tide. Elsewhere, it becomes the knife that cuts through the fog of addiction and the armor of the Nick Cave persona forged over many years, where life with The Bad Seeds was forced to give way to family life.

On the album's cover Cave stands surrounded by pink fire glaring from the shook foil of the backdrop put together with photographer Polly Borland, reflecting the album's night of fire and noise in the chambers of the heart where Cave is both purged and punished. The fresh chaos and abrasive hostility of some songs seems to (sub)consciously overturn the surface calm of domesticity Cave was carving out for himself. "Loverman" descends into demonic organ grind of pure fire and brimstone as Cave succumbs to outright desire, dissecting his frustrations in the anagram of the song's title "L-O-V-E-R-M-A-N." Beyond the middling spark of "Virtue" offering consolation to his carnal drive, a weakness for evil is his true vice. The speech progresses into his demand for total and absolute sexual obedience, anytime, anyhow, anywhere—Cave's fierce howl echoes out the rancor of tangled guitar as the song claws at the shrinking walls beating within his chest.

Martyn Casey is the secret hero of *Let Love In*—the first notes of the album on "Do You Love Me Pt. 1" are his R&B-infused bass vibes that fool the listener into an upbeat ride, laying down the spine of the album around which the other Bad Seeds would create a more haunting atmosphere. An ex-member of the Melbourne band The Triffids, Casey's bass groove stands as the core of several of Cave's most iconic songs, holding things down in the eye of a storm. He casts strident lines through "Red Right Hand," adds a knotted bounce to "Stagger Lee," and edges into poised restraint of "We No Who U R"—all led by his slinky, smooth, understated style. For his part, Casey said that Suzi Quattro inspired him to pick up the bass, quoting her: "Guitar is for the head, drums are for the feet, and bass is right between the legs."

Since the Bad Seeds' first album Cave's songs have personified the dangerous tipping point of love—veering from passionate fascination into full-blown obsession. The ceiling watcher in "From Her to Eternity" is a prisoner of his desire, staring upward, hearing "her" footsteps on the floorboards above his head. Andrew Male calls the song "a monstrous, ever-escalating Dostoevskian love song,"[15] carrying echoes of his novella *Notes from Underground* and the tortured masochism of Kafka's *Metamorphosis*.[16] Cave is reduced to a desperately lusting scuttler held under the heel of rage and desire. The mordant lust of the track, which was cowritten with Anita Lane, suggests a fiercely male fantasy where Cave's jilted would-be "lover" resides in a shrinking world that narrows into obsessive thinking. Envy and jealousy are often turned back against the beholder, while for the victims of his songs beauty often becomes a curse. Warren Ellis noted how all the instruments build toward the song's cataclysmic payoff, front-loaded with the phallic thrust of the chanted lyrics the guitar's searing drone cuts through the mind—the overwhelming power of love that drives us to do terrible things in its name.

Sharing the same obsessive drive in the softly intoned "Watching Alice" Cave explored the forced perspective of the watcher at the window. He sees the girl in her apartment across the street dressing in her uniform on a warm summer's morning, he notes the detail that she brushes her hair a hundred times. His longing stare might be innocent, but such is his obsession that he cannot turn away. A sedated, marching ballad with a slow, breezy harmonica, it is quite out of character for The Bad Seeds. Cave's vocals pour sweetness into the listener's ear, as his eyes run over her glowing body. Though vaguely titled, the song's arch intentions give a firm twist to the line of good taste. The power of its setting comes from the uncertainty Cave rests in the heavy breathless pauses: Does Alice secretly know she is being observed or does her watcher want to be caught, simply to be noticed in return? The song also offers the hope of some fantasy scenario in which their eyes meet and they fall in love, but under the heavy address of Cave's unflinching stare the possibility of romance seems nothing more than a dream.

In the twisted passions of "From Her to Eternity" we find Cave stalking the ceiling as the indoor rain of tears runs trough warped floorboards; he howls out the song's title like a crooked mantra. In sharp contrast the lilting piano of "Watching Alice" paints her silhouette into the window frame, unaware of the watcher's shadow cast over her.[17] Speaking about the song Cave was keen to clarify his objective authorial stance: "I am a songwriter, storyteller and hence a voyeur—that's what all my songs are about." With the writer's discipline he reaches toward deeper transgressive feelings, no matter how shameful or confrontational, to uncover burning desire that speaks to love, real or imagined.[18] Cave would later push back on the idea that his songs were so opportunistic, arguing that they moved deep within the perspective of a given character to inhabit the blood and guts perspective of the moment.[19]

In Berlin, Cave kept a small box of women's hair as well as long locks hanging from the walls. The locket of hair as traditional keepsake starts to look more like a horrorshow of scalped conquests, the murder trophies of the Texas Chainsaw Massacre or Ed Gein's interior decoration. Were they all cutoffs gifted by former lovers or weird curios of other lives that Cave picked up along the way? In The Birthday Party's

"Say a Spell" the deranged murderer makes a leap from the lustful hex of Screamin' Jay Hawkins' "I Put a Spell on You." As if under a curse, he keeps his victim's hair close to him.[20] Now that she is gone it keeps them invisibly bound to one another, coiled about his finger like a ring. As Cave would fascinate on with his breakup from PJ Harvey and in romancing his future wife Susie Bick,[21] the image of black hair remains an enduring presence in his songs. Perhaps still haunted by the motions of two souls moving as one in the "Henry Lee" video, we find him lost in the dense, dark image of her, the minor world around which he gravitates.[22]

At various times Cave would be both encouraged and vilified for his treatment of women in his music, attractive targets either used and abused or raised onto a pedestal of unreality as the impossible dream woman. Cave would mine several key relationships in his life for the raw material of songs, as alluded to by Susie Cave and Nick himself. Since his earliest days he claimed inspiration from some idea of the mythical muse, always implied as feminine, with songs arriving from the non-place of the ether, but also through women he has known along the way. From The Birthday Party and into the beginning of The Bad Seeds Cave would find himself almost overshadowed by the brilliance of his collaborator and then-lover, Anita Lane. A girlfriend since their art school days in Australia, she was an active member of The Bad Seeds, heading with them to London and later on to Berlin, though Cave would sometimes say that they followed in thrall to *her* breadth of ideas. Moving in and out of the band's recording sessions, she existed in her own artistic world, a private universe some might have said, and also contributed lyrics to key early songs.

Lane seemed to embody the ideal of the natural, pure artist, almost naive but defiantly unpretentious. Cave referred to her constant doodles as incidental masterpieces sketched out for their own sake, not to be seen or sold, instead expressing a fantastically original energy, and in this sense, she was perhaps an unwilling or accidental muse figure. Cave would argue that her rare artistic ability outshone the capacity of the band's limitations: "There seem to be three parts to the creative process,"

Nick Cave said, "the not knowing, the sudden knowing of what to do, then the doing of it. Anita was great at that middle part." What she lacked, Cave explained, was the latter stage: to finalize a song to completion so that it could stand by itself and be laid down to tape, left alone in its final iteration. His description suggests someone whose life was their art, more than they ever thought to record it for posterity, to dance with no one watching.

Her swansong with The Bad Seeds would be "Stranger Than Kindness." In its ice-slow luster we hear broken romance and physical sensuality slurred and slowed to a crawl, surviving surface tension but never getting beyond inertia. Cave drawls her line "grind my soft cold bones below" suggesting a removed intimacy at the symmetry of two pelvises stuck in coldhearted coitus—all sensation but no feeling—finally arriving at a terminal relationship. The lyrics were written by Lane with Blixa Bargeld's layered guitar lines crawling over one another toward a fidgeting insectoid hum, needling wires that cut across the itch of blood beneath the skin.

Cave first saw Bargeld performing with Einstürzende Neubauten on TV while The Birthday Party were touring in Amsterdam. He described the music as "mournful," Bargeld as looking "destroyed," and his screams as "a sound you would expect to hear from strangled cats or dying children," managing to make his instrument sound "unlike anything other than a guitar." Blixa admitted he was more of an overdub musician, there to disrupt any notion of a guitar solo and to help dirty up The Bad Seeds' sound. After describing his slide style as a left-handed person playing right-handed guitar, Blixa would notoriously declare: "I did not get into rock and roll to play rock and roll guitar!" His scraped guttural guitar sound is all over the outro of "The Good Son."

The song was seemingly produced without Cave's songwriting input; he called Anita Lane's words "beautifully obscure," noting that like all great song lyrics "it can reveal more every time you sing it." His vocal says enough, half-drunk, walking a whole step behind the beat, his come-lately delivery enriching the song's druggy, subterranean dirge. It is only in the chorus where Bargeld's guitar slides sweep through the ice that we hear Cave yawn from the depths of his introspection. Crucially

"Stranger" offers us a female perspective rarely heard in Cave's songs. We get the sense that the woman in the song is being *done to*. In giving pleasure the man is really pleasing himself; she is at once necessary but also incidental to his needs, hence the bittersweet, sometimes brutal tone of the song's lyrics. In her way, Lane wrote the epitaph to the early Bad Seeds and her relationship with Cave, marking the indelible influence they left upon one another. After Lane's death in 2021 Cave said in tribute, "It was both easy and terrifying to love her," describing her natural and infinitely various talent as that rare thing of trying to catch lightning in a bottle, and to be willing to release it freely, once its moment has passed.

The album from which "Stranger Than Kindness" emerged, *Your Funeral . . . My Trial*, presented a major creative leap forward for The Bad Seeds, with Lane one of many losses from the band's future sound. In 2009 Cave said it was the band's favorite album: "We really hit on something there. We found it really beautiful—to me there's some really delicate, strange, abstracted kinds of songs that I loved."[23] The split phrase of the title track leaves space for the listener, perhaps referencing the deeply uneven marital strife of the 1964 Sonny Boy Williamson and Memphis Slim song "Your Funeral and My Trial," where he calls for his wife to return home to him, or else. Cave presents himself as both murderer and mourner/victim, borrowing the habits of Kafka where the trials of life are exaggerated into the language of justice and crime toward a kind of reckoning, leaving a song about relationship troubles open to more abstract and metaphorical allusions that defy description.

On the title track Cave offers himself up to his "little lamb"; tender and vulnerable; he is the predator made meek, returning to his place as the steward of his beloved's heart who will later claim revenge on her for being unfaithful. In Sonny Boy Williamson's song, he praises the woman as earthly muse that should fulfill his ideal of godly perfection: "She can love to heal the sick and she can love to raise the dead." Knowing she will cheat his heart; he loves her still. To borrow from the blues of Blind Lemon Jefferson, even romantic life remains a series of ongoing trials, for some more than others. Williamson blames his wife for pushing him to murder, threatening that if she cannot mend her ways: "it's your funeral" this becomes a cry of blame and self-pity, knowing that in losing her he will only make himself suffer more.[24]

With The Bad Seeds' Berlin days given over to increasing drinking and drug use producer Flood remembers that despite the cohesive mood and sound of *Your Funeral . . . My Trial* it was the band's most fractured recording process yet: "The band was in a very strange place. Nick was going through a very dark period in his life." Often strung out and distracted, Cave seemed to be slipping away; from the album's cover we see his ponderous, watery intonation, as if trapped behind glass, looking in on his own life of a washed-out gray world.

Cave must have recognized something of himself in Anita Lane's struggle to articulate a rich seam of ideas, in part due to shifts in The Bad Seeds' lineup with Barry Adamson leaving partway through *Your Funeral . . .* the conclusion of his own "dead man walking" phase of drug issues. Meanwhile Thomas Wydler had badly cut his arm in a fall and could only drum one-handed. Mick Harvey was stretched thin covering many instrumental bases at once to push through on completion of the backing tracks, fighting to keep the band together as a functioning unit while they limped toward 1988's ever more strained *Tender Prey* album. *Your Funeral . . . My Trial* remains an album of shadow imagery, the vital memories of love, body horror, and betrayal from a person no longer living.

With his more recent albums Cave would admit to aspects of his homelife with Susie becoming inspirations for his songs, from the more oblique elements of the love song; the private emotion universalized, to the deeply private minutiae of a relationship. In the *20,000 Days on Earth* film Cave describes himself as a cannibal, devouring detail and expanding them into greater symbols and set pieces, admitting to his own surprise when they seem to work their way into his songs: "I feel that I know her better in the songs that I write about her than I do in real life." Cave noted the turns of phrase employed by his wife, occasionally adopting her voice alongside his own to become a third perspective, staging mirrors through his songs in which to better see himself.

Susie Cave spoke of being a visitor who walks in and out of her husband's lyrics, much like the scene on the album cover of *Push the Sky Away*. Cave cites the specific experience of the shifting of furniture in "The Sorrowful Wife," a seemingly throwaway line that becomes the emotional fulcrum of the track. In reality it is a much more benign nervous habit of Susie's that Cave noted was sometimes considered an outlet for unfulfilled creative impulses. He joked that he would return from a tour and find that the couple's entire bedroom furniture had been shifted to another room, like a shipwrecked house.[25]

For her part, Susie Cave would reject the outright definition of herself as a muse, admitting that Cave's songs "look after me," perhaps embedding the depth of their emotional bond, though not without criticizing the precarious and brittle position occupied by any muse: "To be honest, I find the word muse to be a little demeaning. I haven't really got time to be anyone's muse." Cave's most romantic songs exist at a midway point of consolation, where each partner holds their side to meet the other, love bridges an invisible divide.

Cave would acknowledge his own concerns with the term: "I have never been all that comfortable with the term 'muse' either. I think the problem with the word is that traditionally 'muse' feels female and takes a secondary position, as the source of inspiration for the male artist—a kind of sanctifying of a subordinate role." Though he would admit that both he and his wife fulfill an inspiring role in each other's lives, with Susie offering thoughts on his songs and Cave looking over fabrics for The Vampire's Wife fashion projects.

Cave would worry about desertion of the creative muse in the classical Greek meaning of a wan spirit who gifts otherworldly inspiration to mortals. If too closely defined "she" would feel taken for granted and simply disappear, the spur of fear behind "There She Goes My Beautiful World," which Cave would describe as "a protest against loss of potency."[26] But beyond the relatively simplistic figure of woman-as-muse Cave's interest becomes more complex, invested in damaged people whose idea of love skirts the limits of obsession. This moves even his most romantic songs toward a darker place, where abject desire becomes a growing need for possession and ownership, and where his feelings are unrequited, curdling into the vengeful nature of hatred. From the earliest Bad Seeds albums Cave attracted accusations of misogyny in which women, beloved or benign, were often the victims of his songs. The deflection through characters veers toward a kind of corrosive chauvinism where the lovelorn voyeur destroys the one he claims to love above all else.[27]

In her book *Apple: Sex, Drugs, Motherhood and the Recovery of the Feminine* (2022), the journalist Antonella Gambotto-Burke, then using the pseudonym Antonella Black, recounts her interview with Cave for *Zigzag* magazine in January 1985 following a gig at London's Electric Ballroom. Making explicit reference to his drug use, the interview began badly with Cave shooting up in the toilet and emerging with blood on his sleeve. She described the challenge of trying to speak to him: "the drooling, the slurring, the nodding off" along with his aggressive junk-sick tone. He objected to her line of questioning about the death of his father and his relationship with Anita Lane. Shifting from bad to worse the interview collapses, along with Cave, into a series of broken thoughts and unfinished sentences.

In a later interview with Bill Black for *Sounds*, Cave, as if in revenge, would refer to Antonella as a "a grub-street groupie" who arrived at the interview ready to make a pass at him, failing at this, her write-up devolved into a character assassination. This claim was later disproved by Antonella's interview tape, causing an apology from *Sounds*. While this might have been more of an exchange between journalists and their factual integrity, in Gambotto-Burke's view, the personal and professional damage against her was already done, with Cave acting as "an abusive narcissist and a liar." She would be mentioned in Cave's broadside single "SCUM" aimed at her then partner and fellow housemate to Cave and Anita Lane, the journalist Mat Snow. She notes, "Cave claimed that he was our 'creator' and lied that I'd performed fellatio on him." Following the account of the interview written by Ian Johnston in his biography of Cave, *Bad Seed*, Gambotto-Burke, then nineteen years old to Cave's twenty-eight, felt she had been written off as a crying, unprofessional little girl. Snow would remember her being deeply disappointed by the experience of meeting Cave, who had been a musical hero to her.

At the most turbulent part of his career in the mid- to late 1980s, mired in the depths of addiction, Cave observed that much of his songwriting, like a section of his audience, drew upon "troubled women," such as the lost girl of "Deanna" and the murderous Loretta in "Curse of Millhaven."[28] Driven by the need to sin, break the law, and live outside of social conventions, Cave suggested that listeners found a kind of wish fulfillment of themselves in the songs. This was perhaps also a vague form of tribute to fans he no doubt courted as part of the hypereducated bad boy persona thrust upon him and often fully embraced. In "John Finn's Wife" a small town's fascination with a mysterious and beautiful tattooed woman, a sexually provocative figure surrounded by an air of infidelity, she inspires lust in men and enmity in their women. The tension explodes into ugly violence, as if by the click of her fingers, descending into a barroom brawl of the wild west saloon style with high drama of straining orchestral strings and frantic guitar as the community turns itself inside out—all eyes remain fixed upon her.

Cave referred to such tracks as picaresque set pieces of vulgar humanity, but delivered in a jaunty, bawdy fashion well served by the vigorous intensity of The Bad Seeds' music: "I do have a love of violent literature, and I do get a kick out of writing violent lyrics as well. I guess when those two things get together, love and violence, it makes for some nasty songwriting. But I never see that as being gloomy or depressing. I see it as quite lively."[29] While the craft is real, we should not take him, or the song, entirely at their word. Cave stated a preference for "man-sized violence"[30] against women as a more shocking creative event but was quick to point out that at least in metaphorical terms men and women suffered just as much in his songs through both their innocence and the wages of their sins.

The subject of sexualized conflict and violence would return in a 2009 discussion with author David Peace about Cave's new novel *Bunny Munro*. Cave would repeat his frustration with the myopic limitations of the term "misogynistic," this time used to condemn the book, where bad literature and moral corruption were thought to be *sympatico*. In the same way Cave would often be damned by critics for the nihilistic scenarios in his songs, charged with exploiting shock value, of style over content, something Cave did not entirely resist.[31] The book, of course, delighted many hardcore fans, though *Bunny Munro* is less of an anti-hero than the lead characters of Cave's songs, so often made synonymous with their singer. Bunny is an outright failure without mystique, his shabby life devoid of romantic adventure—he offers the conflicted view of a deeply flawed single father doing his haphazard best while struggling with the fallout of his own amoral demons.[32]

When Cave is asked whether or not "there's a little bit of Bunny Munro in all of us?" he responded frankly: "There is in me." Cave pointed out that many male readers could identify with the fantasizing thought patterns of Bunny's internal monologue that became his jilted worldview: "So I guess what I was trying to do with the Bunny Munro character was to create something that was monstrous, or became more monstrous as the book went on and that we recognized and we were shocked to find that we even sympathized with." Cave recognized that the casual chauvinism of his protagonist, often amusing, at times hilarious, would dip into darker misogyny but offered the book as his effort in expressing, exploring, and confronting that mindset, an objective author taking "a good look at it." For Cave, the book becomes an exploration of the crisis of postmillennial masculinity, where some men found a need to reassert baser attitudes. Cave argues that there is a "predatory" instinct in our DNA that men must learn to control and overcome in order to live within society. Whether this process is defined simply as a form of self-denial or emotional growth, it manifests as an expression of our deeper humanity.

Cave would be at pains to point out that his songs were creative exercises; he was not the characters within them, though they certainly expressed his preoccupations with sex and violence repeated across his work and the collaborations he is drawn to, where love and morbidity are so often intertwined.[33] Distancing the author (himself) from the book he pointed to a harsh reality behind his invented protagonist: "I think what's in Bunny Munro is innate in all men, but we learn other things. We learn to be intimate and empathetic. The predatory way and violence of the character are innate. It's in our DNA. It's in our horrible reptilian brains. It's not going to go away."[34]

Bunny Munro became Cave's argument that in spite of his character's distasteful attitudes he should be allowed the same creative leeway as other transgressive fiction authors (such as Bret Easton Ellis, after initial controversy surrounding his book *American Psycho* it would later be acknowledged for its enduring literary worth), in some way validated or proven "right" in their willingness to go further out than the writers before them.[35] As Cave would state in a 2022 interview with *The New Statesman*, art that pushed boundaries in form or theme has its place in breaking new ground, even as it sometimes brusquely dragged sensitive issues into touch: "I don't think art should be in the hands of the virtuous," pushing back against a forced perspective that limits creative potential through moral censure.[36]

These darker influences are suggested in 1985's "Say Goodbye to the Little Girl Tree." The crooked guitar riff and slide guitar reveal their menace slowly, while bounding bass tips us into unhinged territory of a roving eye and twitching, restless hands. A warped sense of love finds a man struggling to contain his terrible desires for a girl-child who may or may not be his daughter. The "daddy" figure of the song is torn between protection and exploitation, hinting toward the pedophilic, and later incestuous, desire of *Lolita*. As Nabokov the lepidopterist (butterfly collector) had his own passion for the delicate, sensual form of butterflies, Cave's song hums to the tune of the nymphet creature in the novel and its emotionally encumbered narrator, Humbert Humbert, who is struck by the downy hair on her skin, caught between vestiges of childhood and nascent adolescence.[37]

Cave's narrator is torn between wanting *his* girl to remain the idealized child but also to assume some male prerogative in his desire to have sex with her and ease his carnal stress, knowing he can never prevent the inevitable loss of his perfect girl's virginity, he perhaps wishes to take matters into his own hands. The song hints that he might feel the need to kill her, walk away, or even end his own life by hanging, of course, out of assumed guilt and in order to keep himself away from the girl. This is the point at which any standard notion of love is overwhelmed by ego and twisted desire, the need to contain or destroy something (someone) beautiful in order to possess it. Either way, her fate realizes the death of innocence.[38]

As with Bunny Munro, Cave neither condones nor condemns his dark male figures; their actions simply express their nature, showing them for what they are without denying their feelings—all too human. For the serial killers and heartsick murderers motivated by a twisted kind of love, he lays their crimes bare, but with no small romantic embellishment in the telling of the tale. It is interesting that Cave and Warren Ellis would soundtrack the 2022 Netflix series *Dahmer–Monster: The Jeffrey Dahmer Story*, the account of a man driven by the need to perform acts of murder and taunted by desire as he struggles with sexual and emotional intimacy. Where Cave's characters tend toward larger-than-life extroverts exploding into short, jagged vignettes, Dahmer's real life exposes the "born evil" introvert, increasingly alienated from society and perpetually unfulfilled by 'normal' life.[39]

Back in 1986 Cave seemed willing to step into the role of agitator, neither apologizing nor ducking the charge of misogyny: "It's so obvious. Still, I've only recently realized that all my songs do have a streak of that."[40] In a tour brochure of that same era he refers to himself, no doubt with tongue firmly in cheek, as the "misogynist." Much later in 1998, "I've never been annoyed about being accused of misogyny," he says, "because it's probably true. At times I have felt a seething hatred towards particular women in my life, and at the time of writing the song, quite possibly towards all womanhood as well. If you're going to censor your thoughts because they're offensive or unpolitically correct, then you're not being true to yourself."[41]

Speaking in a 2006 interview Cave flipped more toward frustration with the banality of the charge: How could the listener *not* hear the misogyny of those earlier songs, when it was so blatant and unhidden? Cave argues that the darkest elements of his lyrics express a kind of hard truth about the world, a more honest expression of the duality and contradictions of human behavior. Cave did not repent or seek to defend his themes because he felt they were prima facie and not simply one-dimensional. As with the question of the muse, Cave would later seem to deflect, defuse, and demure, embracing the shaping force of context of the times, which have radically altered since. Instead, he holds up his hands to profess mystification at the wonder of women, the "lovely creatures" whose blood and bones were used as grist to his songwriting mill. Taking the position of being brought to his knees at the foot of woman as inchoate mother, muse, and lover seems a slightly faux-naive defense, with adoration putting Cave at a distance from criticism.

Speaking from a position of further deference, Caves admits to a fondness for Valerie Solanas' SCUM Manifesto (Society for Cutting-Up Men),[42] where she referred to the male creature as a "walking abortion," damaged and deficient: "[Solanas] wrote a very angry and very precise portrait of what she considered the male to be: something between a human and an ape; an unresponsive blob only concerned with physical sensation and without the capacity for empathy or self-knowledge or intimacy, and at the same time full of hatred and jealousy and shame and guilt."[43] Cave allowed that "her description is beautiful and on some level, I think, entirely accurate." Elsewhere Cave would align himself to intellectuals who became nonconforming feminists such as Germaine Greer and Camille Paglia. Admitting to the social dominance wrought by male entitlement, Cave seems to undermine patriarchal control. Though in his songs, and perhaps in spite of himself, man is often shown at his worst, he nonetheless remains on top.[44]

For all his earnest praise of love, Cave paints a similar image of romance as something that both ruins and rescues us from life, echoing the doomed romance of his songwriting forebear Leonard Cohen. There is rarely such a thing as a straight love ballad in Cave's music; tainted by conflict and lascivious overkill, he finds that love must always bear its thorns. On the album *Let Love In* (1994) Cave forces the listener to question the value and meaning of love, where the emotional exposure of letting someone into his life left him open to being hurt.

In a 1994 interview Cave would explain that the *Let Love In* album was an expression of the bonds of married family life and the ongoing struggle to live up to its demands.[45] On "Thirsty Dog" he paints a stark picture of the constant push and pull of marital arguments exacerbated by alcohol and the drowning of further sorrows, marking the battle lines of a four-year war begun since his marriage to Viviane Carneiro in 1990.[46] Cave plays on the old phrase "Love is never having to say you're sorry," making so many half-hearted and sarcastic apologies the word loses all meaning. Though not always living in domestic bliss, Cave would praise the security of marriage and the obligation of being a parent to his son Luke to steer him further away from addiction, perhaps hoping that family might save him from himself.

The album's heavy themes suggest Cave was undergoing some second thoughts about the duty of love, and his willingness to be loved in return—from fidelity to selflessness. On "I Let Love In" Cave lays himself bare; a victim to the contrariness of past loves or his newfound submission? He leans on heavy metaphors of being gagged, tied, castrated even; where the spiritual weight of love has brought him low, toward the madness of self-abasement. The language of spiritual bondage and the violence of emotional abuse would return in a more melancholic light across the pained confessionals of *The Boatman's Call*. Cave finds himself sinking into the trials of openhearted obligation toward a new kind of loneliness. Elsewhere the us-against-the-world stance of "The Ship Song"[47] presages the sinking apocalypse of "Straight to You" but also shows how love immures us to other experiences. On later records Cave seems to reflect more on how this binding, especially with the wrong person, can become a trap. The knife that first breached Cave's hard exterior turns from blessing into curse, "I Let Love In." It ends by reaching through to the heart. As with Cave's views on the challenge of faith, love is expressed more as an open wound that leaves him permanently vulnerable.

In "Anthrocene" Cave reflects upon love as a blissful state that always lives under the threat of loss, articulating the difficult knowledge that the people we hold closest are those we are most afraid of losing. Cave would refer to the Spanish poet Federico Garcia Lorca's definition of duende, which refers to the heightened state of feeling bound to honest creative expression. This struggle it speaks to a deeper melancholy the inherent sadness of the human condition, combined with its great joys and wonders. With the shared passion and sincerity of the songwriter, Lorca's idea presents the affirmation that to love is also to lose, such that the very precariousness of life, love, and liberty are the things most worth fighting for.[48]

In Cave's more recent songs love is vulnerable to loss and becomes something precious and truly sacred, to treasure and defend. On "Love Letter" (2001) Cave shows how easily the language of love fails us as we trip over our words, where so much feeling cannot be written down or is otherwise left unspoken; elsewhere we are made vulnerable, stumbling into dead zones of unrequited feeling. He sets this against a gentle cascading run of piano notes that lure the listener into his plight, even in melancholy or because of it, he manages to express as much yearning as he does regret. The song's mode speaks to the very writing of a letter meant to console, apologize, and reassure both the lover and the object of their love. Cave laments the many times when words come out the wrong way and cannot be withdrawn once they are said. Where the letter is meant to heal the rift between lovers it could as well be a silent prayer met by deaf ears, its emotional cadence gone to ashes unread.[49]

So many of Cave's love songs draw upon the twist-turning push and pull of relationships, particularly in the tragedy of older country ballads. At love's extremes the heart has to be broken in order to understand what is most important to us. Cave's 1986 cover of Tim Rose's "Long Time Man" (1967) throws us straight into the aftermath of a man who murdered his wife and now wanders from town to town telling his story, the song's wounded swagger is fueled by his regret that sometimes love is only realized too late.

If *Murder Ballads* was the consummation of violence and its excoriating power of aliveness, then *The Boatman's Call* is the language of love only fully realized in its aftermath.[50] Where before Cave told wild stories, secondhand narratives transmuted through larger-than-life characters, he now admitted defeat, binding himself to his music, deaf to his critics and ready to go down with the ship. Until *Skeleton Tree*'s haunting passage of grief and desolation it would remain his most openly autobiographical album that would edge him closer toward the position of establishment singer-songwriter status.[51] As with "Long Time Man," the revelation of what is lost comes too late; Cave can only find the words in praise of love once it has passed him by. He now exists in the rueful clarity beyond the twilight of his relationship; the good and the bad twinned through hindsight, there are no new horizons beyond the vacancy of its ending.

The Boatman's Call is often considered a piano-dominated album, leading to the more recent musical restraint of The Bad Seeds. It remains Cave's private instrument for composing songs and the driving force that leads much of the band's creative input.[52] *The Boatman's Call* initiated a new kind of band dynamic where Cave would bring his playing to the fore and sometimes move it back into the shadows to let the band shine,[53] an approach that would flourish on *Abattoir Blues/The Lyre of Orpheus*, *Push the Sky Away*, and *Skeleton Tree*: "It also pointed a way to a more poignant, raw, stripped back way of performance—the suspended and barely supported vocal," he continued. "The Bad Seeds, to their eternal credit, stepped back and just let these piano-driven songs be."[54] However, we hear the band all across the record enriching the songs: Conway Savage's organs bring warm spirit to "Brompton Oratory," the sweeping folk slides of acoustic guitar in "West Country Girl," and the subtle dynamics that illuminate the emotional fog of "Idiot Prayer."[55]

Though Cave's later love songs offer consolation that we can learn from our mistakes and how the heart might yet be mended. *The Boatman's Call* finds something of a companion album in 2001's majestically wounded *No More Shall We Part*, recorded after Cave's marriage to Susie Bick in 1999. The conscious return to a fuller band sound, it is still Cave's piano jabs and trills of notes that suffuse it with a forceful but conflicted melancholy. On "Hallelujah" Cave flips the writer's fear of the blank page into sudden horror at the scale of the room-swallowing instrument. Marching through heavy chords he stares back at its black-and-white grinning teeth, daring him to try and play at the cost of losing his hands as a kind of creative castration.[56]

Cave would later consider *The Boatman's Call* an act of oversharing, a breakup album that straddles the disintegration of Cave's marriage to Viviane Carneiro as it bleeds into his brief but intense four-month relationship with PJ Harvey. In the video for their 1996 duet "Henry Lee," part murder ballad part love song, Cave and Harvey dance about one another in a blur of long black hair, pale skin, and funereal suits. In close-framed shots they cast a tangle of fraying limbs touching, holding, and breaking apart; throwing downturned glances their lips come close but never touch, they breathlessly mouth the word "moan," their incestuous motion becomes a subconscious act of mirroring. Within the subtle slip of hands, an invisible knife is passed back and forth, neither wishing to step forward as the other's killer, until Cave switches out of the young man's body into third person and makes his short stabbing actions to camera, punctuating the song's murderous line: "She plugged him through and through." Unfurling from passion into death, the curse of jealousy is also revealed to be a lament for love lost.[57]

In a 2008 *Guardian* interview, Cave explained that it was in the process of making the three-minute music video that he and Harvey were falling in love, the fiction merged with reality in real-time: "Fucking hell! That's a one-take video. Nothing is rehearsed at all. We didn't know each other well, and this thing happens while we're making the video. There's a certain awkwardness, and afterwards it's like, oh . . ."[58] Almost as soon as it had begun their affair was over just four months later. Seeing the couple seem to fall in love in the video, knowing it was not to last now, makes it all the stranger and harder to watch, like we have intruded on a private moment. The viewer can only "stare as the wounds open up on their hearts."[59]

Cave would remember that as much as they had drifted apart into their own distinct musical worlds, there was more distance driven between them by his heroin use. Harvey called to break up with Cave over the phone; he was equally shocked and numbed, making the half-hearted joke that he almost dropped his syringe in surprise.[60] He would cite addiction as a split interest pushing them apart, indicating that Harvey gave up on *him*—and was perhaps right to do so. The lyrics to "Far from Me" seem to refer to this incident, with Cave certain that the split was coming before it happened. Harboring a difficult self-knowledge, his feigned surprise was only to make light of its true impact. The song imagines Harvey's voice traveling down the line as a distant call across a great sea, the ever-expanding gulf between them.

At the time Cave decided that the breakup was all one-sided. Abandoned at his most vulnerable; he mourned it as a kind of death. Cave would note in 2020 that love is a perilous thing "and travels surely towards its devastation. A broken heart—that grief of love—is always love's true destination. This is the covenant of love." The breakup would fill him with new reserves of "lunatic energy" where *The Boatman's Call* features some of Cave's most personal and emotionally direct songs, with "Green Eyes," "Black Hair," and "West Country Girl" invoking PJ Harvey in both body and spirit. Cave is still audibly in thrall to her and now openly grieves her absence. Though the album marked the rise of a new maturity in Cave's technical songwriting, its tenor also revealed an emotional shortfall.

Hanging over the songs is a sense of fatalism that paints Cave as the victim of the relationship; suffused with the tough love of sometimes brutal honesty, it is a two-handed expression of praise and condemnation. For many listeners, the album resonates with their own broken-hearted backlash, striking out against someone they still love and care about. This sparks a knowing self-loathing within Cave, through the songs he sees the worst of himself brought to the fore.

Cave feels taken apart in a character assassination exposing the depth of his bitterness which he counterpoints by singing sweet praises of loving moments. The massed recriminations of "Idiot Prayer," while masquerading as revenge fantasy against the former lover, also reflect back upon him, where love "takes two to tango" they are equally condemned to meet again one day—in hell.[61]

Set against this emotional turmoil, Cave would undergo the drawn-out growing pains of more trips to drug rehabilitation centers, uniting several strains of autobiography into a strained confessional.[62] On "Where Do We Go Now But Nowhere" Cave is served a cake full of glass, bleach, and his old razorblades; we feel the ache in the pit of the stomach caught between sickness and knifelike anxiety with all of our little hostilities returned to us. Undergoing detox in a sterile, clinical, loveless place, he is forced to confront the parallels between withdrawal from heroin and being left without love.

In an almost knee-jerk response driven by underlying sadness Cave would admit to an acidic touch in the lyrics that surprised even him: "I think *The Boatman's Call* is in a certain way a rather cruel album. Some songs can hurt the ones whom I feel hurt by. In 'Far from Me,' for example—my favorite song, I think it's the best I've ever written—there's such a strong unconscious violence. . . ."[63] But in this last album there's still a lot of living pain, and it's incredible. It's incredible to tour with such living stuff."[64]

In 2003 he would confess to a degree of disgust with the album as being too autobiographical; putting too much of himself into the songs he is overexposed, perhaps even sentimentally "showing his belly." Cave would again find "his hand forced" by a sense of urgency behind the songs, emphasizing the cathartic power of the album as a combined divorce and "breakup" record.[65] Writing in 2021 Cave realized that his "disgust" was simply a reaction to his own feelings of fear and shame exposed on the record.[66] From the stark black and white of Anton Corbijn's cover image to the album's title we find the anguished "boatman" alone at sea. These songs are his call to the shore waiting for his lover to summon him back, but knowing he will never hear her voice again.[67]

For Cave, the love song presents the ultimate form of worship, becoming a force that expresses the best of us. Borne from the physical world but always reaching toward a transcendent feeling that leaves one floating a few inches just above the earth. Cave acknowledged the enduring power of the lovers' gaze, a deeper connection that persists long after they have parted ways. On *The Boatman's Call* song "Green Eyes" he frames PJ Harvey's searching stare as one of the defining images of her, evoking the briefly snatched looks they share cutting across the video performance of "Henry Lee" less than a year before. On her 1998 song "Angelene" Harvey would explore her own image through Cave's eyes, with the lines "Rose is my color and white / Pretty mouth, and green my eyes" noting the bright red lipstick she often wore as an armor of exaggerated femininity—vulnerable but also tough—taking up her place in the world.[68] Perhaps in Cave's songs she is seeing herself painted as the objectified beauty or a figure of blind devotion; either way the song becomes a subtle arrest of her own narrative on the brief affair.[69]

In many of his recent love songs we see Cave celebrating his wife Susie by praising the reflective power of her green eyes that reveal him to himself. The love song goes some way toward bridging the inexpressible and inchoate sensations of romantic connection[70] impossible to contain within words. Cave's music continues to shape and revisit moments in the shared lives through which their relationship is refracted and intensified, like sunlight striking a mirror.

On the album cover of *Push the Sky Away* we see Susie Cave skip across Nick's eyeline. His constant and adoring stare is realized in her as a sustaining force that anchors both hope and desire, reminding Cave of his own need to love and be loved in return.[71] Much like "Wide Lovely Eyes," where Cave evokes the depth of his wife's eyes, bright bottle green, glass dissolved into the infinity of sea and sand.

Writing in 2022, Cave would explain the formative power of the loving stare: "My safe space is in the regard of my wife's gaze. By this I mean when I look into the eyes of my wife I find a beauty, and this beauty has a moral value, of goodness; a goodness that manifests as a kind of benevolence. . . . Put simply, we see each other, and through that seeing we want the best for each other, without condition—she has me and I have her."[72] This need for mutual understanding and belonging is implied in a passage that Cave quotes from Antoine de Saint-Exupéry's *The Little Prince* (a children's book for adults, if ever there was one), where the prince tries to make friends with a wild fox, the fox explains, "One only understands the things that one tames."[73]

Later Cave points to the world, in dire and urgent need of the healing power of love, where small acts of kindness can become a saving grace among life's challenges. Love serves to ground him and return him to a sense of homecoming. This is a concept absent from earlier albums—the rootless, wild, fated crazy love. Cave later welcomes a more reciprocal notion within the symbolic unity of marriage: "You will discover that love, radical love, is a kind of supercharged aliveness."[74] This opens us up to awe and wonder, even though love is doomed to end, that makes it all the more precious.[75] Now the wiser lovers realize a private chaos between them, held within the storm of life's endless vortex.

EGON TSCHIRCH, *SONG OF SONGS*, 1923.

BAD BLOOD

Of man's first disobedience, and the fruit
Of that forbidden tree, whose mortal taste
Brought death into the world
Sing heavenly muse.
—MILTON, *PARADISE LOST*

"I am not afraid to die." The last words of a condemned man forged in a fever of howling, shivering violins and hammered piano chords, wild quicksilver guitar thrashes overhead as throbbing bass is drawn ever tighter into a narrow loop. A relentless lyric runs away like a racing heartbeat fighting to keep pace and be heard above the noise of a song that is almost all chorus with no breaks or free breaths, each line whips back around the staccato marching drums that push relentlessly ahead. A ruthlessly linear song surges ever onward as if trying to avoid the prisoner's inevitable fate so the listener becomes tangled up in his spiraling tale.

"The Mercy Seat" is one of Cave's most notorious and beloved songs, a sermon delivered from atop a jilted throne of blood-steeped gold, tangled wire, fierce heat and brittle chill—it becomes an affirmation of existence for a man held in the jaws of death.[1] The song is haunted by the disembodied voice of a convict sentenced to the death penalty; we are never told his crime but are left to assume it must be murder. The biblical image of "a tooth for a tooth" demands blood for blood under the all-seeing eye of God.[2]

The accused man's speech is full of broken and conflicted thoughts. Determined to rise above the difficult self-knowledge of his own twisted nature, he declares that he told the truth, avoiding the shadow of guilt he cannot admit to himself. Cave plays with the character's ambiguity; for all his strong words, this is a man with nothing left to lose (but his immortal soul). The listener is left to make up their own mind.

Part of the song's feverish intensity comes from the sensation of being boiled alive within the accused's "burning head," expressing his most intense final thoughts as they are eaten away out of his consciousness. Ultimately "The Mercy Seat" becomes an anthem of resigned defiance, pushing back against the moral authority of God, and even his existence. The accused man strides fearlessly across the boundaries of society to the outer reaches of mortality, betting against the limitations of justice to uphold the good and combat (or prevent) evil in a world full of random cruelty.[3]

Blixa Bargeld noted Cave was reading many books about serial killers at the time, perhaps also the letters of Ned Kelly, a bushranger who fronted the notorious Kelly Gang.[4] A folk hero Robin Hood figure, he embodied the "wild colonial boy" of popular song.[5] His story echoes that of many other figures from history such as Buffalo Bill or Billy the Kid, blossoming into unreal pop culture figures whose legend often far exceeds the truth. Cave absorbed some of Kelly's rebel vernacular into "The Mercy Seat," imbued with a fiery righteousness and forbidding command: "I am a Widow's Son, outlawed and my orders must be obeyed."[6] As written in the eight-thousand-word *Jerilderie Letter*, Ned Kelly gives a final testimonial blaming his rogue life on a corrupt police system and discrimination against Irish settlers and ex-convicts. In a country still emerging into its colonial identity, Australia had imported the same racial and class divisions so sharply drawn by English culture.

The first few lines that open Milton's classic epic poem, *Paradise Lost*, speak about the fall of man manifest in humanity's crimes of murder. In his songs Cave is less concerned with the idea of 'pure' evil and the rule of God's law, than in actions against other people; seeing life as a daily mass of contradictions. In Red Hand File #196 he argues, "There is no problem of evil. There is only a problem of good." Goodness seems only to emerge in spite of bad and terrible things, not as a corrective. Indeed, what we might call "evil" actions are not prescribed by some other power; individual responsibility remains. As with the tragic farce of Humbert Humbert in *Lolita*; broken by his need for illicit love,[7] his desires have consequences. While Cave's songs of punishment don't suggest that the bad will always suffer, he spends more time in exposing the fallout of their misdeeds, and in that sense the songs throw up moral issues, without passing judgment or demanding answers. The great strength behind Cave's lyrics is his boilerplate ambiguity, giving him moral flex but also a continued interrogating force behind the songs.

Cave's earlier misanthropy and pessimism often indulge wrong against right, where the "good" person is at once both a sucker and a victim. His songs show a creative mind drawn toward aggressive tragedy: "I don't deny any feelings of happiness just because I don't write about them. For me, there's just something more powerful in Man's ultimate punishments—whether they're on a humanist level or a more mystical level—than in his ultimate rewards. The rewards of happiness and contentment and security, I see as mostly drawn out of a routine of things. And they have no aesthetic interest for me, or much lasting value."[8]

The opening lines that begin *Paradise Lost* speak as much about the fall of man through Adam and Eve's temptation as they do to man's crimes against humanity and the first intimations toward original sin.[9] The literary critic George Steiner suggested that the twentieth century would gradually reveal the upended balance of natural Godly law: "If, in the Judaic perception, the language of the Adamic was that of love, the grammars of fallen man are those of the legal code." Adam and Eve's shame condemns them to mortality. The first unconscious rebellion of mankind becomes the hinge of Cave's 1990 song from the eponymous album *The Good Son*. The song begins with a laconic chant, "one more man gone,"[10] which John Mulvey hears as "The Bad Seeds' chorus of rude mechanicals, aping the chain gang ardor of an American spiritual." Cave uses the biblical story of Cain and Abel from Genesis 4:1–18 to explore humanity's first confrontation with murder, setting the pattern of original sin for mankind to follow.[11] The first two sons of Adam and

Eve are Cain and Abel. Cain is a hardworking tiller, whose offerings to God are rejected. The eponymous good son Abel is favored both by his father and God, who only asks that he be righteous and resist the temptations of sin. Cain jealously murders his brother as if to take his place as the only son. When God asks Cain where Abel is he responds with the immortal line: "I do not know. Am I my brother's keeper?" Cain lies to God, knowing his brother is buried in the fields that he had worked on all of his life, just as Abel's "blood cries out from the ground." Cain's declaration divorces him from his fraternal bond, denying the lifeblood shared with his brother, the one who he feels has always moved upon his heel. His outspoken questioning is a choice, a conscious break from God's word and his grace.

"The Good Son" can seem ambiguous, dividing sympathy between both Cain and Abel. Cain, for a time, does the right thing by his family as any loyal son should, but eventually snaps as he is doubly tested by the favor of God and his father, Adam. Abel will always remain the innocent victim, the chosen son who was allowed the easier life of the shepherd. It is Cain's struggle as the firstborn to endure his second-best status where Cave finds, "It's a malign star by which the good son's kept," suggesting his thwarted future.[12]

Again, life for one brother seems to default to death for the other, their fates intertwined. The story presents a stark view of unnatural death, where Abel is killed before his time. But in exposing our more animalistic human behaviors, the story helps to polarize our notion of good and evil and punishment. In the story's aftermath Cain's woes are intensified. He must carry the burden of guilt for all humankind, wearing the "mark" of Cain.[13] God decrees that no one shall lay a hand upon him so that he cannot be murdered in turn. He persists as a martyr cursed to life as a symbol of the eternal punishment of wrongdoing. While in the coda of "The Good Son" Cave and The Bad Seeds again chant the line "one more man gone, one more man" . . . their repetition marks the continued line of murders that follow in Cain's wake.

After the fratricide of Cain and Abel, we later find Abraham ordered by God to put his son Isaac to death as an example of obeying his will. Bob Dylan offers Abe's response to God's command with the throwaway quip, "man, you must be putting me on." The test of faith is sacrifice, where the father would rather die in his son's place, though it is not his choice to make.

"Foi Na Cruz," the first track of *The Good Son*, is drawn from a Brazilian hymn that roughly translates as "it happened on the cross," echoing the chanting pattern of the title track.[14] After the death of Abel we can leap forward to the murder of Jesus, where even after his crucifixion to take on the burden of man's sin, murder continues to happen again and again. Jesus' death is referenced in Proverbs as a powerful moment of procrastination, given to doubt and pain while awaiting the forgiveness of love. Given the song's stark title we are expected to respond to Jesus' love expressed in one (final) day of sacrifice with gratitude and through the affirmation of all life. In his lyrics Cave nods to Leonard Cohen's *Songs of Love and Hate*, "a little love, a little hate," a motion which soon turns into trickery and deceit. The tension of extremes that life demands means that sometimes we blind ourselves to love, other times we are blinded by it.

A primal surge of red inside and out runs through Cave's discography, a rich seam of menace and dread, with his deep red shirt on the cover of *Tender Prey* expressing the bleeding heart of the artist and the violence yet to come. "Jack the Ripper killed women in real life—Nick Cave kills people in his music."[15] This persistent almost obsessive theme rendered the charge of violent hypersexualized misogyny in Cave's music more real, right through into the mid-1990s. Cave began his slow descent into tales of murder with The Birthday Party's "Deep in the Woods" (1983), the knife unleashed from its sheath to bring chaos; Cave offers the pun from "rags to stitches" carving letters into his victim's body.[16]

Cave would remember his father reading him the murder scene of Fyodor Dostoyevsky's 1866 novel *Crime and Punishment* in which the protagonist Raskolnikov kills two people, escapes undetected, and is haunted by his actions: "When I grew a little older my father read me the murder scene in this book and said 'this is what violent literature should be like, son.' He was right."[17] Combined with his reading of *Lolita* we can see sparks flying between twin poles of great literature

for Cave, merging into an artistic fascination with the power of life and erasure of death, where procreation and murder dance between two elemental states.

This sheer bloodiness is partly expressed through the twist and turning of love songs, what music critic Anwen Crawford referred to as Cave's *lustmord* or "sexual murder" of obsession spilling over into violence. She observes that the character of "From Her to Eternity" ultimately blames his infatuation with the woman upstairs on her, as an enchanting siren, "nagging me like a *shrew*."[18] Where his characters predominantly kill women out of love, an attitude to which Cave would later express some regret without rejecting his songs, Crawford finds a career built upon a "metaphorical pile of female corpses."[19]

She writes partially in response to the journalist Peter Conrad, who in his 2009 article "The Good Son" draws out the exaggerations of Cave's persona and his continued fascination with murder, while casting a thoughtful critical eye over his use of language.[20] Occasionally Conrad exemplifies the worst kind of fan who buys into the wholesale myth of the artist through his songs, himself exhibiting casual misogyny and lazy glorification of real murders referring to the "whore-slaughtering Yorkshire Ripper, Peter Sutcliffe." In 1988 Cave would already speak with some regret, knowing he had overloaded his misogyny to the point of parody: "I feel that I've misrepresented women in my songs, and I've actually misrepresented the way I feel about them. I invented a type of woman that I used artistically in order to dump all my ill feelings and suspicions on."[21] Though this admission would not yield a drastic shift in Cave's lyrical direction for some years, the solo artist Anna Calvi would see the extremes of his subject matter exposing deeper vulnerability: "He's honest about the madness of masculinity, showing all the dark corners of it."[22]

Gnashing his teeth again and again at the persistence of evil, Cave pushes our faces up to the ugliest side of human behaviors pitching the question of a fixed human nature where some are "born to be bad," killers by design, and for others to become victims.[23] This sparks the argument for a kind of determinism rather than people being swayed by malign influences. In "O'Malley's Bar" Cave is forced toward a full stop, causing him to wonder plainly on the freewheeling riff of the murderer: "If I have no free will / then how can I be morally culpable?" For all the fatalism that seems to burn through Cave's songs of death and destruction, he asks whether or not the most extreme suffering might still have meaning, even when it becomes surreal and absurd.

On "Up Jumped the Devil" Cave allows that some are born under a lucky star (a benevolent eye?), something they might squander, or fail to catch, where others are cursed by the same sign hanging over them as a signifier of future doom.[24] The song presents the Devil as the very real "bad side" of our human character that leaps to the fore, taking hold of the soul, admitting to the human capacity for evil and leading us astray toward poor moral choices. In keeping with the cartoonish renditions of the soul with an angel and a demon steering us left and right at the shoulders, here he is the dancing, jeering voice of temptation which the song's protagonist surrenders himself to, like a bad friend you let drag you from bar to bar to drug deal to strip club to accidental robbery to skipping out on a taxi fare to spending the night in a jail cell—even though you know you've already had enough.

Cave often preaches transgression, where the extreme individual acts outside of society's boundaries as a kind of destiny. But this does not assume a wider innocence for the rest of the population, we are all part of a bigger lie that we tell ourselves to escape the guilt and universal culpability for the choices that determine the kind of world we live in. This stark view of the human condition is bound to the original state of nature, still red in tooth and claw, and is expressed in the casual violence of the songs gleefully told by Cave: the still-warm gush of blood from a slashed artery that paints the walls of the listener's brain on "Papa Won't Leave You, Henry."[25]

When asked about the inspiration for the pit of wild and decomposing animals kept by Euchrid's father in *And The Ass . . .* in a 2009 Q&A with author David Peace, Cave quipped "just life, really."[26] Only half-joking, this is the same vision evoked in the "scrape/scratch" chanted lyric of The Birthday Party's "Junkyard,"[27] escaping from out of the womb and then fighting through life. These harsh perspectives affirm the darker edges of his songs, where life as existence is always on the verge of becoming nasty, brutish, and short, demanding ferocious acts of self-creation to find pleasures where we can before everything burns itself out. The younger Cave did not expect a more constructive world-view of life, but equally songs such as "Papa Won't Leave You, Henry" broke him out of his backward-staring solipsism to see the everyday atrocities become routine. Drawing upon his experiences living in Brazil, outside of the assumed safety of the Commonwealth nations and the imperialist control of the United States, Cave's lyric reels off a fantastical horrorshow of head-spinning events, playing on the cliches of Western supremacy: floods, mudslides and chemical fires destroy favelas, secret death squads "disappear" citizens, babies are born without brains, alongside fierce weather of burning sun and torrential rain all combine into a state of disaster becoming something toxic in the water.

Cave continued the resonance of Cain and Abel's tale across *The Good Son* album, but it began with the band name of The Bad Seeds.[28] Mentioned in Cave's list of beloved books, *The Bad Seed* is a 1954 novel by American writer William March telling the story of a young girl, Rhoda, who seems the perfect child, while her mother slowly comes to realize she is a sociopathic killer. A story embodying the biblical warning of the bad apple in the bunch, it seems too good to be true not to be a Nick Cave red herring.[29] The book draws its own title from the parable of the sower from Matthew 13:18–23. The seed that falls on thorny or stony ground, representing a spirit not ready to receive God, will not take root in the heart and flourish. The bad seed either rots or grows crooked, like the thwarted figures of Cave's songs; it thrives in the margins harboring a deep enmity for the rest of "straight" society.[30]

Being interviewed for the *Stranger in a Strange Land* documentary (1987), Cave explored his own attraction to outcasts and freaks: "I have a tendency to look at people and say that they are good people, simply because they are interesting." Attracted more to strength of character than moral direction, we can see that the protagonist of Cave's first novel, Euchrid Eucrow, was, not unlike himself, a man of natural extremes: "What's interesting to me in a character are their faults and their problems. So, I'm basically writing about dysfunctional faulty 'bad' people, if you want to use that word and they're all kind of heroes of mine." It is because of Euchrid's often deluded self-righteousness that he holds a strange fascination over the reader, not because we find him sympathetic, half villain and victim. It is this internal friction that delivers such great drama, and like many of Cave's songs we experience the fallout of bad situations, rarely their causes or even their resolution. Cave would be forced to wonder upon the depth of his characters; whether by nurture or defect they perform terrible acts, is there still a singular "identity" behind it all?

The centerpiece of 1994's *Let Love In* album, "Red Right Hand" begins with someone lighting up a cigarette, like the devil had just stepped onto the soundstage of his own biopic.[31] The song is peppered with creepy organs, theremin, oscillator, timpani, woodblock—throwing every sound-bending mirage into a dusty desert backdrop pitched at the terrible sight of a dark silhouette stepping out from the blood-pitched sun. The stranger wanders into town, which for Cave is really his hometown of Wangaratta, dominated by tough rural work and not much play—except a few bars and a haunted roads stretching far beyond the town's main street—it is Cave's own "Smokestack Lightning" of the mind.[32]

The "Red Right Hand"[33] legend bears the lighting strike of violence piercing the land with a harbinger's sense of fear and doom. The color itself is the echo of blood, the abject horror of the insides turned out; confronting the viewer in the light of an open wound, like Jesus pierced by the spear of destiny on the cross. Blood on the hands becomes the aura of guilt; elsewhere trees rise like hands in prayer, the water of life a stain that won't wash.[34] Cave recalls the knowing cry of Lady Macbeth's "out damn spot" line as she tries to remove the symbol of her lingering guilt, the echo of a difficult memory—not unlike the mark of Cain. Cave refers again to the shock issue of blood in the vengeful "Hand of God" from the *Carnage* album.

Despite the foreboding mood of the lyrics there is still much humor in the surreal music of "Red Right Hand" peaking with a throttled organ solo of B-movie schlock quality alongside a mad oscillator, wurlitzer, and theremin sounds, at once breezy and electric without sounding hi-tech. The struck bell that marks the end of each chorus signals the approach of some great unknown, humming with uncertainty, like a new wave horror it drags the listener deeper into the song.[35]

Elsewhere on "The Mercy Seat" Cave presents the hands as tools of crime, one righteous, the other sinister, like skin gloves for God or Satan, balancing the weight of truth and lies, crime and justice. The "kill hand" is marked "EVIL," the other with the wedding band is baptized "GOOD." The two hands measure out morality against good and bad choices. The mention of the marital ring suggests that perhaps the murderer has killed his wife, killing love in the process. He has nothing to hold on to but death as a welcome release from the continued censure of life.[36]

On the 2021 *Carnage* album Cave would return with renewed ferocity in the shadow of the global pandemic still humming with the threat of annihilation. Both "White Elephant" and "Hand of God" echo the megalomania of Kanye West's 2013 song "I Am a God," flipping the roles of deity and subject into pyromaniac heresy—the pathological character who seems to kill on a whim, or because they think they have the *right* reason: protection of property, self-defense, blood sport, and cruelty. It doesn't seem to matter. The song's heavy gospel ending hints that the self-righteous shooter seems to turn the gun back on themselves, to the point where violence begets violence.[37]

> Not a fig shall I care then for all the devils in hell: it is they who will fear me. . . . I am quite sure I am more afraid of people who are themselves terrified of the devil than I am of the devil himself.
> —TERESA OF ÁVILA, *COMPLETE WORKS ST. TERESA OF ÁVILA*, VOLUME I

Cave himself would luxuriate in the shadow of the bad guy character, always attractive, it offered a new liberty in meanness, a freedom coined by Milton: "better to reign in hell, than serve in Heaven" (thwarted father figures as cruel antiheroes and victims of patricide loom large on several Cave albums). For the love of the murderer, it is since the birth of original sin we are all tainted by the human affect for wrongdoing;

the potential to kill, and to be killed. Knowing what this means, evil becomes a verb, to *do* wrong, rather than to be the personification of a higher metaphorical evil, mundane as murder can become.

Cave would find a counterpoint to the outright criminality exhibited in "The Mercy Seat" in the unassuming small town sheriff Lou Ford from the 1952 crime novel *The Killer Inside Me* by Jim Thompson. Responsible for a series of dark, hard-edged books, Thompson leans toward the shade of law enforcement being as brutal and crooked as the criminals they are supposed to be battling against, inhabiting a mirror world of wickedness, whichever way you turn it. Ford is a womanizer of cold, reptilian zeal who is sometimes overcome by "the sickness," an urge to kill that overcomes his fleeting moral sense. Instead, he plays with people, rolling out cliches and platitudes that only half conceal his calculated contempt for others. This form of lazy punning masking macabre intent also spurs along many of Cave's songs, flipping old-time sayings into more nuanced freakish pronouncements. Thompson's protagonist is condemned to stand astride the law, a dual-edged character who can only function through his derision of the society that holds him back.

Cave would lean heavily on the murder ballad tradition (as a record of folk history ballooned into legend) where facts are recounted quite plainly, and life is often held cheap, but the essence of tragedy was also shown to be meaningful and tough, sometimes absurd to the tipping point of tragedy into comedy. For some this is hollow laughter, but it bears the hallmarks of a knowing self-consciousness willing to shrug off artistic reputation for making great songs; it becomes a traditional murder ballad as overkill.

In a 1988 interview, a journalist suggests Johnny Cash as the godfather of the murder ballad, citing the immortal line from one of his earliest songs "Folsom Prison Blues": "I shot a man in Reno just to watch him die."[38] Cave responds with palpable enthusiasm to a cold-blooded song first released in 1955 and delivered with renewed enthusiasm as part of the 1968 live album *At Folsom Prison* performed in front of a crowd of prison inmates, Cave said: "I don't know how politically correct that line is, but fuck what a line!"

A man walks into a bar (called The Bucket of Blood) . . . and kills everyone in the place. From the first trigger pull of "Stagger Lee" Cave sets up the song's joke and delivers its final punchline, taking the comic-book violence of "O'Malley's Bar" to even greater levels of profanity.[39] It began with a white Stetson beaming bright, stolen, scuffed, spat-on; the mark was made and a line crossed from which there would be no return. In other versions of the story the hat is already oxblood red, "the color of cancer," a warning of the carnage to come. The Bad Seeds hammer home a dense piano chord dragged alongside a howl from the gut raked up the spine before Blixa Bargeld's rock-drill guitar marks a hole driven into the head, then slowing into a reverse shriek as he swallows the mic into his whole mouth, pulling the still whirling drill bit out from the skull in a helter-skelter of blood and gore.[40]

Cave found the original song (thought to originate from 1895) in a book called *The Life, the Lore, and Folk Poetry of the Black Hustler*, recounting the half-whispered tale of "Stack O'Lee" or "Stagolee."[41] Greil Marcus notes that Cave's song draws upon the tradition of the prison toast: ritualized declamatory insults become a loose narrative where injury is heaped upon injury; long after the spark of the first insult, they become alternative Americana in the national songbook.[42]

Cave himself becomes the wronged man, growing into the stature of evil as he steps into Stagger Lee's "rat-drawn shoes"—six feet plus of meanness bound up in a whirlwind of "fucks." Marcus notes the wild run of obscenities tumbles into a chain of graphically absurd imagery: "not merely an assault on rational discourse but on English itself." Making a scene as counting coup Lee's swagger grows in proportion to his ego, Cave noted: "Just like Stagger Lee himself, there seem to be no limits on how evil this song can become." Stagger fulfills his nature as only the "meanest motherfucker can—he knows no other way to be."[43]

Recorded as an afterthought to *Murder Ballads*, the track has the air of novelty that goes full circle back to the sickly-sweet tone of "Where The Wild Roses Grow." Between them these two dark stars would come to define the heart of the record, its blacker-than-black sense of humor, they emerge as genre pieces, nudged toward self-parody. Cave would admit to "Stagger Lee" as a strike of inspiration, compared to his normal months-long rate of composition: "I hear people talk about art as being man-made, that it's about craftsmanship. I think that's bullshit. The gods gave us this song and they were pissing themselves with laughter when they did it."

Cave exposes the self-delusion and egotism of many killers who see themselves as existing beyond the realm of normal humanity and above the moral demands of their actions.[44] The narcissistic killer of "O'Malley's Bar" only pauses to admire his own reflection in the mirror. This marks him with the rare ability to dissociate from the suffering in other human lives: they are weak, unworthy cattle, inviting their own destruction—the act of murder validates the existence of the killer. Speaking in 1996, Cave said, "I wanted to get the point across of your archetypical nonhuman being that America seems to produce. As well as the situation where these people who have no identity feel that they have to go to such horrendous lengths to get some meaning to their lives. The killer thinks he's the winged angel of death, but on the other hand, he is, in fact, a moral coward who can't shoot himself at the end."[45]

Mankind's great inheritance from the tale of Cain and Abel was the establishment of the cultural idea of the murderer—born from our potential for original sin. At first a loser and later an outcast, the killer must make themselves notorious and iconic, as Cave would, bound to a nickname and its legend. In the liner notes of *From Her to Eternity* there is credit to "Sutcliffe" for the track "Wings Off Flies," a friend from the Melbourne scene better known by his nom-de-guerre "Pierre Voltaire." In the song Cave presents the casual, childish cruelty of picking apart insects—"she loves me, she loves me not"—as much about morbid curiosity as it is about breaking down another creature's body just to see what happens. Like pulling the petals from a flower, he turns love (and death) into a game of chance, the flower turns and the last petal we land upon determines our fate to raise the question: is this love, or just desire?

Gordon Burn's psychologically penetrating but strictly objective nonfiction book on Peter Sutcliffe, "The Yorkshire Ripper," is told with a novelist's insight. Titled *Somebody's Husband, Somebody's Son*, a nod toward the plea to emotional bonds of family often used in police

GUSTAVE DORÉ, *PARADISE LOST*, 1866.

witness appeals to kidnappings and murderers; this is flipped to consider the killer as normal person (there is no such thing), emphasizing the facts of Sutcliffe's day-to-day life: married with a job, mortgage, and broad circle of family and friends. His fourteen murder victims were all women, some of them prostitutes; many had young children (all of them somebody's daughter). Burn connects the perverse humility, or rather the shared humanity between killer and victim, the ones that got away and the ones left beaten and mutilated and their bodies hidden, Sutcliffe bears the shared stain of a species.[46]

From Yorkshire to London—and beyond—Alan Moore's comic book *From Hell* is a reimagining of the original "Jack the Ripper" murders of five prostitutes in the Whitechapel area of east central London in 1888, carried out by Royal Surgeon William Gull as part of a cover-up seen through the prism of occultist madness. The real killer was never caught or identified—he remains the notorious villain of dark imagination, a blank silhouette into which we can pour fantasy and speculation.[47] Moore explores how these tragedies would become a sociohistorical cultural event fueled by rumor, media speculation, and outright fiction. From this would rise the serial killer legend and a whole horror genre, a further link in the chain beyond the first moral collapse of Cain toward cult celebrity and a hunger for product and merchandise. Moore points beyond the crucial nexus at the fin de siècle period that closed the nineteenth century shortly before the arrival of the modern world took hold, with Gull experiencing a surreal vision of an equally vacant moral future fulfilled in strip-lit offices, screens and people invisibly chained to their desks.

Cave's "Jack the Ripper"[48] is the rollicking ride that ends *Henry's Dream*; a buccaneering live take from the Bad Seeds' 2013 KCRW session blows the album version away. Though it seems to have no real connection to the other songs on the album, it remains a great closer. The song itself seems relatively problematic by today's standards, a thwarted satire of the man behind real acts of horrific sexualized violence. "Jack the Ripper" fastens hard onto the myth and doesn't let go. With all of its gory garlands, it seemed to set the stage for *Let Love In* as snapshots of thwarted and twisted romance, blood on the flowers. Elsewhere in

And the Ass Saw the Angel the local prostitute Cosey Mo, visited by most of the male townsfolk, becomes an object of their hypocritical wrath revenge—she is too desirable and outside of their control; they have to cut her down. Hating and denying themselves, she must be scapegoated and punished for their own moral shortcomings.

"Ripper" manages to be two songs at once. Cave imagines a cuckolded man emotionally beaten down and sexually frustrated as his partner scolds and denies him physical intimacy. She cries out "Jack the Ripper," the accusation of guilt landing like a marketing slogan.[49] Cave's wife at the time, Viviane Carneiro, has said there was a lot of truth to the song, which manages to remain neatly ambiguous as the woman rightly or wrongly believes her man to be the closeted murderer, and having gotten away with his heinous crimes she becomes his domestic punishment as the nagging, cuckolding tormentor. The song alludes to the wider psychic unease generated by Sutcliffe's repeated murders, causing some couples to break up; either through suspicion or acrimony over whether his victims "deserved" their fate. The story blurs further with the wife's rule by an "iron fist" lashing out with a (deadened) hand of lead; where imagery of dancing knives haunts their sleep, and when the husband wakes, he finds a hatchet hangs over him like a death sentence. For good measure Cave throws in the spirit of the viper, perhaps the woman he keeps by his side, or he really is the killer that she says; this overarching ambiguity means the author never having to take sides.

As much as he would focus upon the heresy of crime as contravention against society, Cave indulges the listener in seeing the consequences of punishment. "The Mercy Seat" presents an intensely claustrophobic vision of the "last walk" toward execution and perhaps some of Cave's own views on the nature of retribution. For his role as the killer convict "Maynard" in the film *Ghosts of the Civil Dead* (1988), for which Cave helped to write and edit director John Hillcoat's script and produced the film soundtrack alongside Mick Harvey and Blixa Bargeld,[50] Cave did substantial research, discovering cracks in the Australian penal system: crumbling buildings, overcrowded cells, institutional violence, and abuse meeting the politics of the asylum. Corruption at entry level exposed the hypocrisy of the penal system with management and guards being equally as criminal as the inmates.

The character "Jack" played by Ian Mortimer in the film is a reflection of the 1986 track "Jack's Shadow." A prisoner released back into the civilian world, he is alienated by the light of the sun and frightened of his own shadow, the darker edge of his past following him around. Cave drew upon the story of Jack Henry Abbott, a real-life serial offender in a story that could just as easily have been torn from the pages of a pulp novel.[51] He spent more of his life in jail than outside of it and as such was ill-equipped to deal with the conventions of civilian society. Abbott was a product of systemic incarceration and a symptom of poor rehabilitation—others would argue he was just plain evil. Cave paints a vivid picture of the comfort Jack finds within pockets of his shadow secreted in the corners of his cell, a familiar world he had grown into.

The author Norman Mailer interviewed Abbott and campaigned for his release as a victim of his brutal upbringing, sparking minor literary celebrity for the ex-convict with his memoir *In the Belly of the Beast* issued in 1981 to coincide with his exit from jail. But after just six weeks of freedom Abbott murdered twenty-two-year-old waiter Richard Aden, who refused to let him use a restaurant toilet. The next day the *New York Times* issued a rave review of his book. Cave's lyric suggests that on a metaphorical level the murder was an act of self-sabotage, ruining what was likely his last chance of freedom. Abbott also kills off his shadow, perhaps representative of his human soul, his actions become a form of slow-burn suicide.

The title of *Ghosts of the Civil Dead* refers to inmates stripped of civil liberties where punishment is prioritized over reform and rehabilitation.[52] It opens with a twenty-four-hour lockdown of inmates. Short of solitary confinement, this was the idea of deeper incarceration, speaking also to the high rates of criminal recidivism that sees former inmates committing new crimes, returned back into the vicious cycle of an industrialized prison system. Abbott's political diatribes are long and rambling, but no one can deny his experience of prison life and its environments: "We have no legal rights as prisoners, only as citizens. The only 'rights' we have are those left to their 'discretion.' So, we assert our rights the only way we can. It is a compromise, and in the end, I greatly fear we as prisoners will lose—but the loss will be society's loss. We are only a few steps removed from society. After us, comes you."[53]

In "Jack's Shadow" we see him cast into the solitary confinement of the hole, as punishment for lack of discipline and acts of violence, then returned to a cell with a light endlessly burning, causing sleep deprivation. In the song's crashing chorus Cave imagines Abbott's alienation upon release to the outside world calling forth the infinite, searing light of the sun. He is eclipsed by the light of love (the Christian virtue of kindness), which is shown to be blind and open to all—but also hypocritical and blankly offered without thought or feeling. Haunted by himself, Abbott briefly leaves jail but could not escape the black mark of his shadow. In his final crime he is exposed as a shallow criminal, a hollow man, who cannot survive inside or outside the system. In 2002 Abbott would come full circle and hang himself in his cell aged fifty-eight, having spent almost forty years of his life behind bars.[54]

In "The Mercy Seat" Cave first presents the execution of the murderer as death in return, where this final punishment is thought to equivocate the crime, somehow balancing out the universe. As Albert Camus said, corporal punishment in its final form of execution is revenge masquerading as justice, the performative enforcement of responsibility or blame upon the body and the erasure of the soul. But if, as Cave so often sang in his early lyrics, nature at its most basic is a bloody struggle for survival, then the eye for an eye demands of the Old Testament invoke the bloody tooth of violence to be met with further violence. The New Testament offers the famous aphorism of "turning the other cheek," where if a person strikes you once you offer the other cheek for more of the same. What might be viewed as defeatism is meant to be spiritual overcoming—the virtues of kindness and meekness—what should the fate of the supposed murderer be?

Looking back to *The Firstborn Is Dead*, "Knockin on Joe" tells the story of a prison inmate resigned to his sentence—a man thwarted by the wastes of empty time. Preempting the frantic execution ballad of "The Mercy Seat" by several years, this song keeps a funereal pace led by heavy-footed piano. It could be considered a dirge toward slow self-annihilation or a man reaching the end of his last mile.[55] The prisoner has looked up and down every inch of his cell, familiar as the soles of his feet, followed step-by-step the endless reach of every hallway—each one just like the last—and looking up through a small skylight he finds a piece of blue sky that is his own, reaching out toward infinity. There is no escape but this, nowhere to go but beyond, into fate, pacing out the days. Abbott writes about this experience from his time spent in the hole: "Time descends in your cell like the lid of a coffin in which you lie and watch it as it slowly closes over you. When you neither move nor think in your cell, you are awash in pure nothingness."

The podcast *Today's Lesson* suggests the expression "Knockin on Joe" as prison talk for self-injury to avoid the workday of forced labor.[56] The narrator "Joe" wishes he could tap out, black out, go blind, but he knows there is no escape that will get him off the hook other than completing his sentence or death, whichever comes first. Little wonder Cave's late-night smoky barroom piano makes a few stabbing notes, line for line, then staggers along with long howls calling back to his own emptiness—the track stakes out more than seven long minutes—which might seem indulgent for the casual listener but for the lost soul of the song it is a life sentence that might yet be cut short, though it will never be soon enough.[57]

By its end, the song's title becomes literal when Cave, howling, whining, and pleading, calls for the guard to lay his burden down upon him as hammering fists falling upon the body. His self-abasement is a knowingly cruel joke: inmate and jailer are bound by the same chains, cast as servant and master of one another, a deadweight to life. To keep beating on the masochist "Joe," the guard ekes-out his mental frustration on the other's body as a form of vengeance; the more he beats him the freer Joe feels, transcendent pain delivering him from an endless waiting or terrifying execution, the jailer trapped with him in the cycle of punishment and slow retribution, with no deliverance in sight.

Cave would often dismiss the idea that his music was misanthropic, arguing that he tried to show an honest reflection of the world and how people behaved within it. As angry and sometimes vicious as Cave's early music can be, the deepest expression of his wider misanthropy can be heard on "People Ain't No Good,"[58] a point of resignation nestled in the "love song" album of *The Boatman's Call*, the record that for all its venom succeeded in making Cave and The Bad Seeds a household name. "People . . ." shows us as beings of great potential often found to be painfully lacking. "Far From Me" is even bleaker, where people are too busy getting ahead and fucking each other over to consider the consequences of their actions, let alone breaches of any moral code, a space in which there is less hope or space for kindness to exist.[59] Cave takes his own experiences of being burned and sees it routinely happening between others. Though there is a hint of sardonic forgiveness, where everyone is forced into the harsh evolutionary position of survival of the fittest, should we all follow our blood and 'do it to them, before they do it to you'?

Cave has said "People Ain't No Good" is not about blaming people on the basis of good or evil; it simply exposes our innate fallibility. The greatest challenge against virtue is that we can all make mistakes in the heat of a difficult moment: a careless word, some rough gesture, a loss of control—these are the inherent challenges of being human. While perfection is a religious myth there is always responsibility and the shadow of guilt.

On "Darker with the Day" Cave greets the smiling sun with mutual indifference. The new day appears good but remains infinite in its capacity for evil, it is the contrariness of humanity that mires us in constant conflict. There is a common thread here with another famous couplet from Yeats' "The Second Coming," which reveals human contradiction to be the source of much pain and suffering:

> *The best lack all conviction, while the worst*
> *Are full of passionate intensity.*

Across the song Cave would go on to expose "big" businessmen and politicians as the new devil of the twenty-first century, thieves in the temple mired in the desperation of their greed. He calls them out as creased-up little men with a big ego complex, born to privilege and a narrow worldview, always grappling to rise above their ability, insulated from their failings by money. A cast of everyday monsters, they cause a deeper bitterness to rise up in Cave from which only love will rescue him, fearing that otherwise he too might be absorbed into the monsters' ranks. Almost twenty years later Cave would find the haunted man of *Ghosteen* surrounded by tyrants and fools, like sad clowns to the left and callous jokers to the right, but with graver concerns leaving him sick at heart.[60]

Cave would continue to explore the deep narcissism that lurks behind the banality of evil, shifting the world from a place of life and wonder into industrialized murder and institutional persecution. Cave is angered and frustrated by the stupidity and ugliness of cruelty inherent in civilized societies and the denial of their guilt—it is easier to look away and shut out the dark reality than to admit uncomfortable truths. On "(Are You) The One That I've Been Waiting For" (1997) Cave sees the egos and wills of great men burning through the metaphor of the romantic relationship. Beginning with desire and the powers of imagination we are capable of creating great wonders of science and art, some of which are achieved by expressions of force and exploitation; equally great atrocities are carried out in the name of love and righteousness.[61]

The 1988 track "Sunday's Slave" offers a near-socialist view of the alienating pressure of labor performed as exploitation; Cave suggests a character born of self-abasement and humiliation, being pissed on and abused as a stable boy, experiences that return to him as nightmares.[62] Even in the song's title Cave is perhaps moving beyond metaphor toward the real horrors of American slavery[63] where people would be forced to work all week, from daybreak to midnight, excepting part of Sunday given over for religious observance. From the day of rest Monday comes around again, the days of work give no reward and no pay, they are simply the act of slaves digging their own graves.

On "Rings of Saturn" Cave muses that slavery has already been abolished: "How come it's gone and reared its ugly head again?" His wordplay throws up the open question that since the Emancipation Proclamation and the 1807 abolition of slavery in the United Kingdom slavery was gone from the world but also yields to the fact that it never really went away, from the great buildings of industrial cities and the institutions we still depend on today. From his readings of the nonfiction books *King Leopold's Ghost: A Story of Greed, Terror and Heroism in Colonial Africa* and *Late Victorian Holocausts: El Niño Famines and the Making of the Third World* Cave would discover more concrete accounts where the achievements of empire and civilization are built on the sweat, blood, and bones of other human beings, slaves, migrant workers, refugees and casualties of war, in order to feed the great lie of improving society for all. It becomes an expected or forced demand of sacrifice from our fellow human beings. *King Leopold's Ghost* begins with the powerful moral dilemma faced by young clerk Edward Morel, standing on the docks of Antwerp in 1898 seeing a great wealth of goods brought into the country from the Belgian colony of the Congo—but very little except rifles and stacks of ammunition being sent in return—what he and the world had assumed to be a matter of trade exposes the industry of human slavery in the dirty, dangerous work of rubber harvesting without pay or reward, gathered and carried by thousands of Africans with their families held as a ransom.[64]

Cave highlights the challenge against progressive liberal consensus, which of course accommodates artistic license and freedom of expression, where each new age still reveals its own exquisite tortures. In "Jesus Alone" Cave offers splintered visions of desolation glimpsed alongside flashes of spiritual uncertainty that cut so close to one another as to become interchangeable horrors of broken faith and self-destruction—waking up covered in someone else's blood and wondering how it happened, the lone junkie in the worst hotel in Mexico or tear ducts being harvested for profit.[65]

As W. H. Auden observed in his poem "Musée des Beaux Arts" (1939), "About suffering they were never wrong / The old Masters." He has us watching over the shoulder as visitors flock toward the painting *Landscape with the Fall of Icarus* (c. 1560s) by Bruegel, which shows Icarus' descent from the sky toward the earth. Though no one in the picture seems to notice his passing, it is the implicit focal point of the painting.[66] The image displays the luxury of the living not to stop for death; the people in the painting are too busy, their attentions divided by life. There is the ending of a splash, ripples, and a few feathers on the water, then a return to the surface calm—the world's revolving carnage and all its raging are spent for another day.[67]

Cave begins 2004's "Nature Boy" with a childhood memory of watching TV; witnessing the offhand violence of slaughter and atrocity is normalized by repeat viewings. He would remember sitting in his grandmother's house and being shocked at the report of the 1972 attempted assassination of US Democratic presidential candidate George Wallace.[68] This connects back to "Abattoir Blues" and Cave's musing on the hypocrisy of so-called civilizations and the forces of (self-) extinction. While never explicitly political in his songwriting Cave cites incompetent government, climate change uncertainty, and societal divisions, which in 2016's "Anthrocene" becomes the growing threat of extinction and a posthuman world, perhaps kindled in his reading of *Late Victorian Holocausts* (2000).[69]

Cave finds deeper amorality churning up a gray zone of uncertainty in "Babe, You Turn Me On." There is the returning fear of collapse where "everything is wrong" and the truth of all moral sense has evaporated, where history simply repeats itself and we are caught in the cycle of our mistakes. On "As I Sat Sadly By Her Side" the two witnesses look down from high windows, insulated by the glass. The world beyond is at a remove, we close the curtains or change the channel when we cannot take it anymore. The woman speaks to her partner, noting that God does not notice our benevolence or the lack of it; each person's heart is their own, not the home of their fellow man, pushing self-responsibility back onto the individual.[70] Cave referenced this same decadent indifference; the casual cruelty of the world, on "Push the Sky Away," the almost routine horrorshow of the world can often be brushed off and buried only if we choose to give up and turn away.

From the grand scale of ethnic cleansing to the common struggle for kindness, Psalm 8:5 says, "For thou hast made him [man] a little lower than the angels, and hast crowned him with glory and honour." Man in God's image suggests a pale imitation, or worse still, a rod designed to break before it bends—we bask in God's good grace but the warmth on our face will always turn away into a shade. Nonetheless we can always work toward our better natures, against cruelty. Cave pushes for kindness, if not understanding and patience,[71] then at least positive acts that help others and somehow manage to keep the world turning. In the Buddhist sense we cannot eliminate the inevitable suffering that comes with existence, but we can act not to add to it, and make the world worse than when we first came into it.

In "The Fable of the Brown Ape" Farmer Emmerich[72] is shocked by hyper-evolved creatures having outgrown their animal status. He nonetheless cages and feeds them and when the local townspeople find out they murder the snake in their brute ignorance. Cave sees the good deed punished, the "milk of human kindness"[73] literally bleeding out from the snake's broken body. Some have read the song as a lament for Blixa Bargeld leaving the band, but it works overall as a comment on the madness of crowds, perhaps even critics, moralizing on unholy things such as the raising-up of beasts, like the snake and the ape, minor gods that in their pure strangeness might outlive us.

Philip Larkin is a favorite poet for Cave. His poem "The Mower" speaks to an unfortunate incident where the animal lover accidentally runs over a hedgehog with his riding lawn mower (apparently wearing a D. H. Lawrence T-shirt—his one concession to literature, sex and rock and roll). Waking the next morning after he has buried the poor beast's remains Larkin is reminded again of its absence, as with his poem "Aubade," it serves as reminder for acts of kindness in our daily lives (with an emphasis on timeliness) as if to offset the cycle of cruelty and destruction that can seem to overshadow everything else. Cave refers to his own version of hope as overcoming the cynicism that sets us up to fail with the oblique belief that "that humans are shit and the world is fucked."[74] Cave argues that deep cynicism is one of the greatest evils; to adopt a tired-eyed approach both to wonder and terror, accepting both as a constant and taking life for granted.[75] Cave relates the Stevie Smith poem "Oblivion" where she finds a "human face" amid the empty hopelessness; something sincere in the voice of its pain, and it makes her turn back, both to confront and to console. Instead of walking away she chooses to respond with humanity in kind.[76]

LAUGHTER IN THE DARK

A tall, gaunt man marches onto a stage and yells out "who here wants to die?" The crowd cheers, the band jump into the frantic, slashing rhythm of "Sonny's Burning." Judging the mood just right, the spider-crooked figure calls out "is everybody having a *bad* time?" Turns out death in a cramped, sweaty, black box is lots of fun, perhaps too much fun. Cave wears a crooked smile; half grimace half grin, his songs bear the ironic tragedy of the face bent sinister, every joke in his lyric is delivered askew, twisted and distorted by orchestrated violence, crippled ego and body horror. Only half the audience get it. The rest are shocked into gasping silence: confused by the band, shocked by the lyrics, scared of the singer—but they all love the song.

It was The Birthday Party's display of the upbeat macabre that would give momentum to the dark-winged ship of The Bad Seeds in the early 1980s. Feeding on their bridling reputation of gothic allure, Cave and the band managed to display a practiced contempt for all sides of the musical spectrum: pop, punk, post-everything; critics and audience alike. Cave steered The Bad Seeds toward a more even keel, making his humor equal parts bawdy over-the-top grotesque and burning satire. In The Birthday Party's full pomp Cave was aligned to his own Grand Guignol nosedive—all for the love of live entertainment—but with The Bad Seeds this excess was tempered, moodier, and subtly less assured.[1]

Speaking with much self-effacement about his early years in Melbourne and London, Cave said "I had, without any supporting evidence, a shameless and pathological belief in my own awesomeness."[2] A combination of joie de vivre and positive nihilism spurred Cave into the act of fulfilling his artistic desire—writing songs and being onstage was simply the mode that stuck. There is much theater in Cave's pure spectacle of bodily performance: leaps into the air, bringing forth the ecclesiastical weight of preacher knee drops and backflips, landing just right, disbelieving of his own luck; or crashing in a heap on the floor, collapsed into failure.[3] Behind all of this was the tension of a band at the edge, jerking their way through songs, edging out of tune and only just holding it all together—reaching for the great sublime of the united front. The audience love to see the bloodsport thrust headlong in forward motion—the horrorshow must go on.[4]

Cave's first band The Boys Next Door was formed too late in the 1970s beyond the Saints-era of the Melbourne punk scene that Cave treasured, becoming an art school reaction to the purposefully offensive punk band names, with original drummer Phill Calvert leaving to join The Psychedelic Furs' new wave optimism in 1983. The Birthday Party took on a more cruelly ironic tone between their band name; the atrocity exhibition of the band's live show met with the death, drugs, and mayhem in their songs.[5] Rowland S. Howard claimed the name expressed the band's celebration of extreme realities, as Cave's lyrics sought to ruin false illusions of the "normal" everyday world. The band aimed to bring revelation to the bored and bourgeois setting of their upper-middle-class Melbourne neighborhood, dragging behind them the dissolute free spirit of St. Kilda Beach. Cave argued that in spite of their ferocity the band combined the spirit of being both "aggressive and intelligent."[6] The band's bassist, Tracy Pew, embodied this dichotomy: an avid reader who seemed to absorb the damage of drink, drugs, and fights, he is often seen strutting about variously in leather trousers, string vest, frilly pirate shirt (a la *Seinfeld*), a ten-ton cowboy hat, and a pencil mustache, deflating the band's hard and heavy themes. Though Cave cared less about audience satisfaction the band was trapped together in the radical experience of deconstructing the music gig where "having fun" was not necessarily everyone's idea of a good time. Baiting the audience to engage, Cave would refer to live gigs as a "full-on attack" using tried and tested performance method of throwing striking silhouette shapes, climbing the rigging of the stage. After being darlings of the Melbourne scene, and much later in London, Cave was forced to return fire from objects thrown onstage, concluding the exchange by making a kamikaze dive into the audience.

One of the major reasons the band fell apart, aside from physical, mental, and drug-fueled exhaustion was the intensity demanded of them in live performance. People went to the gigs expecting to see a car crash or start a fight, either with the singer or each other.[7] While the band could sometimes be viewed as props, cracked actors channeling the uneven motions for Cave to get lost in self-flagellation, he praised them for holding the performances together. Speaking of The Birthday Party years later, Cave observed, "Our audiences were starting to make demands on me onstage, it made you feel like some sort of geek, with chicken blood running down your chin . . . covered in feathers."[8] Cave paints himself into the 1932 movie *Freaks*,[9] a living spectacle, but he became the voyeur's dream by choice, while later trying to shed the persistent caricature that grew up around him, playing to the crowds but always moving forward on an artistic level.

As early as The Birthday Party's "Deep in the Woods" Cave manages to create horrific, haunted imagery while the song revels in cartoonish acts of torture and mutilation, bringing the grotesque and the ghastly to the limits of good taste. Acting out in wordplay and exaggerated vocal snarls, the characters speak through the song, while others hear his most extreme lyrics as promoting violence against women. Speaking in 1988 he said, "But I find a lot of my work grotesque and tasteless in a lot of 'Mutiny,' that particular song, and 'Sad Waters.' Just a couple of moments here. Things like 'Deep in the Woods' are diseased with grotesqueness."[10]

Elsewhere, the band offered agitation without physical propaganda. On the *Mutiny/Bad Seed* EP Cave produced his own cover art. Surfing the wave of easy rebellion, he painted a winged skull, thorny heart, crucifix and swastika, garlanded with full blood roses—Cave stalled as the final finishing date for the artwork grew closer. Already pushing at the locked doors of controversy for its own sake long after the forced outrage of The Sex Pistols in 1977, on the song "Kiss Me Black" he sings of a girl who "sleeps like a swastica [*sic*]." It's unclear if this is simply a case of crazy distracted posture, two bodies curled up holding another, or just a tasteless and self-serving nod toward aesthetic symmetry, the image association is both striking and pungent.[11] Opening "Saint Huck" with the militarized phrase: *"Achtung"* (warning/look out) a post–Birthday Party indulgence, the same phrase in English would not carry the same shock value, but by 1983 it was a shallow pose already out of date.

Nick Cave and the various Australian members of The Bad Seeds have long traded in behind-the-scenes joking, used both to provoke and defuse tension, which many non-Australian musicians who passed in and out of the band sometimes found to be refreshing and other times isolating.[12] Barry Adamson would recall the shifting intensity of relationships within The Bad Seeds, a fraught studio atmosphere, where everything happens fast; pieces of a song come and go.[13] In the *20,000 Days on Earth* documentary Cave would observe the process of song and lyric writing: "Counterpoint is the key. Putting two disparate images beside each other and seeing which way the sparks fly,"[14] an expression that for Adamson could also apply to studio working relationships. His bandmates impress upon him their arch sarcasm, half grins, and shifting eyebrows; he marks the intense chemistry of the studio as a place for mistakes with no right answers, only the intuition of feeling out the song that would absorb the atmosphere this dramatic and hard-nosed work ethic: "They used conflict as a means of creation, negativity as a source of power."[15]

For his part, photographer Bleddyn Butcher would remember the shared spark behind The Birthday Party's Rowland S. Howard and Cave: "Very funny, very fond of teasing. They'd tip over any situation if it was getting po-faced, bring to it that Australian sense of humor, brutal and harsh."[16] When questioned about his mocking address to God on the *Abattoir Blues/Lyre Of Orpheus* album, Cave would respond: "I consider myself to be first and foremost a comic writer. . . . That's not to say my songs are not addressing serious concerns and things that are very meaningful to me. But a necessary part of it to me is the humor."[17] The album's range of maudlin piano, pop, and extreme gospel-tinged rock was forged by the balance of power divided across the band's rhythm section, adding a distinct character to each "side": "We have two drummers. We have a really heavy drummer and a light, jazzy drummer. [We can safely assume Cave refers to Jim Sclavunos and Thomas Wydler, respectively.] I see it as two separate records in that you only have to listen to one of them to understand that particular record." Despite Cave's claim the two records share a use of overkill and restraint that make both 'sides' melodically rich and full of fire.

Walking a highwire divide between stand-up performance and laughter at the funeral party, Cave's songs demand that above all we are able laugh at ourselves. "Hiding All Away" throws acts of extreme sexual violence against small-town mundanity: police with greased truncheons, paper-thin dresses, and greasy-eyed chefs clash with big-fisted butchers; comical ranks that could have appeared in Franz Kafka's kinkiest nightmares, all emerge from the shadows as we hear Cave trying to escape from a sado-masochistic fever dream.

Elsewhere, Cave is more subtle and deceptive in landing his punchlines. The 2001 track "Oh My Lord"[18] is presented as a confessional for a man demanding redemption as he wanders through a broken life, alienated from his family and himself. Having a haircut at the barbershop and watching the world go by, pedestrians stare back at him like a goldfish in a bowl. Suddenly he is noticed by a man wearing plastic reindeer antlers who presses his naked bum up to the glass, to the narrator's great shock and bemusement. Cave would admit that this was a true story: "As with most of my absurd lyrics I just wrote it down as I saw it." After a panic attack on all fours on the barbershop floor he calls his wife, who doesn't even recognize his voice, thinking she is receiving a prank call, and tells him to go away.

The song highlights the ridiculousness of his situation while making light of his suffering, the perfect balance for the holy sinner as fool. There is a suggestion that the song shows Cave racked under the pain of addiction: sneaking out, becoming someone else under the night, estranged from his former life—a different man seen through a glass darkly. It is a powerful touch of humor that is used by Cave touching upon greater depths beneath the surface.[19]

In his graphic novel exploration of Cave's life and music *Mercy on Me*, Reinhard Kleist offers the view of "Hallelujah" as a hymn to Cave's addiction. A lonely patient wanders off into the snow in his pajamas, leaving behind his invalid life and the worries of what his nurse might say. Kleist sketches her in full cliché, bursting out of her uniform as the bosomy, smothering matron, who watches Cave wander off from rehab and into the wastes of temptation. But as ever, the lyrics are sung with guarded smirk, the man's position is absurd, and he knows it. A beautiful woman bathed in light offers him shelter; she might be the temporary warmth of getting high again, where the next fix is never the last. Eventually the pajamaed runaway returns to base and the familiar arms of his nurse. The song seems to be about nothing, a nonevent, but perhaps for Cave it carries much deeper personal meaning and is a parable on desire, wants, and needs, so the closing chorus chants about buckets of tears—wherever you go you carry your sorrows with you.

On "Oh My Lord" Cave uses similar language to Leonard Cohen's suicide attempt masquerading as a dry shave "Dress Rehearsal Rag," a lament fully poised upon self-pity. He dances the fine edge between making himself presentable to the world that fits his self-image, realizing that he did not have far to fall in reaching his lowest ebb. The commonality of his complaint is echoed in his surroundings, of New York's famously louche Chelsea Hotel, befitting the album title from which the song springs. Without love he only finds hate projected outward then internalized where it comes home to roost.

The Bad Seeds' great inheritance from punk was the willful urge to antagonize and expose the weakness of people's sense of morality. Often built on outrage, it was too easy to bait and spur them on, if only for the sake of a knee-jerk reaction. Cave would later argue that people who hold to their ethical or political principles with absolute conviction are often guilty of a deeper uncertainty, unwilling to bend or entertain alternative points of view, otherwise this embeds a polarizing extremism.[20] Amid the shouting down of cancel culture, the murky waters of his songs entertain bold ambiguities in our moral characters, not unlike Cave's own idiosyncratic spirituality.

As a humoristic writer, Cave uses flashes of the absurd and surrealist derailment to counterbalance ideas that might otherwise weigh down his material. His pitch-black comedy offers some of his most memorable lines, which jump out from the songs like a quickfire comedian taking shots from the stage. He borrows the dark sardonic tone of Jonathan Swift and his (still) notorious satirical pamphlet *A Modest Proposal* which suggested the poor eat their young as a solution to hunger and poverty.[21] The strength of such bleak comedy is that it is wrought from serious tragedy; we are dared to be amused but equally touched at the plight of others. Cave further entangles the extravagant ridiculousness of life with genuine pain, the bleeding edge of emotional complexity— the listener is often left unsure whether to laugh or cry at his songs.

Cave's creative dilemma echoes the Greek myths and biblical suffering; where individuals work against fate or in denial of the "divine" will (and mistakes) of the gods; suffering the fallout of their own hubris, where so often elegiac tragedy can turn to bathos.[22] With an artist as established as Cave we know that sex or death is around the corner, waiting for the hammer to fall; Cave delights in confounding the listener where desire collapses into disgust, the beautiful die young or even become murderers themselves.

Reading between the lines, Cave is funnier than many would allow him to be. Beneath the dark cloak there is a veiled amusement at the madness of it all, where a prolonged seriousness would make a misanthrope out of anyone. On *Skeleton Tree* this surrealist edge is heightened, even when Cave breaks into bizarre imagery of spiders, stars, or the night as spilt ink, it is only in cathartic release with no release of humor at the end. Instead of throwing us lyrical cannonballs to mentally juggle, keeping the listener on their toes, The songs sink into a deadweight, the arch playful mood returns on aspects of *Carnage*. "White Elephant" presents the man on his porch with a loaded gun willing to lay down his life in defense of property or a stone-dead statue as a righteous target for mockery—until the song's overblown heavenly farewell.[23]

Looking back to 1986, Bleddyn Butcher would note of Cave and The Bad Seeds: "The band were full of sound and fury, but there was a great ironic intelligence to their work, which I found inspiring." Where humor invites questions of how we could live differently it becomes strangely useful.[24] In his foreword to the new edition of Nick Cave's *Complete Lyrics* Will Self sees a consistent sharp satire at play, by turns a scalpel or a blunt instrument, used to prick at or explode the pomposity of arrested attitudes and constipated moral preoccupations. The overtly hostile transgressive act becomes the enervating force of (benign) cultural shakeup, but often falls short of revolutionary social change.

Cave's mirthful vitriol would find its peak in the 2001 song "God Is in the House." After his marriage to Susie Bick in 1999, Cave and his new wife would visit America on their honeymoon, driving through several states along the way. After so many years of writing about the country as a distant subject viewed through the tour bus window, dank alleyways and across the dark mass of an audience, Cave would finally come face-to-face with the country's crushingly conformist rebels and everyday naysayers' civic pride inflated into hyperbolic dictatorship, that in Cave's hands ballooned into a domineering grotesque.

Finding a new source of "the evil within," "God Is in the House" sees the closeted hellfire behind the gated community as the new homesteaders—immured by wealth to wider social ills—bristling with fear of the outside. An alternative musician born of rock and blues musical traditions; Cave would now find himself dancing across the political fence. He gives full vent to a series of minor annoyances, the little things that get up your nose until they become a brain hemorrhage of major grievances. Cave would admit that some of these frustrations were his own, others invented, though he refused to state which was which. In the song they rise up as jagged vignettes born from his American travels as a double alien: a deeply Anglophone Australian with his own very personal conception of Christian faith and traditional conservative values. The song speaks from an objective position to witness headless chickens driven to insanity by tokenized notions of equality in suburban towns with names so forgettable they merged into the meta-mythic zip code of *"Anywhere, USA."*

The song begins as a laconic examination of the peaceful little town taken a Lynchian hard turn—and coming full circle——exposing the hypocrisy of its (neo)liberal facade. Cave takes a stab at the political correctness of the homegrown-made-perfect, the American experiment tamed, enclosed by self-righteousness. He cites a woman mayor who keeps drugs on the wrong side of the tracks, with brightly lit monuments and kittens painted white, a place where there is nowhere for the guilty to hide from the mob, except as the bearer of the light.[25] Cave lifts the lid on the repressed need for social controls met with double standards of local government—clashing with the extreme challenges of Cave's own pagan poetry.

The song subverts the idea of God as the foundation of a home (perhaps even his own beliefs). From the perspective of church as a communion of belief and spiritual imagination beyond walls and old stone, Cave takes a sideways slant, skewering the "utopiate" of liberalism delivered by "teetotalitarian" autocrats.[26] Certainly the song confirms his more recent views delivered twenty years after the song was written—arguing against the postmodern religion of the (elite) masses that sees factional group rights tread on the individual: how the freedoms of democratic culture lean upon equality but create a new straitjacket around freedom of speech and creative self-expression.

Cave's lyric delights in setting loose the mice into a bag of cats, squaring-off the rival tribes of gays, homophobes, and lesbians in open warfare, not a clash of perspectives, reaching the fallout of an intolerable situation where nothing is right and everyone is wrong. The song's power stems from Cave's exacting tone of mockery, exhausted by the monotony of monolithic thinking. In the song's closing bridge Cave gives a torturously exhausted, whispery-whined vocal, teasing out the clipped vowels of listed moral demands, inviting the congregation to "quietly shout" for deliverance with one throttled voice.

At the song's close Cave repeats his call for God to "come out," either daring him to magically appear and embrace the town's brave new world, perhaps to confess or to invoke his wrath and quit the hollow vampire's castle of narrowed-down secularization—just as Cave rejects the singular Christianity of self-righteous judgment.[27] If Jesus was the example that would set us free from tyranny, God has become co-opted as the false figurehead of muscular Christianity turned inward against the truth of humanity's conflicted natures. The Conservative Christian soldier is the new bigheaded bigot, and the fiercely self-loathing liberal their shadow opposite; both reaching around from behind to stick their finger further into muddy waters. The house of the song's title has its walls cast so high it becomes a prison of forced conformity camouflaged as modern neoliberal tolerance, as if predicting Cave's fears of the culture wars of embattled censorship and political polarization that would begin in the short decades following the song's release in April 2001.

In his songwriting craft, Cave has always worked to inflame and subvert the melancholy pessimism of his public image, away from misanthropy, much of his lyrics always start with the beginnings of a smirk edging into shadow. His deft and determined approach is to shock us out of normality and one-way feeling, deconstructing the singular purpose of a song to embrace jarring dynamics: we are soothed until we are slapped across the face, kissed then bitten—lifting us up only to cast us down again. The journalist Mat Snow would note Cave's measure of poised madness: "The linguistic relish of the tale and the eye-rolling, blood-curdling conviction of its telling were always more the point than the storylines themselves. Revisiting his recorded repertoire from that perspective, such a song as 'Mutiny in Heaven' now jumps out as a Fabergé egg of erudite and intricately worked design whose elements—hellfire preacher, Catholic peon, ghetto junkie, sea shanty buccaneer."[28] This marks out Cave like any other great artist: 100 percent sincerely inauthentic; depth of feeling met with artistic construct, rather than trying to be entirely one or the other.

Cave is well-known for his wry sense of humor that enables him to find the lighter edge to the dark side of life, to see the marital strife of the accused cuckold in "Jack the Ripper" and the Ku Klux Klan furniture of "Deanna." So many of his jokes are pitch black, drawn from the mania of his wordplay and extreme physical violence to the

The fire of the mind agitates the atmosphere

LOUIS WAIN, 1875.

point that it becomes absurd. The dandy and wit Sebastian Horsley called Cave a "Troubadour of Trouble," exploiting comedic settings that could only arise from tragedy. The Quietus founder Luke Turner who has interviewed Cave several times cites the small but pertinent detail of the haplessly seedy young man of "Jangling Jack" who on entering a bad-time bar asks for a drink with a little "rinky dinky" cocktail umbrella and ends his night finding death at the wrong end of a gun.[29] Cave, the arch-sensualist, is happy to see poor Jack advance on Lazarus to lose himself inside the sexual dissipation of cunnilingus only to end up shooting himself, allowing Cave to cutely rhyme "vulva" with "revolver," piling on the innuendo with a gravedigger's spade.[30] On "Lay Me Low" Cave has great fun pulling a Huck Finn and Tom Sawyer, indulging himself to watch over his own funeral, no doubt with a chuckle. "Idiot Prayer" takes this a touch further: with the emotional death of a breakup, Cave is taken down, beyond the grave, to hell, floored and beset by troubles that keep him there. It is an empty cry from a sinking man.[31]

Andrew Collins believes that "it is plausible to revere and mock Cave." The ability to hold this seeming contradiction shows us Cave constantly reaching within the ridiculous highs, and lows, of the sublime, perhaps at the same time, the tragically dark and the hilariously surreal. Perhaps against our better judgment, we embrace the cognitive dissonance of the holy fool; dancing along the wire of high and low taste. He gives us permission to get down and dirty, to share in the sick joke and feel happily vulgarized along with it.

In "We Call Upon the Author" Cave tosses out names like scattered pages—Bukowski, Berryman, and Hemingway—the so-called greats, not-so-goods, and most sinful of all—the merely average. Cave finds a running joke in the great artist falling short as a human being; occasionally he finds himself standing alongside them, a haunted portrait in a gallery of noble fools, trying to write so intensely about human experience while failing to notice that at that same moment life has already passed them by. By contrast, the curse of the rock star is too much hard living compared to the writer's cloistered retreat of introspection. Cave often finds himself divided between the two; except for the self-effacing insight of "Easy Money" he has managed to avoid writing songs about the *travails* of the rock star's lament.[32]

In Charles Bukowski, Cave sees a myopic imagination working within a very narrow worldview, although much of his work is often glorifying romance and self-loathing; misogynistic and misanthropic, it is not unlike many of Cave's song characters.[33] In "We Call Upon the Author" Cave arms himself with a pair of scissors calling out the prolix wordiness of long-winded navel gazers unable to self-edit. He is determined to set an example and fix them by pruning words, cutting-off their effete fingers and grinding away the overkill of purple prose, perhaps even castrating the much-venerated dirty old man—taking a wrecking ball to his risible sex scenes and sentimental detachment from reality. The minor gods are easily toppled and ripe targets to be taken down, if not excised from the canon altogether, where the artist must fight to earn their place, or else be forgotten.

For every well-meaning ballad of humanist lament and broken hearts The Bad Seeds' songs also jump forward to shock the listener, rubbing them the wrong way in true contrarian fashion. On "Papa Won't Leave You, Henry" Cave finds his protagonist waking up to "a fag" dressed in a corset laying his dick on his cheek. Whether a flaccid slap across the face or a prick up your ear, it is an act of provocation. The narrator murders him in sexual horror at the thought of being pinned, pegged, and roundly violated, if not already.[34] While Cave would later reject the song's lyrics as trash, they present a wonderful storm of surreal imagery, vividly terrifying; this remains a hilarious scene. Though the joke doesn't lean on the homophobic slur with Cave making use of his character's voice, to some ears the term can as morally jarring as the "N-word."[35]

Cave has even more fun with later examples of abject body horror where innards are turned out into the world, designed to unseat the listener through a warped reality, ill at ease with itself. 2013's "Jubilee Street" embraces Cave's seedy surrealism that happily lapses into double entendre: we see a man in tie and tails wandering about a real-life street of Brighton, arriving at his own carnival of flesh that presents a fetus on a leash, a sack of of sludge, and a man made of meat—the human creature dissected. Dragging around his "ten ton catastrophe on a 60-pound chain," Sisyphus-like set against wild and weightless body horror; urban ghost stories cut through the pages of *Viz* magazine.[36] Veering from the ridiculous to the sublime it hits the sweet spot of angst and bittersweet folly, a bellyful of love is haunted by "butterflies": a case of nerves or intimating pregnancy. Cave echoes Will Self's novel *How The Dead Live*, where the (dead) female protagonist Lily Bloom is followed about by portions of old body fat and a stillborn child who taunts her with pop songs from the era of its death, we trail the burden of our sins behind us.[37] As the lyrics and music of "Jubilee Street" coalesce in the outro, reaching off toward outer-body elevation, we see Cave looking down on his life, as if it were happening to someone else. Amid the epic power of sinuous violins and a rousing backing chorus Cave manages to combine catastrophic hyperbole with intense ridiculousness.[38]

In 2006 Cave would make a conscious break from the assumed seriousness of his earlier music under the guise of Grinderman. The bratty garage rock of 1994's "Jangling Jack" set the scene for the now older and wiser man grown disgracefully immature by the day. Though Grinderman manifested more as a tangential psychedelic freakout from The Bad Seeds' music, Cave would mine familiar lyrical preoccupations. As if realizing the unfiltered freedom of self-expression as art promised by The Birthday Party, an uncalculated post-rock project, the two bands from opposite ends of Cave's career offered a more direct form of music. Cave spoke about the writing of Grinderman's "No Pussy Blues" delivered as free-range ad-lib, giving him the spur to shake loose his subconscious: "At some point in my career, I've managed to flip this little switch in my head which says 'It doesn't fucking matter' and go in with a certain sense of humor about it all." An easy, unpracticed surrealism comes to life through Cave's libidinous tongue that never stutters or trips over graphic depictions of the body as lustful object to be both seen and acted upon. On "Mermaids" "the match that would fire up her snatch" moves beyond embarrassment and shame toward pure outspoken joy, singing the body electric. Cave would seem to expose something of himself in his characters' flaws, holding them up as kind of a mirror to mankind, equally flawed and broken and seeing the humor in it.

The more recent Bad Seeds albums of the 2000s would demand further reflection on aging and mortality in navigating the rough ride peaks and troughs of midlife crisis.[39] Through Grinderman Cave threw himself into this aesthetic of domestic disaster,[40] suggesting that one is never too old to change and learn something new.[41] Hyping up his obnoxiousness to eleven, this renewed persona gave him even thicker armor to hide behind. This "Nick Cave" was merely the singer in a bar band; ostensibly there were no leaders, though Cave remained the songs' chief architect. With suitable perversity, the outspoken nature of Grinderman would score a new legion of female fans drawn to the unfiltered, down and dirty, gross-out gaudiness: a younger, happier crowd beyond the "troubled women" Cave had courted in his earlier career. These were fans who enjoyed the unbridled sleaze and brazen sensuality of the songs in an industry that prioritized younger and younger female pop singers with short skirts, and even shorter career paths. Cave was able to work in utero and go retrogressive as he moved the stripped-down band into a more open-ended jamming form of songwriting. The oversexed fixations recur in the characterization of *The Death of Bunny Munro*, once a middle-aged lothario, now thwarted pervert, Bunny is increasingly taunted by visions of impossible sexual fantasies. The book features exaggerated, in-depth descriptions that imagine Avril Lavigne's vagina as well as obsess over the revolving golden orbs of Kylie Minogue's hot pants from the "Spinning Around" video, the two infatuations gravitating about Bunny's growing disassociation.[42] He would carry these torments about his swollen gut like a bellyful of strife as he heads toward the seemingly inevitable conclusion of a terrible secret that threatens to destroy him.[43]

A few years later Cave finds new sirens and doomed mermaids in the emergent pop culture, ending "Higgs Boson Blues" with the alive-or-dead figure of Miley Cyrus "floating in a pool" in Toluca Lake (a wealthy area just north of LA), the latest addition to Cave's burgeoning cast of pretty girls lost to watery graves. Earlier in the song Cave seems to satirize her Disney alter ego, Hannah Montana, going on a colonial tourism safari and finding false paradise of simulated rainfall and toilet queue frustration, perhaps hinting at the mediated roles the manufactured young ingenue is forced into performing. Cave leaves her fate open-ended: lying face down or supine on an air mattress, he claimed the latter as the more devastating image, in keeping with "the nature of the song and the absolute spiritual collapse that's happening all around her."[44]

With the increasing number of wildfires sweeping across Californian hillsides, the song's apocalypse would have the haunted air of a premonition, where we have seen images of the rich sitting at a safe distance watching successive environmental disasters unfold as the world burns around them.

By the time of *Push the Sky Away* Cave would bring the power of perspective to the tensions between sex, aging, and creative renewal. "Water's Edge" creeps in on a sonic undertow of dense rumbling bass, the pulse of tides. Cave sees young girls on the beach who flaunt and entice with their bodies, held captive in the hard and horny stares of the local boys high on summer heat. It is the chase of wanting to be wanted, breaking themselves apart for lust without love, only to have to put themselves back together again. No doubt inspired by the rowdy Brighton nights out Cave must have heard and witnessed beneath his high windows, amused and nostalgic for the ungenteel side of English binge-drinking culture in the regency seat of former aristocracy, minor worlds colliding in small town dissipation, the frisson of sex edging somewhere closer to romantic love.[45]

This track meets with the failed romanticism of "Mermaids." Cave paints a divided portrait of frustrated lust and sexual resignation. The girls possess a knowing power that is only theirs so long as they keep their admirers at a distance; the coquettish mirror of flirting is a harsh and fleeting glimmer like a splinter of sunlight. Carrying echoes of T. S. Eliot's *The Wasteland* (written farther East, along the coast in Margate, Kent), the sea maidens threaten to become sirens, as in "Water's Edge" we dash ourselves against one another, driven by mystical urgency, not knowing where the rocks are hidden. In the permanent vista of the sea Cave finds the endless push and pull of the tides' roiling infinity, playing with the limits of his certainty and self-doubt.

Like many rock stars, where Cave's earlier songs had persisted in the young man's game as adventuring conqueror, he now faces up to the cult of youth that overtakes age, the precariousness of bodies and passing pleasures. Cave once noted a Martin Amis comment that after the age of forty women seemed to stop noticing him, no longer a sexually attractive candidate. Slightly shocked on behalf of his friend, Cave attested, "Martin Amis is a good-looking guy." This becomes the middle-aged man's perennial fear—when will the mermaids stop singing for me? On Cave's song he has aged out of their reckoning, though he cannot break his gaze. When they wave to him now, it is both "hello" and "goodbye," the "drowning" person of Stevie Smith's famous poem, poised at the knife-edge of an ending.

The meaning of the line "fired from her crotch" could go either way; steeped in past-tense resignation, Dorian Lynskey hears sexual inadequacy and rejection. It could also refer to the passionate fire of sex but, equally, the womb as the cradle of life. Turning from this image to Cave's spliced collection of vintage pornography cut up with icons of female saints, you can feel Cave channeling the weight of Gustave Courbet's notorious painting from 1866, *L'Origine du Monde* (The Origin of the World), a close-up vulva as part of a reclining female torso. The eye is drawn to focus on the pubic mound, presented willingly to a lover or voyeuristically exposed, reconnecting the idea of sex to birth-as-rebirth and the future child.[46] The viewer is challenged to take up their own point of view on the pained voyeurism of the situation. He has become a spectator to his own decline, the cuckold cut off down below while the mermaids continue to catch his eye. On "Higgs Boson Blues" Cave looks up from his basement patio hotspot toward young women in summer skirts, "their roses all in bloom." His perennial condition confronts the viewer with the compound adjective of being "cunt-struck,"[47] not unlike the conjoined agony and ecstasy of St. Teresa of Ávila. This would invite the reflex horror of the vagina dentata, which smiles back before it devours you, inciting the castration fears of Freud.

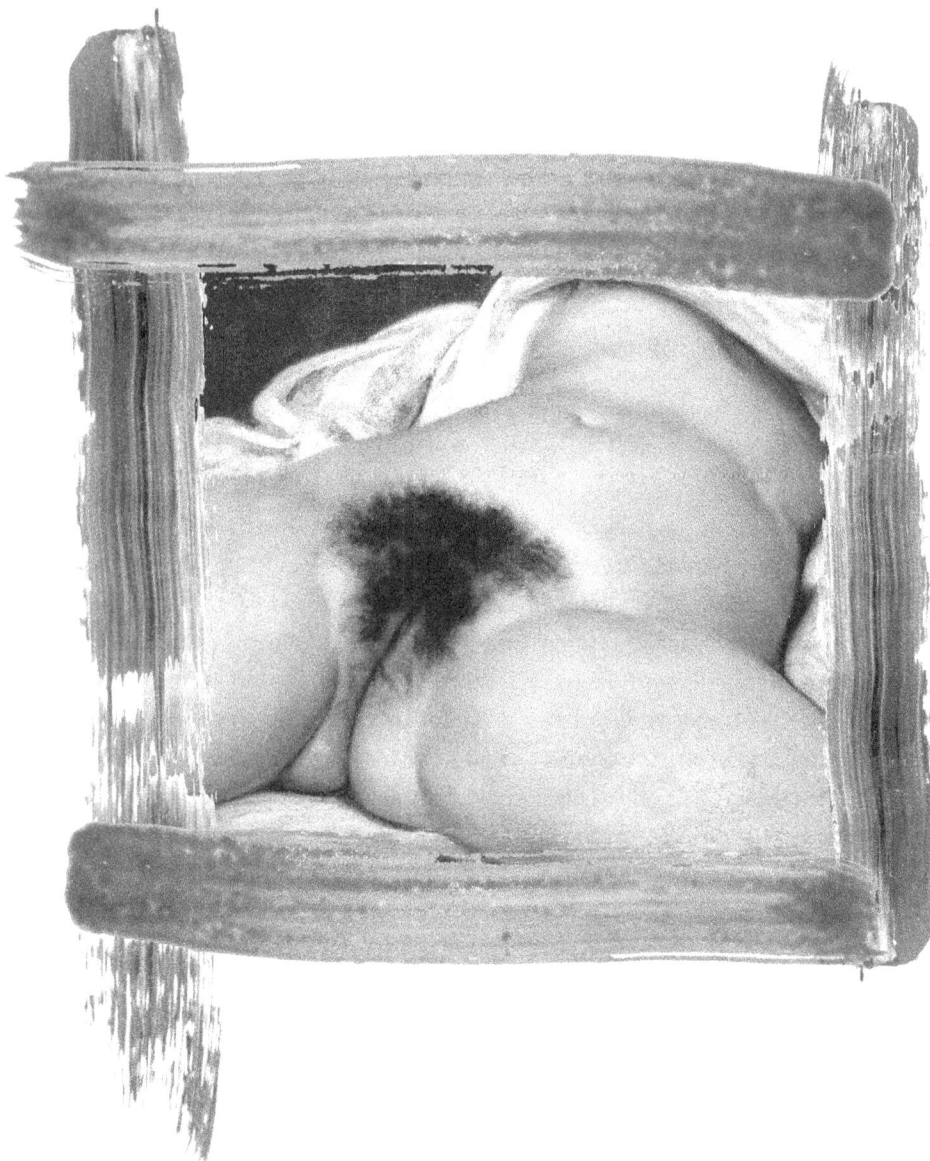

GUSTAVE COURBET L'ORIGINE DU MONDE 1866

The constant tensions of love played out across "Water's Edge" "chill, thrill and will" are scattered across memory to haunt the present. Cave lets these simple rhymes do the talking. Older and colder, the younger world is full of light but demands a cold hard shoulder turned upon the aging man who feels himself sinking with the horizon.[48] The album's tenacious sense of lust is always in decline, stalking a vicious circle of desire, and being desired, cooling in the blood and going to seed—a wave of personal crisis rushing toward breakdown. Cave recognizes his own aging as the loss of vital youth; getting older, but not growing up, the perennial condition of the rock star, but finds affirmation in his hard-won knowledge that only time and experience can bring.

Not unlike Bunny Munro the strength of the Grinderman project was to openly get down and dirty in the gutter of masculinity and repeat sometimes uncomfortable truths, exposing the stone-cold "real" man, an overdriven stereotype of insecurities masquerading as sexual threat—under perpetual fright of being replaced by a younger, stronger alpha male. On "Kitchenette" Cave yowls the chorus like an alley cat with its penis caught in a trap, plays on the classic theme of the backdoor man, pure lascivious Jim Morrison, wanting someone, who is really a "something," we cannot have. There is no love, only overriding lust that causes him to lose his mind.

"Spiritual yearning" defines much of Cave's work in regards to love. This might not seem apparent on several Grinderman songs, like "No Pussy Blues," but lascivious feelings are part of being human, the orgasm a heightened state, the lack of it, another form of yearning—even sexy songs reach for something divine, beyond ourselves. The songs would still bear traces of Cave's piano and The Bad Seeds romantic verve. The near ballad "Palaces of Montezuma" is gorgeous, bound to its surging vocal melody nestled around the French kiss of tongue-twisting lovers' tryst between Marilyn Monroe and JFK, the two conjoined by the image of a spinal column draped in a barely there negligee that embodies a mutually destructive sexual affair almost stripped of naive romanticism—meeting in eroticized fetish of the death wish.[49]

Grinderman would become a great reset as rebirth for Cave and Ellis, and in turn The Bad Seeds. The same duo who made those albums would also score numerous films of extreme and sometimes shockingly confrontational material: *The Road, Blonde,* and *Dahmer.* While embracing irony at half-tilt, Cave managed to unite feeling and the abstractions of a cultural wasteland washed up as broken anthems for a freshly alienated and thwarted generation.[50]

Amid Cave's twisted sense of humor and surrealist lyrics there is a more transgressive spirit that drives toward self-expression as resistance from censorship and a defense of fierce individualism. As exercises in control and restraint, so many of The Bad Seeds' songs are liberally bawdy Chaucerian tales of not giving a fuck and the consequences, or not, thereof.

Through the characters in his songs, Cave has declared himself a strong opponent of bowdlerisation and its sanitizing effect upon dangerous art. Already back in 2008 he noted the shift of cultural mores from the old days of sexual innuendo in the blues: "There are lots of things you can't say these days that you could say thirty years ago," a statement that would be echoed by Cave and others in the present.[51] The reason so much of The Bad Seeds' early music succeeds, and upsets, is the audacity of imagery. Cave would argue for hard psychological portraits, getting into the full guts and gore of horrific acts and terrible people to be brought into the harsh light—to show the blood-ridden hands alongside the still-warm bodies. His challenge would be to distance himself by association, half in shadow to retain some hackneyed "Prince of Darkness" edge that the more punk and goth-eager section of his audience bestowed upon him.

More recently Cave's argument for the independence of the artist from censorship has seen him advocate for the right to free speech in the creative realm and in the open discussion of social issues. Cave would own his persona as someone who grew into notoriety first, and more mainstream fame later, set within his retreat from the contemporary culture of celebrity and harsh individualism.[52] While Cave seems to push for marginal voices to be heard, he speaks against what he sees as a new age of entrenched perspectives, such as tension between antifascist and far-right groups, also the so-called "woke" gag-reflex action of cancel culture denying a platform to ill-considered and abhorrent views.[53] As if citing a wider death of affect, Cave suggests a deeper lack of awareness that many of the worst crimes against humanity are blinded by a self-righteous, neoliberal complacency, avoiding responsibility by blaming external evils. The struggle here is to make space for the "good faith" conversations, Cave suggests through the Red Hand Files, a website on which Cave invites fans to communicate with him, sending direct questions, song suggestions and even cries for help. While some messages are openly critical or hostile, though Cave rarely seeks to defend or excuse his views, merely to explain his own perspective and to accommodate others. Given the controversial material of his past music it might seem hypocritical, but Cave often presents a strong front on being secure in his own attitudes, while his songs inhabit a kind of extreme moral relativism.

On "Loverman" Cave closes each chorus with the repeated chant: "i am, what i am, what i am, what i am." It is both an excuse and unapologetic acceptance for his character's deviance, suggesting the unrestrained voice of difficult self-knowledge. In the Gospel of Mark, Jesus once asked his disciples, "Who do men say that I am?"[54] shortly after performing a series of miracles. Their reverent replies suggest he is John the Baptist, Elijah, or simply "one of the prophets." Academic Cullen Murphy noted the disciples were disingenuous and knowingly humble; they avoided mentioning the many slurs that surrounded Jesus: blasphemer, false prophet, madman. Equally they did not mention that others thought him to be Christ, the son of God. For his part Jesus was keen to shrug off his doomed fate as the savior of mankind (and its universal soul). In his struggles, Murphy sees Jesus as "a man who wishes to disturb but who is also himself disturbed," a self-flagellating rebel.[55] Cave clings to this affirmative power in the lyrics of "Red Right Hand," jostling with uneasy definitions of his seemingly enigmatic prophet. So much like the devil, he is a god/a ghost/a guru in human form become the great destroyer; taking away more than he gives, his seeming benevolence is born out of a cruel vacancy meant to test, try, and break us. There is a reason his right hand remains stained red long after the blood has been washed clean.[56]

Cave admires the writing of Flannery O'Connor, who once said, "I write because I don't know what I think until I read what I say." This quote is variously attributed to Joan Didion in a slightly altered form: "I write entirely to find out what I'm thinking, what I'm looking at, what I see and what it means. What I want and what I fear."[57] This is a sentiment shared by many creative people and echoed by Cave where he would find his positions on certain things revealed to himself in song, such as the diatribe of "God Is in The House."

Though this might sound autobiographical, confessional even, there is an aspect of deflection through the characters such as "Red Right Hand"[58] that Cave would appear to embody. Being tall and dark, a kind of bogeyman, he casts the stranger as a "handsome" figure but never tells us what he actually looks like. Put more simply Cave's songs are often expressions of his anger, rage, and humor. In this we are perhaps seeing Cave wrestle with his own demons around faith, judgment, and self-image and actively challenge himself in self-discovery through art.

A daughter of the South, O'Connor grew up in 1950s Georgia, a world that inherited the sustained racial attitudes of the past, along with land, wealth, and divisions, cultural and physical, of its recent past of slavery and conflict of the American Civil War. Cave would note the "canceling" of O'Connor after some of her work was recently removed from US libraries in 2020, in his eyes watching her "driven to the margins by an unforgiving present, taking part of me with her." Cave noted this as a form of cultural carnage; O'Connor's overt racism, recorded in her use of the "N-word" throughout her letters, though rarely in her fiction writing, marking the divide between private life and the artistic work.

Cave doesn't shy away from this himself. The only slur in an entire discography occurs in "Saint Huck": "bad-blind-nxgger at the piano."[59] Consider the use of the "N-word" throughout *The Adventures of Huckleberry Finn* (1884), which contains the word over two hundred times as a commonplace term of its time, and employed in service to Twain's overriding message of anti-racism, manifest in the relationship between the slave, Jim and young, open-minded Huck. Cave's immersion in the "Swampland" concept of the Deep South becomes a further manufactured and distant imagining of the American vernacular, a deeper work of fiction.[60]

Elsewhere Cave would criticize the BBC's decision to cut the word "faggot" from Shane MacGowan and Kirsty MacColl's Christmas song "Fairytale of New York."[61] For a song written about the pure experience of the drunk tank, with all of its ugly realities of pissed-up outbursts, it is fair and accurate to its subject, though from Cave's point of view it is simply a confrontation with hand-wringing censorship.[62] He would regret the inability of radio stations to play "Stagger Lee" boasting more fucks given and discarded than many hip-hop or punk tracks can muster.[63] Given the final come shot of "lead" that closes the song after multiple, more literal, shots are taken, Stagger's murder by ejaculation, *le grand mort*[64]—further precludes the song from mainstream airplay. "Papa Won't Leave You, Henry" with its own mention of the word "fag" is problematic, simply because the joke does not entirely depend on the slur—so why say it? Cave would play the song unedited as part of his live *Idiot Prayer* performance in Alexandra Palace. Already in 1999 Cave argued against a bloodless "hysterical technocracy of modern music" that did not allow for sorrow and pain, but more importantly irony and the right to produce an authentic voice for horrific characters.

Cave's defense of his lyrics would amount to an argument against a blanket ban of moral censure on creative work, offering both mystical and practical points: "Songs are divinely constituted organisms. They have their own integrity. As flawed as they may be, the souls of the songs must be protected at all costs. They must be allowed to exist in all their aberrant horror, unmolested by these strident advocates of the innocuous, even if just as some indication that the world has moved toward a better, fairer and more sensitive place."

Cave's response is not reactionary but it is absolute: free speech for art, but like actions, individuals must be prepared to face the consequences of their words. Perhaps rightly critiquing an overly sensitive contemporary culture, with which he claims to have uniquely fallen in step as an arch-agitator, Cave overemphasizes: "What songwriter could have predicted thirty years ago that the future would lose its sense of humor, its sense of playfulness, its sense of context, nuance and irony, and fall into the hands of a perpetually pissed-off coterie of pearl-clutchers? How were we to know?" By turns songs are bombs of truth and also delicate slivers of artful wonder. What is problematic for fans of Cave is his being taken up as a new big-C conservative saint by idiotic, anti-"woke" libertarian media who argue for extremist freedom in all areas of life.[65]

In Grinderman songs the funny, angry man voice comes to the fore. On "Kitchenette" Cave yells at goofy-looking kid in the streets, letting the id run riot, unwilling to check himself. Many of those songs go full frontal in sexual lasciviousness and innuendo in the grand old traditions of the blues and rock and roll. While in the voice of the angry man he won't be held responsible for his actions and wants to say whatever he thinks or feels, happier to cut out his tongue than to check himself. Cave's argument is perhaps simplistic—letting the horrible aspect of older songs stand and fall for what they are. As with his openhanded retreat from the question of the muse and the place of women in his songs, Cave invites barbs of criticism but doesn't feel the need to renege on or repent for his work. In his blank-faced admission he makes the subject ahistorical; there is nothing we can do, now, the song has already exploded, we live in the aftermath. Cave's argument seems to be that it is wrong to continually regret or seek to alter the creative past, as if the song had never put a foot wrong in the first place. In the Red Hand Files entry #149 about hope from May 2021, Cave responds that it is not possible to separate the artist from their work, nor should we wish to. But there must be layers. Where the "Nick Cave" onstage, in the studio, or writing songs, is never entirely Nick Cave the private person, though a part of him touches everything he does. When bad people make good art it is its own form of transgression, as Cave says: "to make beauty from the unbeautiful" there is no need for distancing; to do so might be considered an act of artistic cowardice and insincerity in the first place—it is enough to love the song but not the singer.[66]

Cave would invite controversy from his fellow musicians in 2017 when he and The Bad Seeds decided to play two concerts in Tel Aviv, Israel, a state that many other acts from Western liberal nations have proactively boycotted in protest against Israel's human rights abuses. The ex–Pink Floyd singer and full-time egotist Roger Waters is a firm critic of Israel and its militarized occupation of Palestine. He would write an open letter, entreating and cajoling Cave to join his cause, citing the human rights breaches and acts of violent persecution carried out by the Israeli state and its settler communities.

Cave would praise Israel and its people while also criticizing its government's military-industrial state of violence, often exacerbated by the conscripted members of the Israeli Defense Force.[67] Though Cave debated the idea of not playing as a form of artistic censorship: it was his creative self that he wanted to put forward to audiences, not his personal views. The concert would be for the citizens of Tel Aviv as people: "I think it's not my place as a musician and an artist to put forward my political points of view within my songs. I don't trust artists who use their creative impulses as a platform to push their particular political agendas down the necks of their audience. I find that gross, to be honest. I don't want to go onstage and preach to people about things. I try to stay outside of that—which is not to say I don't have my own political opinions."[68] Cave would later joke that rock stars are perhaps the most ill-informed to comment on social issues, coming from the worst position of power and influence, regardless of the content of their opinions.[69]

Cave would affirm his position around separation between church and state, and art and politics when questioned about controversially outspoken figures such as Kanye West and Morrissey. In a 2022 Q&A event with Sean O'Hagan at the Southbank Centre, Cave would praise both, citing Kayne West as one of the greatest living artists[70] and responding to an audience question about Morrissey's support for far-right political groups. Cave wrote off Morrissey's views, supporting his right to expression, again stating that he should expect to be challenged, though he defended Morrissey's (past) musical track record: "He has created original and distinctive works of unparalleled beauty, that will long outlast his offending political alliances."[71] While Cave was also quick to acknowledge the musical brilliance of Kanye West's songs,[72] with his more recent abrasive works an influence on Cave and Ellis, he acknowledged that West's idiotic views put him off and again were to be openly criticized and for their intellectual weakness to be readily exposed.[73]

Certainly, Cave's earliest music is purposefully transgressive. The Birthday Party was not intended as a project of contempt against the world, but as resistance to the narrowing of culture that the ideal society can sink toward. After this, The Bad Seeds Cave continued to play with language, controversial concepts, and ugly imagery. His songs are works unto themselves—inexplicable to overanalysis. In much the same tone Vladimir Nabokov declared that everything he wished to say about his books was there in the work, and the rest would be propaganda.

Cave declares himself a conservative person with a small "c" in this, he again enjoys the position of an arch-contrarian.[74] He explains that he errs toward traditional values but is economically liberal. As many aging artists hold more firmly to their convictions, so Cave praises the strength of the family, the unity of faith where the congregation of a church, in the broadest sense, is a way of bringing people together but not under a banner of sameness. Elsewhere he talks about children needing free-range childhoods, reflecting on his own experiences of growing up in the countryside with less rules and more opportunity of adventure.

Cave would argue for the sovereignty of the individual as an embodiment of free speech, which includes the freedom to be wrong, and to admit to our mistakes.[75] As stated in *Faith, Hope and Carnage*, Cave is keen for rhetorical exercise, to talk through concepts and beliefs rather than to have a conversation prematurely closed down. Not without some humor, Cave would cite Jesus as being canceled upon the cross; a controversial figure and corrupter of the youth like Socrates, he willingly drank the hemlock, just as Jesus walked the stations of the cross toward the hill at Calvary—dying to make a point.[76] Cave states that like his purposeful agitation, a heretic to social conformity, these once-dangerous ideas might yet save the world.[77]

The need to speak loudly, born from a desire to be heard, noticed, read, or understood, is a freedom worth saving. For Cave in particular this feels like a hard-won journey of self-discovery: "My sole intention all along has been to access my voice about things and not to dilute it. From all that a unique voice has emerged . . . but it's taken a very long time."[78] Listening back to the 1981 live version of The Birthday Party's "King Ink" we hear Cave rolling and roiling on the floor, yielding to the song's midway maelstrom. He continues to yell, "Say something" "express yourself, express yourself!" squared against Tracy Pew's hip-thrusting bass to Rowland S. Howard's tight angular riffs.[79] This is performance overriding common sense, the duke of confrontation fighting to get a reaction and short circuit the numbed everyday—the enervating power of art as autodestruction of the voice.[80]

For all Cave's argument on the sanctity of artistic free speech—including the right to transgress rules, codes of convention, and the boundaries of good taste—he longs for a return to the joyful play of language where art can be made new, unbound by tradition. Where the audience can decide what makes something good art purely by the emotional reaction it evokes in them—becoming an invitation to share in the crooked smile—the last laugh is ours, and the joke is on us.

BOOK II
MIDNIGHT

ONE EYE ON DEATH

Life is very sweet, brother; who would wish to die?
There's the wind on the heath, brother;
if I could only feel that,
I would gladly live forever!

In his script for *The Proposition* Nick Cave quotes from a novel by George Borrow as the final words of John Hurt's dying bounty hunter. So much of Cave's early music is similarly preoccupied with death, the dirty wretched business of dying. The continued challenge of his songs is to overcome the existential hinge of life as incommensurable to death and realize a future outside of morbidity. Through The Birthday Party Cave first tried to overturn the withheld promise of seizing each day as a new sunrise. A group of manic males in their early twenties with nothing to lose (but their lives) in the name of art, the band pursued a pseudo death drive, presenting themselves as constant revelers in sex, alcohol, drugs, and violence in pure Dionysian overkill. The Birthday Party would be cast as an autodestructive force captured on tape—"We created a monster" Cave told *Zig Zag* in 1985. Their inbound fatalism was enshrined in live shows where the band embodied acts of living theater that often came to outshine the mood-driven nous and rigorous dynamics of their songs. Tracy Pew's bass throb that sounded like a death rattle banging the coffin lid from the grave and Rowland S. Howard's searing guitar lines, shrieking and swooping arcs of white noise, would saw the songs in half, while Cave was forced to scream beyond singing just to make himself heard. Where Cave cries "flame on, flame on,"[1] he becomes the dark herald of the burning house as mutual death—we are all going to die here together, dancing in the snowfall of our ashes: "I felt a genuine rage in those days, a disgust at myself and the world around me."[2] Years later Cave would reflect upon this sentiment: "Pissed off at the world, disdainful of the people in it, and thinking my contempt for things somehow amounted to something."[3]

Death was a straw man, always held at a remove; death is for tomorrow, life is for the good times, here and now, though The Bad Seeds' early music would not necessarily reflect this undercurrent of tailspinning joie de vivre. Ritual death was normalized into the mechanics of the band's songs, with only the murderers of ex-lovers left behind. Their mindscape became a barren earth, its endless blood-dimmed tide sweeping across the land with every revolution from sun turned into moon—though few have the time to stop and take count—death goes on with or without our watching. We hear the same rhythmic laps run across news feeds of blood into ink, snatches of broken tongues lick about your ears, a voice you can't shake long after it has moved on. Cave's songs merge the cycle of love, death, and birth into a single pulse, a relentless, unstoppable wave.

The opening track from 1996's *Murder Ballads* album "Song of Joy" returns us to the image of Milton's "red right hand" in baroque spine-tingling piano and cymbal splashes. We hear of the husband and father of a murdered family turned drifter who presents himself as a wandering victim sharing his sorry tale, seeking shelter with another family.[4] But in his repeated allusions to *Paradise Lost* we hear the same phrase[5] painted on the wall in the victims' blood, it is slowly revealed to us that he is actually the killer, making himself an echo of the vengeful and jealous God. Cave's song carries a strange resonance with the "Manson family" murders where "PIG" and "HELTER SKELTER" were written around the house at 10050 Cielo Drive in the victims' blood.[6]

On the same album "O'Malley's Bar" takes this appetite for ultraviolence to its limit. The song's monster narrative accelerates hung, drawn, and quartered into the cadaver of a minor epic.[7] On the B side version of the song, split into the three parts, the violence would only increase, with the rising damp of bloody murder creeping up the walls. "Crow Jane" nestles blasé honky-tonky lounge piano with a pastiche of the brutal 1970s revenge movie genre, depicting the eponymous girl gang-raped by twenty men. She takes revenge by murdering them all, marked by the small town's population being slashed in half. This excess death would become parodic: the body count of *Murder Ballads* eventually stacks up to sixty-six people and one dog.[8]

Cave is often tagged with a deep pessimism that overshadows his music, but the songs do not collapse into dirge; they remain energetic, vital, the sonic force of The Bad Seeds making Cave's words live. He would reflect on the inner struggle between light and shade in his most melancholy songs: "I often think that the violence in my songs is really a metaphor that speaks about the darker side of my personality and I feel very much split in two. I have two very strong sides to my character; one is a definite tendency to self-destruction and one is quite austere and clean and spirited and I think the violence in my lyrics is a representation of that side."[9]

By virtue of the blacker-than-black vibes of their music, it would seem inevitable that The Birthday Party (and to a lesser extent the freshly formed Bad Seeds) would invite comparisons to the aesthetics and themes of goth music, drawing upon the more traditional history of gothic culture and the maudlin sensibilities of the Victorian era that romanticized the arcane mirror world of death and dissipation, set against their own strict Christian morality. The new goths went beyond this decadent spirit and made it their own; it was as much inflamed by the extreme drug cultures of heroin and absinthe, but equally pints of snakebite and cheap speed along with occasional LSD drops—a psychic cocktail that could be equally applied to The Birthday Party in those early heady days. Fueled by a furious naivete—taking the shortcut to nihilism—the music of both bands might seem world weary before its time but also freakishly alive to reality. Even the band's po-faced demeanor was self-mocking, while the brilliant racket they made was pure horrorshow spectacle.[10]

Writing about the single "Release the Bats," Andrew Collins notes there was division over whether The Birthday Party were there to "praise or to bury" goth, a trend that gathered force into a snowball from hell by virtue of this momentum becoming known as "positive punk." The song remains a postpunk pastiche, a staple of future goth compilations, though it was released partly in jest at the band being labeled by association. Cave admitted, "We thought they were barking up the wrong tree. But we were in no position to pick and choose. A little bit of attention, perhaps wrongly applied, was better than nothing."[11] Alongside this was Cave's short but profound fascination with American Southern Gothic—veering away from its historical roots via a mutation of the American Deep South to the late twentieth-century manifestation that gave off the stink of unholy bliss, it was inherently dark, death leering, and decadent. Often death is attached to sleep—echoing Hamlet's immortal lines—The Birthday Party track "Deep in the Woods" hints at Edgar Allen Poe's call for the "big" sleep as descent into peace, free from the struggles of life.[12]

The Birthday Party carried their own unsettling aura of shock and awe, with half of the band standing over six feet tall, they loomed larger than life. Now a recognized producer, in 1983 Nick Launay was a tea boy at London's Townhouse studios. He remembers being asked to give the band a lift: "They really did look like vampires. Very ill and pale, mountains of black hair, elegant and wasted. Really cool."[13] Particularly in the first-sight domineering figure of bassist Tracy Pew,[14] the band carried a foreboding sense of invulnerability and self-belief, manifest in the fresh hell of blood and aggression that arrived once they took to the stage.[15] The band's seemingly nihilistic escape from "real" life concerns of the mundane soon burned itself into their extreme profile, foreshadowed by their reputation.[16]

Cave's tall but scant frame seemed to worry on the weight of its shadow, unfurling like a spider burgeoning with gangling menace. Mat Snow would note the "predatory glamor" that stalked alongside him.[17] Speaking in 2014 Cave would find the aura of his persona chased into the "one-line drawing" of an iconic silhouette, an unbroken thread binding the rock star to their audience. The public image of the poised and composed Nick Cave would stand in stark contrast to the wild man, broken back snapped in the throes of performance, overreaching toward Iggy Pop levels of flex. Cave switched from stillness to explosion, sweat-ridden hair swept across his face in a matted black wave, like The Birthday Party, always threatening implosion, a courtesy to which they would eventually oblige. Cave himself seemed to possess a rare quality of being separate but engaged, compellingly universal and universally compelling, allowing him to light out on what initially began as a solo career but would become the gravitational core of The Bad Seeds.[18]

As if marking the break away from wilder days, by the 1990s Cave adopted the wearing of a dark "rarely black" suit as a pointed mark of professionalism.[19] Tony Dushane would compare the more austere Cave style to Grinderman's increasingly risqué practice of gradually undoing shirt buttons toward the navel as their stage time drew closer, forever "toeing that thin line between looking like a well-dressed preacher or a high-end pimp." When Warren Ellis first joined the band wearing a bomber jacket and shorts made out of flour bags by his then speed freak girlfriend, Cave made a mention of his "sartorial" appearance, forcing Ellis to look up the word. The rest of the band would soon fall into line, sometimes resembling a gang of rangy undertakers. Chris Bailey of The Saints observed, "Nick is fairly cosmopolitan, but has an Australian larrikin element—and not just because half his band looks like Ned Kelly."[20]

From the start of Cave's career with The Bad Seeds, a gothic-tinged masochism was present at the heart of his songs, edging toward an inner self-loathing eating away at the outward defiance. Opening *From Her to Eternity* with a cover of Leonard Cohen's "Avalanche" from his 1970 album *Songs of Love and Hate*, Cave placed himself under the aegis of bodily degradation as a fading spirit, undermined by its own cruelty. The album was a major influence on young Cave; from the very first line, the song seems to encapsulate Cave's career:

> *You who wish to conquer pain*
> *You must learn what makes me kind*

"Avalanche" works through its latent suggestion of emotional and physical violence continually threatened during Cave's career. It suggests the wearing of another's flesh as brutal dysmorphia of damaged souls expressed through body horror—submerged cruelty that becomes overt at the failure of kindness.[21] Cave's vocal would leer on these lines as a further twist of the knife:

> *Your pain is no credential here*
> *It's just a shadow of my wound*[22]

While Cohen's original featured his sinuous fingerpicked acoustic guitar creating rhythmic urgency behind the words, The Bad Seeds' cover begins with a rumble of snow and ice, less a thaw than a surrender to fate collapsing down upon their heads. Their rendition is struck by the jittery slides and snarls of Blixa Bargeld's guitar, acting as a precursor to "Stranger Than Kindness." Suitably tortured, Blixa also fingerpicks the strings of his electric guitar, layering several tracks into a dense tangle of wire that creates a biting mesh around Cave's lonely vocal embodying Anita Lane's lyrics at the song's fragile heart. The song seems to feed on the same energy as Cohen's hymn to (self-)abnegation and the rigors of being caged by the body—desperate to escape from the feeling of one's own flesh. Much heavier and denser than the original "Avalanche," Cohen would offer sardonic praise: "I guess you could say Nick Cave butchered my song, Avalanche, and if that's the case, let there be more butchers like that."[23]

Inviting the grotesque, Cave loves a casual deformity in his songs; where Cohen uses the "hunchback" figure, the freak outsider is nomadic but always held within society's judgmental gaze. Cave embraces the mixed perceptions of ugliness inside and out, as in Kafka's *The Trial* we meet a lawyer's daughter and her webbed hand described as "a pretty little paw" and in Carson McCullers' *The Ballad of the Sad Café* where a person with a "hunchback" (kyphosis) inspires love in the town's cruelest matriarch, only to betray her. Feeding on these awkward and jilted moments of connection, many of Cave's lyrics from the early 1980s are fed through the mangle of a crooked man's perspective, haunted both by the uncertain and difficult miles ahead of him and the shadowy path that stalks him from behind. Finding imperfect beauty in the fucked-up, the flawed and the freak would inspire Cave in his musical efforts to bring the circus to town and make it his creative home.

"The Carny" takes this motion toward extreme dark parody as Cave establishes an excess of horrific spectacle and tragedy reminiscent of the 1932 film *Freaks*.[24] A "carny" is a slang term for carnival or circus folk, but in Cave's world he is at once both servant and king; the shadow gear behind the ringmaster, he runs the show but is also stuck in the grind of carnival life. Producer Flood remembered the recording process at Berlin's Hansa studios: "That was the first day of recording *Your Funeral . . . My Trial*, and that kind of set the tone for the whole record. In some respects, it encapsulated everything about that album on one track. This was in Hansa, Berlin, so it seemed perfectly suited to the location. Berlin was part of 'The Carny,' without a shadow of a doubt. I abhor opera, and I abhor musicals even more, but it's theater. The whole Kurt Weill thing, that is much more what Nick feels at home with."

Mick Harvey would deliver the guts of a piano to the studio, plucking the strings with a guitar plectrum in time with Cave's piano chords, a heavy bass *blomp* dropped into their lap with tingling vibraphone and marimbas, each note clawing its way up the spine as the hurdy gurdy organ lurches on in seasick curves that pitch and roll the song into psychedelic indigestion.[25] Every instrument is beaten as percussion becomes an act of punishment, with every note another stab at brokenness. Pieced together from a series of "oblique sounds," the song arrived as an outpouring from Cave's brain to realize the orchestra from hell.[26]

His double-tracked, sing-speaking vocals made Cave sound both eerie and soulful. The ghost cry of the horse, Sorrow, is taken up by Blixa Bargeld's whinnying shrieks of guitar cutting through like a razor. "The Carny" exits the scene as a shadow, passing the storyteller on his way out. No one saw him leave as the song spirals down into helter-skelter maelstrom of the oompah organ dancing over the muddy pit of Sorrow's grave.

The morbidity of Cave's early music would become nestled into the drugs and alcohol depression of the perpetual hangover among The Bad Seeds, with heroin central to Cave's growing complaint, he was either high or working on getting high. As early as 1983's *Mutiny* EP Cave would point toward his struggle with addiction. As Australian outcasts in London, bitterly disappointed by the food, weather and the advent of post-punk indie jangle; the band reacted with consistent hedonism, delighting in the Rimbaldian derangement of the senses. This merged into a deathly pale air, constantly on the verge of sudden illness or physical collapse, sickly seeming forms become a mere host for Cave's tenacious spirit, held together by resolve and unfettered ambition.[27]

"Mutiny in Heaven" offers a brazen nod to the fatalism of *Paradise Lost* and Milton's imagined outrage of heaven at war with itself, Cave would cast himself as the disconsolate outcast of Lucifer, never entirely angel or devil. The Birthday Party allowed themselves the contrarian liberty to chant "if this is heaven—I'm bailing out!" nailing down the hypocritical abuses of the priesthood and enshrining the freedom to fix up heroin—trauma, spiritual tribulation, and self-medication dancing hand over fist.[28] This key early track hints at the doom-laden vibe that the band began to embody in their nocturnal look and the insidious junkie aura that gravitated around them. Cave noted the band were less political than aesthetically radical, living in a squat for lack of funds, drifting from room to room in each ruined house; haunted by failure stepping over the remnants of other lives, people who never meant to stay. An early photograph by David Corio in 1981 shows the band inside a disused church in Kilburn, London. Standing amid collapsed pews, dust scuffed from breaking and entering or kneeling in supplication, they clutch an old banner "Surprising Where You Find God," shadows inside the ruined house of broken and uncertain faith.

Not unlike David Bowie, Cave's most drug-sick era seems to have been lived almost nocturnally but still functioning within a fierce work ethic. Often studio bound or writing in his notebook first thing in the morning, he worked prolifically throughout the 1980s at a breathless rate of production regimented by Mick Harvey toward intensely focused studio time, laying down basic tracks within a few days, moving by instinct more than rational overthinking. The Bad Seeds managed to record almost one album a year in the 1980s, a rate of production that must have been as exhausting as it was exhilarating, dancing along the knife edge of collapse and creative endeavor. Accordingly, Cave still claims to this day to have only missed one Bad Seeds show in his entire career.

In a 1994 interview with Joe Jackson, Cave admitted to darker, destructive impulses in his life, particularly around 1988 and the *Tender Prey* era in Berlin. Doing lots of speed and heroin, he assumed the role of the outcast within his own band. In the crooked shuffle of "Brother My Cup Is Empty" (1992) Cave declares himself "the captain" of his pain, taking command as the agent of self-destruction—if he must be made to suffer, it will be by his own hand.[29] In a celebration of decadence for its own sake, the cup doubles as a spiritual symbol but equally the vessel of renewed solace for the faithless until it suddenly runs dry.[30] Speaking to *The South Bank Show* in 2003, Cave observed that excess seemed to come hand in hand with band life: "We drank a lot and experimented with drugs" before becoming more candid: "I took a lot of drugs for a long time."

Cave's pattern of addiction would verge on a kind of ritual observed with almost religious dedication. "Sunday's Slave" (1988) has Cave perform a slurring waltz through his nocturnal grind, carrying the metaphor of addiction with him through the sinking song, in and out of doors to nowhere. All days come back around to more of the same—life made deathly dull—like a permanent Sunday. Cave would be divided over the rights and wrongs of heroin use; like many before him, he saw himself as a responsible addict, talking himself into the corner that he managed his drug-taking routine. The transience of "Brompton Oratory" finds him drifting as he floats in and out of music making as serious a commitment as he can, chipping away at new songs.

Cave once compared the experience of heroin to riding a bike over a road of banana skins without brakes or handlebars—at times he was happy, engaged, ecstatic, while elsewhere he could barely keep awake through his own life. Although he always maintained creative activity, heroin became its own crutch that enabled him just to feel okay again, a coping mechanism. As the intervals grew shorter, scoring, shooting up, and fighting sleep became a single blurred state, punctuated by making music. Like Bowie's "Always Crashing in the Same Car" speaks to the vicious cycle of his own cocaine and alcohol addiction, where the drug life becomes a ride you have to exit before you lose control and somebody dies. Undermined by his addictions, Cave dug himself deeper, stuck in a kind of recurring snow blindness as he struggled to escape from himself.[31]

Heavy drug use became another confrontation with death—to repeatedly cheat and even mock death.[32] Mark Mordue notes how many friends of Cave would recall his good fortune at never coming away seriously injured from his many scrapes: riding on the top of stolen crashing cars, overdosing, drunken brawls—he seemed to float just a finger's breadth above his troubles without a physical scratch. In the (mortal) words of Emily Dickinson, "because I would not stop for death,"[33] young Cave simply did not have the time, suggesting a form of constant escapism: "There was just an accelerated pace to my life where I didn't allow things to affect me. I didn't stand still long enough. I was too busy to die, although I came close, overdosing on several occasions."[34]

For many years Cave seemed to race toward this great blind spot of uncertainty, a chain smoker who miraculously endured decades of self-abuse. Though Cave maintained a liberal attitude toward recreational drug use he would also admit the self-deception of the functioning addict: "I have no problem with drug taking, I never have. I was a junkie for twenty years." Asked why he stopped, he replied, "Well it is impossible to function on every level so I basically had to stop."[35] In *Faith, Hope, and Carnage*, Cave would advocate for shooting galleries as a system for people to take heroin in a controlled and safe environment, as a potential step toward getting clean.[36]

Cave would later explain that after repeated stints in and out of rehab, often ordered by the court to avoid a prison sentence, he finally kicked heroin in an Arizona rehab facility with the support of Susie Bick, after an ultimatum that she would no longer see him if he didn't get clean.[37] Cave acknowledged the value of the twelve-step program of Narcotics Anonymous, not unlike the moral examples he found in the

life of Jesus Christ "as a series of suggestions as to how to live a life—the original 'antidote to chaos.'"[38]

Cave would later criticize his original view that good creative work demanded a conflicted and self-destructive private life: "What I get a lot of creative stimulation from is the chaos of confusion. When my life is chaotic and confused and destructive, I fill up with a lot of ideas. I find that when my life is ordered and more disciplined a lot of the ideas that I'd drawn into myself come out. I think there's a lot of pain and unhappiness in my confused and destructive side but there's a lot of genuine happiness and joy that is in the other side and when I'm writing, it's when I'm elated and happy."[39]

Though Cave would routinely admit all through the 1980s and 1990s that he essentially saw the world as a punishing place, he claimed this did not push him toward despair, though it would draw him toward the darker edges of life casting long shadows across his music.[40] Increasingly Cave argued that his songs offered a sincere connection with the world as it really is. Speaking in an interview about the release of *Lyre of Orpheus/Abattoir Blues* in 2004: "I don't see them to be miserable songs. Or nihilistic songs even. They're songs with a lot of heart and a lot of belief in beauty." Even as "Abattoir Blues," "Cannibal's Hymn," and "Messiah Ward" would share a comorbid perspective, offering a sickly gloss as anthems of dislocation, carving a hard line between those who choose to fight on further into life while others are too busy trying not to die. As noted by Mark Mordue, Cave's family home in Wangaratta was down the road from the local abattoir, which Cave elsewhere refers to as the "blood factory"; these songs speak to the rising smell of death. The Bad Seeds' music behind the songs would often prove a revelation—where searing organs, fierce drum sounds, and roaring guitars met with Cave's ascending piano lines, a crooked staircase that points to a way beyond the claustrophobic of aura of decay as the song sinks into the mass of rising bodies.[41]

In Red Hand File #190, April 2022, Cave would criticize his former "disdain" for life emerging from the position of someone who did not yet know what loss truly meant. He said, "I know this because much of my early life was spent holding the world and the people in it in contempt. It was a position both seductive and indulgent. The truth is, I was young and had no idea what was coming down the line."[42]

Already an album of dark subject matter, the emotive force of 2016's *Skeleton Tree* would be further complicated in the wake of Arthur's death, marking it as a record of internalized conflict. Real-life events overtook the record, with Cave feeling compelled to return and amend some lyrics, though many of the songs would remain unchanged. A powerful and beautiful album, it would bear the brunt of what Cave would refer to as the annihilating force of grief that would come to mark a rupture in time. The song "Jesus Alone" would take on new meaning both for Cave and listeners, the album itself becoming an affirmation of what it is to lose someone close to you and in turn to reflect upon our own mortality.[43]

Connor Harrison writes about Jesus walking with his disciples after the Last Supper, already knowing he will be betrayed; every step of his walk to the garden of Gethsemane at the foot of the Mount of Olives brings him closer to his own crucifixion. Jesus stops to pray alone, exposed in his humanity: "Fell on his face, and prayed, saying, O my father, if it be possible, let this cup pass from me." The cup is a poisoned chalice of his burden and responsibility to God. In this Harrison finds, "He admits to experiencing that most human crisis: he doesn't want to die." Jesus asks his friends to keep watch over him; several times they fall asleep and several times he goes to pray. As he would later be deserted upon the cross, Harrison sees Jesus spiritually and physically isolated: "someone who didn't know they were so alone." He can only count upon himself and must admit to his own responsibility. "Jesus Alone" suggests a vicious crash landing into reality; human mortality is a wreckage from which we must resurrect a meaningful life. Cave's voice dominates the song, seeking connection only for his call to echo back hollow. With no kind word to reach him, he underlines the isolation sometimes felt in our distance from God, inviting doubt into an already uncertain universe. "Jesus Alone" would come to mirror Christ's own tragedy of being abandoned, his trial cast against the lives of the humans he died to save from themselves.

Where *Push the Sky Away* delivered a widescreen breath of life, *Skeleton Tree* withdrew into a needle point of intensity, a dark mirror to the illumination that would later flow from *Ghosteen*. It embodies the day-to-day struggle of living through grief, where the future is marred by uncertainty, nothing more or less than a point in time collapsed into itself. Cave's lyrics are shot through with sudden blasts of gloom and memory; he looks for a shape to the songs veering between presence and absence.[44]

Cave would describe the vulnerability and grace under pressure demanded of him at being forced to grieve in public as akin to having his shell ripped off. The 2016 documentary *One More Time With Feeling* was commissioned by Cave to be directed by trusted collaborator Andrew Dominik on the agreement that they would address Cave's experiences of loss and that Cave would be given final cut. Produced to avoid a series of interviews in which Cave would be asked the same difficult questions by different journalists, he broke free of the media cycle, allowing the film to do the talking in an honest and measured way.

Shot in stark, high-contrast black and white, it seemed an honest portrayal of a world drained of color. Cave is clearly vulnerable; he largely avoids the camera's gaze, where before he would meet it head-on. Dominik shoots in a way that orbits around Cave at the piano, moving through the operations of the performance with certainty; it created a safe space for the *Skeleton Tree* songs to be heard, removed from judgment. Speaking to the *Guardian* in 2016 Andrew Domink describes how the film became an act of "self-preservation" for Cave: "Nick deals with everything in life by working, if his heart is broken, he can turn it into a song, everything is a grist for the mill. But I don't think the film, or the songs, helped him with his grief. Perhaps momentarily. But this thing is so big, you can't even get your arms around it."[45]

Loss remains a recurring theme throughout Cave's songs; cutting across love and death it becomes the arbiter of existence. An English teacher who helped to encourage his son's love of art and learning, Colin Cave would read *Lolita* and other key books to Nick, marking a fundamental step toward the artist he was to become. In 1979 Cave's mother was summoned away from his jail cell to be told of her husband's death, just as she had arrived to bail Nick out from St. Kilda police station. In shock at the news, Cave would remember two police officers in the background discussing the murder of a prostitute, a strange but also very Cavean moment.[46]

His father's death in 1979 seemed to spark a personal crisis in the young Cave, who would first leave Australia in 1980 never to resettle there: "He was here one minute and gone the next." Although Cave brooks the idea that his father's death was the catalyst for his self-imposed exile and extreme risky behaviors (he had already been using heroin since his late teens), his father remained an undeciphered, totemic ache: "I see that my artistic life has centered around an attempt to articulate an almost palpable sense of loss that laid claim to my life. A great gaping hole was blasted out of my world by the unexpected death of my father when I was 19."[47]

His father remained a spirit of influence who came and went. Colin Cave would be mentioned in interviews and alluded to in songs, at different times criticized, praised, or shooed away, Cave appears to express things that he never had the chance to say to him in life.[48] The Grinderman song "Man in the Moon" shows Cave tap-tapping away on the typewriter, with roles reversed his father the teacher is somewhere else receiving Cave's words as faint signals. The son looks less for approval than keeping some broken connection alive, haunted by the "presence of distance"; loss is a void filled with longing that cannot be bridged.[49]

From the mourning of the fractured relationships that defined *The Boatman's Call*, Cave would later explore the idea of love as a compact with life, where in loving someone we must be prepared to let them go: "It seems to me, that if we love, we grieve. That's the deal," he writes. "Grief is the terrible reminder of the depths of our love and, like love, grief is non-negotiable. There is a vastness to grief that overwhelms our minuscule selves."[50]

"The Weeping Song" is an early Bad Seeds track from 1990's *The Good Son* that first pushed toward a new sincerity around loss; becoming a hymn to cathartic struggle, the song extends the idea that throughout life moments of sadness will inevitably find us out. It was sung as a duet between Cave and Blixa Bargeld, and many people missed out on the exchange of perceived wisdom being passed down from father (Blixa) to son (Cave) caught up in the willful tragedy of the *saudade*.[51] The father suggests that children cry without understanding what it really means; though Cave responds, "I won't be weeping long," he knows that sadness continues long after our tears have run dry. The roles are reversed partway through the song when it becomes the father's turn to cry; there is a shared bond where they come to feel one another's hurt.[52]

The song "Sorrow's Child" from the same album continues the conversation in its swooping and swooning chorus spiked by orchestral flourishes. Like the endless rain of "Papa Won't Leave You, Henry," Cave throws up the idea of drowning in his sorrow that falls upon the singer like a hail of tears, where the last sadness will only end when it is washed away by the next. In 2001's "Oh My Lord" these tears become answered prayers, a foreshadowing of being careful what you wish for. These ripples of sadness are hurled into extended time, sparking the apprehension of future pain we know "is yet to come" while remaining anchored to reflections of the past—it never goes away.

The album *The Good Son* continued a gradual shift of perception for Cave. In 1990 he married the journalist Viviane Carneiro, and they had a son together, Luke, born in 1991. The sudden interruption of the relative chaos of making music by family life changed Cave's perspective (alongside The Bad Seeds) and the expectations of a rock and roll star persona. Cave would state, "I feel more a part of the world," a major shift in both his music and in his personal life.

For a time, Cave would find life in Brazil relaxed and easy. Where before he had been happy in his alienation, people were more or less dispensable through the prism of addiction, the lack of heroin supply in São Paulo at that time enforced a cleaner period, though he would increasingly rely on alcohol. He told Australian *Rolling Stone* that his initial positivity and loved-up mood were present in the São Paulo recording sessions of *The Good Son* album. With generally brighter and more openly melodic sounds on tracks like "The Ship Song," Mick Harvey would wryly note that Cave's wild rage had given way to a "gentleman muse."[53] Shedding the druggy heaviness of the 1980s Bad Seeds albums, Cave observed, "I was quite happy there. I was in love and the first year or two was good."[54]

The conjoined state of bliss and disquiet would manifest in 1992's "Papa Won't Leave You, Henry": "It's this sprawling, lyrical thing. That song was composed over a long period of time and something that I would sing to my little son, Luke. It was kind of a nasty fucked-up lullaby":[55] A mad fever dream of sadomasochism and extreme violence casually performed alongside the threat of being swallowed up in the jaws of the night. Cave claimed that the song was written more or less in his head, exposing the deeper fears and concerns for his newborn child common to so many parents, suddenly made vulnerable by new life in their arms.[56]

In a 2010 interview Cave pointed out that his homelife did not "center" him, although it certainly changed his outlook on life, particularly where his marriage to Susie Bick suggested a second chance at family life. Where before Cave's preoccupation with death and mortality were presented as a challenge, life was something to be confronted or overcome, the second half of his career maintains a more celebratory and elegiac mood that works alongside darker but equally sincere material. Cave would conclude *Murder Ballads* with a cover of Bob Dylan's "Death Is Not the End," suggesting a life beyond, in heaven: "just kind of a jokey little punctuation mark to the whole thing. There's tongue-in-cheek to that song, even though I think it's quite a beautiful rendition." Speaking in 1999, Cave would admit that as he grew up, he gained renewed perspective: "And now, at 40, I do have a fairly clear idea that I'm going to die at some point; I wake up with an understanding of that, and that's something that affects the way you live, your relationship with people and with life. But it's not something I think young people should need to understand. [smiles] It would just ruin a good time."[57]

In *Faith, Hope and Carnage* Cave admits to the fact that we are all due to experience greater suffering in our lives—it is simply in the post.[58] It is the incommensurability of death to loss that defies understanding and shows the limits of our language. Cave would continue to reflect upon the challenge of articulating grief, where both sides of the conversation are afraid of saying the "wrong" thing or to make themselves understood. *Skeleton Tree* would highlight the crushing surrealism of life in mourning, veering between sadness, anger, self-doubt, and reams of unanswered questions.[59]

This uncertainty is explored in the music of *Skeleton Tree*; less open and assured than *Push the Sky Away*, it echoes the neurasthenic ambience of early Cure records. The songs are battered by troubled visions, bass swells and ebbs, guitars scratch away, drums shuffle and skitter like jagged claws; a thwarted vision held through a palimpsest of wounds. Melodies are carried by Cave's voice against minimalist song settings. Like *The Boatman's Call* before it, The Bad Seeds provide more atmospheric, less rigid, song settings to highlight Cave's words.

Occasionally Cave is dragged back to a kind of normality with a sudden horrific "thud," an empty-hearted terror where the ground is always threatening to fall away through the bottom of your stomach. On "Magneto" grief returns as an acidic shock exposing Cave caught up in the struggle of the everyday, from the urge to kill someone to the deep blues of queueing in the supermarket. Cave describes this sensation manifesting in his songwriting for "I Need You" where "time and space all seem to be rushing and colliding into a kind of big bang of despair. There is a pure heart, but all around it is chaos."[60] The latent swagger of "I Need You" becomes a ballad of hurt before unfurling toward healing and resolve where Cave is swept up in the vision of his wife in a red dress: "This song is just improvised completely. Most of it doesn't really make sense. And I just didn't fix it up, because it's a one-take thing, it just has this pull."[61]

In the album's penultimate song, "Distant Sky," Else Torp, a Danish soprano, appears in duet with Cave. On a largely vocal track the song speaks to the dream of escape and release. It is delivered like a prayer, their vocals winding in and out of one another toward an absence, reaching far and away but almost close enough to touch. Cave got to know Torp talking over the phone, a conversation she described as the need to establish a "safe space" in which to collaborate, so she knew the limits and pitch of what Cave was aiming for.

The song would open with an allusion to T. S. Eliot's poem "The Love Song of Alfred J. Prufrock"—"Let us go now . . ."—though Torp never asked Cave the exact meaning of the song, fearing it would be wrong to try and fix his words to a singular interpretation. Like many of Cave's songs "Distant Sky" dances within its ambiguities, as Torp described: "If you start being too specific in a creative situation you kill it. I'm like the listener, who creates their own meaning. It could be a very cathartic statement from lovers, walking into the sea and dying together. It's a song that exists in its own right." The idea of freeing "Distant Sky" from the context imposed upon the album is generous; though the song alludes again to the concept of a great unknowing, it carries with it a pained sense of drift resigned to an inevitable flow.[62]

Cave would reject the idea that the loss of his son[63] Arthur was a "theme" of autobiographical subject matter. It remained a "condition of being" where grief subsides but loss is never resolved.[64] Through the music it became both a cathartic expression and symptomatic of his personal situation, highlighting the extent to which loss drastically altered him and his worldview, shattered and then reborn.[65]

Cave explains his own sensation of loss—for a parent to outlive their child—as a particularly brutal form of grief; furthermore he would point to the specific struggle of a mother losing her son.[66] In several interviews he returns to an image from the Holy Bible, Matthew:27 where upon being taken down from the cross Jesus is deserted by his twelve disciples, while Mary Magdalene and the virgin Mary stand at the mouth of his tomb long after everyone else has gone: "This silent, helpless vigil is, for me, the single most moving moment of the New Testament."[67]

Alongside his wife Cave would come to realize a new fearless state of mind, a form of defiance that accommodated grief as a universal experience. Speaking to Mark Mordue in 2017 Cave said, "I feel I have turned a corner and wandered onto a landscape that is open and vast. The 'sweet prairies of anarchy' as [the English poet] Stevie Smith says!"[68]

For Susie, this would become The Vampire's Wife fashion label she created, for Cave it would form a renewed intention behind his music. This conscious act of rebuilding and reimagining the world, was their reaction spurred on by the fallout of loss, overturning the intense negativity into a new perspective of saying "yes" to new possibilities—creation was a revolt in spite of sadness. Cave cited the song "Night Raid" for evoking this renewed state of consciousness.[69]

From a place of darkness Cave would move into a more open relationship with his audience. After the gradual thaw of *One More Time with Feeling* Cave would do a live Q&A tour in 2018, sessions that revealed a divided man, sometimes lost for words. Born out of these sessions Cave would start the Red Hand Files in September of the same year: an invitation for people to email him questions with the sole instruction "Ask Me Anything" writing considered responses and posting them online, becoming a "public declaration of the private life." It would become a space in which to actively engage with his audience, where in the exchange Cave would reflect upon his own grief. The long "anti-memoir" discussions during lockdown between Cave and his friend, the journalist Sean O'Hagan, would give rise to the book *Faith, Hope and Carnage*, a conclusive step in taking control over his personal narrative, as an open conversation with the reader. In his 2020 concert film *Idiot Prayer* Cave would debut a new song "Euthanasia." Described by one reviewer as "like a seance" the film was shot during the lockdown of the COVID-19 pandemic. Cave sings and plays the piano solo to an empty Alexandra Palace in London.

"Euthanasia" would suggest a musical point of closure for Cave. His lyrics describe looking for a missing person, or seeking their presence. Instead, he finds himself lost in his own retreat from life into deeper alienation, its own kind of dying. In the end Cave is reunited with his wife. Framed again at the kitchen table of the family home first introduced at the close of "Spinning Song" he is greeted by a smile of enduring love.

BROKEN TONGUES

He is risen. Bedraggled, half-awake, loosely clutching a mug with a cigarette dangling from his lips, limbs unfurled from a body beyond lean, framed inside a cloistered space nine feet by eight hands high, a garret room within a room too small to stand in. Stripped to the vest and rail thin except for the black shock of crow's hair nest, every inch stretched out toward the cliché of death for art's sake. When people asked where or even *how* he lived, the space was cast variously as a shoebox, a coffin, or a prison cell. Ensconced in his premature tomb, Cave's "office" would embody the romantic impression of the man writing himself into a corner, lying among his words at night staring back at a ceiling of black-eyed stars.[1]

A portrait of the young man posing as an artist: this photo, taken by Bleddyn Butcher in West Berlin, 1985, has become synonymous with the popular image of Nick Cave. Exposing the interior walls of Cave's mind, it presents a wild palimpsest of imagery plastered across the walls and marshaled into teetering columns of books. Setting himself among cultural touchstones, Cave rubs up against the clash of ideas with steadfast determination, where religious iconography is set shoulder-to-shoulder with vintage pornographic postcards and Cave's own lurid sketches, looking down from an already low shelf: a photograph of Elvis, an ancient print of the three virtues, Faith, Hope, and Charity sitting snugly on a shelf together.

Stacks of paper piled heaven high revealed the mental filing system of the autodidact caught halfway between a Brigitte Bardot LP and a bottle of vodka where removing a single sheet would cause utter collapse. These pages became circulating ideas and set pieces tapped out on the typewriter and continually edited in Cave's spidery hand. Fistfuls of this spiraling work in progress would be stuffed into carrier bags, carted around rowdy bars and salubrious cafes as "quiet places to be seen writing in," the distended stomach would then spew its contents to be furiously edited and reedited again then; blood, ink and heroin absorbed into the lifestream of Cave's hermetic existence.[2]

After much hard work, self-doubt, and consternation, this mad shuttling motion would coalesce into Cave's first novel, *And the Ass Saw the Angel* (1989), a one-line hurricane, its feverish text is shot through with glimpses of Cave's work-as-living headspace. Overgrown into a years-long writing project, the book began life as a film script *Swampland* cowritten with Evan English, which from 1985 began to merge with Cave's Bad Seeds lyrics to become an all-encompassing *gesamtkunstwerk* that threatened to swallow up all of his attention away from music retreating further into the wreckage of his personal life. Lurching from writing trips to studio comedowns, Mick Harvey remembered the *Tender Prey* album sessions: "If Nick was on speed or heroin his mind was either racing or nodding off." His concentration waning by extremes, in spite of fervent self-discipline, Harvey was encouraged to play piano along to Cave's guide vocal, to keep The Bad Seeds machine rolling.

Cave's West Berlin world, like his room, was equally small and focused. Not unlike Bowie before him, he kept an almost triangular existence bouncing back and forth between Hansa studios by the wall, hovering around Kreuzberg and Schoenberg districts, and the band's favored bar Risiko. This hermetic intensity distilled these experiences of the city into greater extremes. Die Haut drummer Thomas Wydler, who would later join The Bad Seeds, remembered meeting them on tour around 1982 and later in West Germany: "They were kind of exotic, and Nick was a wild singer. Here in Berlin, we didn't know much about Australian music at all. They just came here with this strange, upstart-blues music." Filtered through the prism of Cave's speed-seeped acceleration this was the era when West Berlin discovered its second, third life toward a better postwar future, haunted by the shadow of World War II and the new specter of Russian communism. Cave is nestled in the dark heart of a divided city, trying to find a new musical language—to reach for the speech that he knows is his.[3]

One of the most openly literate rock stars, Cave would rewrite classical themes into modern contexts, spanning the crossover between the ancient and modern centuries. Cave returns to key canonical texts of Western civilization, the Holy Bible and the Greek myths, for their lyrical and allegorical power.[4] Standing tall as the first stories of humanity they fulfill our hunger for raw matter of both dream and nightmare, the twinned masks of sadness and joy helping us to cathartically sort through our feelings: broken down into passion, loss, betrayal, and depression in much the same way that the greatest songs chime with universal experience.[5]

Cave's earliest lyrics of fire-and-brimstone hyperbole draw upon the high drama of the Bible's liturgical power. Ostensibly the "good" book, it offers stories to teach moral truths and lessons exploded into cycles of creation and destruction, delivered in poetic verse that is memorable and sharp enough to "hook" the mass audience. The poet Andrea Mbarushimana would note that on albums like *Henry's Dream*, Cave exploits the moral shorthand of biblical tales hardwired into the popular consciousness of Western democracies, from which our legal codes and moral behaviors are derived. Cave's close reading seems to accept that these classical texts are as good as real, otherwise imaginative interpretations of true events. Gravitating around love, sex, crime, and death they explore perennial concerns offering a natural history of humanity. The extremes of our behaviors are framed within the struggle to find meaning through the reflections of heroes and monsters.[6] Evan English would note that Cave preferred to work in the direct extremes of the human condition, where good and evil were carried within the simple metaphors of God and the devil, dividing lines that would become blurred in the near future of Cave's twenty-first-century songwriting, a world of conflict and compromise first brought to bear in the good and evil dichotomy of 1988's "The Mercy Seat."

Cave's earlier fondness for neoclassical narrative and more recently the fragmented modernist poetry of his lyrical style draws upon the innate human desire to apply meaning, no matter how disparate, onto our human lives. The writer Joan Didion stated, "we tell ourselves stories in order to live,"[7] where narrative brings a greater sense of structure beyond random chaos. For Flannery O'Connor this went deeper, toward a spiritual imperative: "There is something in us, as storytellers and as listeners to stories, that demands the redemptive act, that demands that what falls at least be offered the chance to be restored." The choices made by the protagonists of O'Connor's novels come to define their moral character but also have a wider impact upon the world of the story. Although a natural autodidact, Cave does not just repeat what he has read but applies interpretation, taking old stories further into the future.

It is his enthusiasm not to stand in the way of a good story that emboldens Cave to borrow the title of William Morris' socialist allegory for the 2004 song "More News from Nowhere," crash-landing it into a retelling of Homer's *The Odyssey* where the shipwrecked warrior adopts the mantle of Larry's (Lazarus') own shortfall shaping the trajectory of the album. In the course of eight brief minutes, Cave blinds the Cyclops with a pen (!!!), the ship's crew are turned into squealing (long)pigs, and for seven years Odysseus becomes the sexual prisoner of a muse trapped on an island. The music video features Cave recounting his tale alongside The Bad Seeds as a strip club house band, gyrating onstage complete with a porn-star mustache and red St. Kilda T-shirt while in the lackluster audience there is a star cameo of studied disinterest from the author Will Self who never looks up from his newspaper—he finds no stories worth listening to. Played out to a groovy surf riff and jiving handclaps, it is a neoclassical redux that other singers could only dream of writing. The enduring power of such songs is for us to listen to the same track and hear the words we know by heart and to still be moved by them every time, swept up in the tow of language and wordplay toward deeper meaning.[8]

Through his songs Cave expresses his deep passion for books and words themselves, becoming the art of self-knowledge as they help us shape our view of the world. In the early 1980s Cave would collect self-made dictionaries that soon merged with his lyric notebooks, aiming for lost words that "no one else knew." His precociousness is amusing, a seasoned immaturity shared with contemporaries such as Will Self, both transgressive authors would often keep a thesaurus close by when writing a novel. The notion of words as fuel is common blood to Cave who would list Roget's Thesaurus and David Whyte's book *Consolations: The Solace, Nourishment and Underlying Meaning of Everyday Words* among his lists of selected books.

This is clear in the mock–Southern gothic tone of *And the Ass Saw the Angel*: the idea of accent and sight-read phonetic sound show Cave's parodic imagination in overdrive. The echo chamber for Euchrid's "mongrel language that was part Biblical, part Deep South dialect, part gutter slang, at times obscenely reverent and at others reverently obscene," overloaded by "hate inspiration straight from God," as Euchrid puts it. Again, for Cave he is "Jesus struck dumb, he is the blocked artist, he is internalized imagination become madness." In the mental realm his obstruction is removed and he lets rip with unrestrained cathartic flow. There is also humility in his approach to know the limits of language: after writing at least one hundred songs Cave described the book as forcing him to "reassess everything and begin again." Later on, Cave would have his own laugh at the expense of the sincere but overserious young artist he once was in the shallow portrait(s) of "We Call Upon the Author."

Early in his career Cave would joke that "cliché is my game;" he borrows phrasings and puns on famous lines, acknowledging the common forms that unite us and the struggle to subvert these assumed wisdoms into something new. Where so many of his songs would work to fulfill or subvert our expectations, where some outlive death and evil goes unpunished, we follow narratives without conclusive endings and are forced to embrace the sometimes-absurd consequences of tragedy. Playing into this, Cave would be at pains to emphasize the use of other "voices" in his songs, borrowed like archetypal masks. He plays the part of murderer, doomed lover, and crazed victim, but always deflecting away from the private person at his core: "The characters are all auto-biographical in a sense. I tend to prefer to use a character as a vehicle for saying something about myself to actually talking about myself in the first person."[9] Not unlike the old "traditional" songs, rarely attributed to one single author but passed on from person to person, its spirit is present in whoever sings it. Gathering new voices and mutations along the way, it admits to adaptation, and in that way the song continues to live, the words subtly shifting over time.

At the request of fans Cave would list several of his beloved books and a rundown of fifteen favorite poets. Collated at a time when much of his personal library was on display in Copenhagen for the 2020 *Stranger Than Kindness* touring exhibition,[10] Cave's reading spans more modern fiction and poetry, as well as books around Christianity and language, though barely any music books or biography, a genre he has little time for.[11]

Much like David Bowie's well-publicized list of one hundred books[12] Cave's lists are not definitive and in no particular order. They include a diverse range of writers from across the early to mid-twentieth century and a few much older classics.[13] Cave would be keen to point out that the books which meant a lot to him were those from his youth, works of art and ideas that helped to shape his creative spirit today, books that Cave said, "introduced me to worlds that were strange and fascinating and new." He would absorb works on various aspects of his songs' interpretations of Christianity, particularly Butler's *Lives of the Saints*.

One thread to pull upon would be the oral storytelling traditions that infuse so much of Cave's music and his verbal style in singing and lyrics. One of his chosen reads is *The English and Scottish Popular Ballads*;[14] folk songs of lives that carry their own meaning, they imbued his words with a strong ear for melody.[15] Alongside this Cave's interest in the blues would draw upon the vocal traditions of spirituals and African American gospel music, a twisted blend of catharsis, religion, and escapism. The traditional British (English, Irish, Scottish, and Welsh) forms of verse, along with Scandinavian forms, helped to establish what we now know as popular songwriting; for example, the Scottish poet Robert Burns penning the lyrics and melody for "Auld Lang Syne" (Happy New Year), one of the most famous examples of common song. Cave's awareness of the roots of contemporary English language grounds him in tradition such that he was then free to break away from its forms. The singer Richard Hawley noted that The Bad Seeds' album of covers *Kicking Against the Pricks* mixed a contrarian sense of traditional mainstream music with more edgy countercultural bands, from Tom Jones to the Velvet Underground: "He bit a big shark's chunk out of the classic school of songwriting."[16] The record was an attempt to destroy people's expectations of The Bad Seeds, while highlighting the breadth of Cave's musical taste; a continued iconoclast free from fashion, creating his own brand of cool.[17]

Reading widely across contemporary and international poetry Cave would explain that he reads poetry almost as fuel to fire the brain and spark the imagination. If songwriting is a craft but also work, then words are the tools, each time reimagined, that make songs happen. Cave made clear his debt to the artists that have gone before him: "I have always read a lot of poetry. It's part of my job as a songwriter. I try to read, at the very least, a half-hour of poetry a day, before I begin to do my own writing. It jimmies open the imagination, making the mind more receptive to metaphor and abstraction and serves as a bridge from the reasoned mind to a stranger state of alertness, in case that precious idea decides to drop by."[18] Though he would admit that he was selective in the writers that most appealed to him: "Sometimes the reading is something of a chore and there are many 'great' poets I find boring, inscrutable, long-winded and painful to read. They can be bad news for the imaginative process." He was tactful to name no names, dead or alive, poetry being a subjective matter of taste that nonetheless carries a common thread of emotional resonance in a way that no other art form can.[19]

Elsewhere Cave pays direct tribute to authors in his songs, on "Supernatural" he embraces W. H. Auden's poem "Funeral Blues," made famous by Stephen Frears' 1994 movie *Four Weddings and a Funeral*, borrowing the lines "my North, my South, my East, my West," which serve to ground him within his love. Where in the past, love was often a tragicomic affair, Cave now finds it his securing anchor to the reality of normal life, framed in the diurnal routine, where the sun rises and sets with his love, and the planets must move around them.

Where the metaphysical poet John Donne, much admired by Cave, began to overturn the rigidity of poetic subjects with brazen affirmations of love and sex and question the nature of belief in God,[20] Cave would remember an adventure from 1996 in a rowboat on Hyde Park lake. After falling asleep he awoke stoned and slightly dazed to find Warren Ellis reciting John Donne's poem "The Flea." Speaking of "one blood made from two" mingled together in the wee beastly body, it becomes the metaphysical, almost parasitic aspect of love in sex and procreation, the merging of blood and sexual fluids. When asked to dash-off a poem at the request of a fan Cave delivered the opening couplet:

> *God is love but love gets weird*
> *Said the flea to the ant in the devil's beard*[21]

Increasingly Cave's lyrics shift toward the blank verse of modern twentieth-century authors who move in and out of form at will. Unmoored from standard rhyme schemes (falling at the end of a line to chime with the last) he finds precedent in the creative liberties of Milton's *Paradise Lost* where the focus was upon hooking the reader with powerful imagery, not meeting the demands of poetic meter.[22] Speaking about "We No Who U R" Cave would note a decline in reading and writing standards: "Texting is apocalyptic on some level. It's a reduction of things. Maybe the last book, the last thing that ever gets written is just a 'bye,' you know, goodbye in text speak."[23]

Cave shifts between the poles of John Betjeman's suburban verse, Larkin's bitter but sensitive poetry, and Emily Dickinson's use of dashes as punctuation, while alluding to e. e. cummings' use of ellipsis and enjambment; frayed lines that seem to come out of nowhere, wrapped about the body of the poem blurring where one thought begins and another ends.[24] Some of Cave's lyrics on his most recent albums can seem more like spoken-word monologues, halfway between singing and whispering, where he reaches beyond "I" and into a more open-ended dreamlike state.

Cave would stress the work done behind songwriting, explaining: "I also have an affinity with artists who treat their craft as a job and are not dependent on the vagaries of inspiration—because I am one of them. Like most people with a job, we just go to work. It never occurs to us not to work, there is never a moment when we don't work because 'we are not feeling it' or 'the vibes aren't right.'" Waiting for ideas is perhaps the need to sit down and start writing, becoming the act through which inspiration happens,[25] Cave would describe songwriting as the pursuit of the "exquisite idea" naturally imperfect and elusive. It was about trying to create something that held onto a lasting impression of an image or sensation, just as it was slipping out of reach.[26]

Cave would claim that he never set out with a definite image or style in mind for each album. He would simply select a "start date" and begin with a fresh notebook. This ground zero approach would be a conscious act against what Cave calls the deceit of the "residual idea," where in the initial stages of writing old ideas would return, seeming new and interesting, but needing to be excised to clear his head,[27] allowing for the negative capability of the blank page as a "point of deprivation" trying to get toward that "twilight place" and allow the songs to come.[28] For example Cave would admit that "Into My Arms" was a very conscious act of craft, of working things into place. He explained that he got more resonance from the listener's reaction to the song than he did personally—drawing a hard line between the art as work and the singer's private life.

The deluxe edition of the *Push the Sky Away* album comes with a facsimile of the notebook in which Cave worked out the album's lyrics. He explained: "Some of it's dreadful and painful to read, but I just thought—what the fuck. Pages and pages of absolute shit. . . . And just every now and then something, little tiny ideas start to come out."[29] In much the same way that Cave takes a partisan line on being politically aligned to a single movement or party, he argues against being steered by his audience: that way lies artistic death, and inevitable disappointment on both sides—the artist as individual is key—maintaining a creative and expressive independence. Equally, Cave would note the need to cannibalize his life for raw material; as life progressed, he would feel his songwriting evolve, writing himself into the future and trying to outrun the legacy of his back catalog: "The good song is always rushing forward. It annihilates, to some degree, the songs that you'd previously written, because you are moving forward all the time."[30]

Sometimes a more spontaneous, absolutist approach worked wonders. *The Lyre of Orpheus/Abattoir Blues* albums would become a great experiment with the band often recording all together in a large, wooden live room. Where Cave observed some of his albums had been slightly morose and stiff affairs, the back-to-back records had allowed the individual Bad Seeds more musical space to work within. Arriving with no lyrics or chords, writing and adapting songs in the studio, the sessions thrived on the immediacy of the present moment, an attitude that would continue to work its way into future records such as *Push the Sky Away*.

The recorded versions of The Bad Seeds' songs represent just one performance from many variations explored, the song's mutating shape is finished as the perfect idea imperfectly realized; the best, and most honest, music that could be produced at that time. Many of the band's songs, such as "Tupelo" or "Jubilee Street," would explode in their live incarnation outgunning the studio version.[31] Both Cave and Warren Ellis task themselves as quite ruthless and concise self-editors, unafraid to "kill your darlings," doing what was right for each song and ditching parts that simply didn't work, no matter how much you might want them to. Working on *Push the Sky Away* producer Nick Launay found a real brevity to the process, with the main work done in four to five days: "We recorded *Push The Sky Away* in the first week. In the second week, we did overdubs. In the third week, we took the overdubs off."[32]

There is a definite sense of hypergraphia, compulsive writing or drawing, to some of Cave's lyrics. Naturally verbose, he lets lines run both ways in order to indulge a pun or a reversal at the expense of a cliché. In "Loverman" the "devil" admits that the woman he is stalking has answered his prayers just as he becomes the answer to all of hers. Speaking to Sean O'Hagan, Anita Lane once joked that if Cave was hit by a bus he would be compelled to write about it—in his own blood—before he died. Accordingly, Jessamy Calkin remembers Cave on the London Underground once writing a letter in blood using the hypodermic syringe he'd just ripped from his arm as a pen.[33] In many early Bad Seeds songs Cave's lyrics could stretch to several pages, the written lyrics of "Tupelo" cascading down, chopped into some poetic meter to become increasingly fragmented verse. The sometimes-overwritten lyrics that dominate The Bad Seeds' first album *From Her to Eternity* (1984) would feature a nine-minute title track, already a bold move, and would close with "A Box for Black Paul" at ten minutes. Though Cave would note a gradual refinement in his songwriting from the early days of The Birthday Party to The Bad Seeds where "lyrics became more focused, words weren't just used as weapons."[34] On "Rings of Saturn" Cave takes on the form of a madly phallic octopus consumed by the need to verbalize inner feelings, he squirts ink all over the blank page of white sheets, overcome by an excess of ideas. This is the burning fount of creativity in meltdown, where life is absorbed to become just another story as self-obliterating pleasure. Elsewhere there is the double perspective image of older Cave knowingly mopping up the messy mistakes of his younger self that he was always bound to make, featured on the cover artwork of the *Stranger Than Kindness* book, a painting by Ben Smith knowingly titled *Ink and Solace*.

In 2008's "We Call Upon the Author" Cave marches through a stream of ideas opening up his wounds in public, which sees him falling from a ladder of literary influence and condemnation, hitting every rung on the way down. The song becomes a witty confrontation with the shared cannibalism of the reader consuming the writer as their work, just as their words gradually suck-in and absorb the reader. Cave stands in for God-as-Author, creator of his own world of pain, writing lives in and out of existence but devolved of authorial responsibility for their fates—God's will as wild muse.

Like any great artist, Cave makes the case that created work is inextricable from itself; the world is what it is, his characters' actions are the expression of their own nature, all delivered as a series of hard and soft truths. In keeping with Barthes' theory on the *Death of the Author*, Cave allows the removal of artistic intent and encourages the reader to determine their own meaning from his songs. In the Red Hand Files Cave says, "I find that many of my favorite lyrics are those that I do not fully understand. They seem to exist in a world of their own—in a place of potentiality, adjacent to meaning."[35] Even the most seemingly straightforward or direct lyric affords other possibilities, just as the reader who seeks good or evil will find it.

Cave's more recent songs embrace ambiguity as a kind of freedom from closed ideas. Where before The Bad Seeds seemed dead set on nailing the darkness of shadows to the floor, or letting blood flow just to reveal its delicious deep red, those concrete images that once hit like a blunt sledgehammer are now crumbling slightly, tempered by a deeper questioning but also an objective removal to let them stand as they are.[36] This is the root of an idea taking flight and become something other beyond the author, the song becomes *for* itself, fighting for survival in the mind of the listener where it now lives.

In "We Call Upon the Author" Cave finds himself beset by cannibal analysts, false disciples who ask Cave for the secret meanings of his songs, answers where there is no question. Setting out to devour their master, to overread and take themselves too seriously in the process. Mark Mordue refers to the bad habit of reading too deeply into biography looking for "answers" to the art, and by intimation the artist, as a whole "Technicolor yawn" of lazy connections. Cave refers the gathered inquisitors to the explosive trail of liberation reaching toward the dynamite inspiration of his father's creative passion. In *20,000 Days on Earth*, Cave declares that one of his earliest memories of his father, the author and English teacher Colin Cave's "performance" as he read the opening passages of *Lolita* to him. Cave would cite his father's passion as the spark that lit the fuse to his own love of language, marking a deeper connection between the two men. Not without irony and some small pride, Cave would later note how this wish would be fulfilled as he sought to establish himself as a man of letters and his work continues to be critically praised.

Cave speaks to the powerful and elevating enthusiasm of his father's reading and teaching style, labeling him an "astronaut" on "Man in the Moon." Cave would absorb the writer's methodology of the 1962 Stanley Kubrick film of *Lolita* Peter Seller's character Clare Quilty drops the phrase "lovely, lyrical lilting name" referring to the teenage girl recast as coquettish nymphet. His heavenly words resonate on the surface, while their true meaning of intent is haunted by pedophilic lust, alluding to the future image of the "lovely creature."

The book remains a touchstone for Cave as an example of art exceeding morality, with its author once proclaiming: "Any work of art is above censorship." Nabokov's high-flying literary style would later be taken up by his controversialist inheritor, Martin Amis.[37] Amis would be part of a generation that praised Nabokov for his writing ability, not the sanctity of his ideas, "style is morality: morality detailed, configured, intensified," where before him Oscar Wilde went full frontal, referring to his own novel *The Picture of Dorian Gray* and its latent suggestion of homosexual "perversion," expounding the claim: "There is no such thing as a moral or an immoral book. Books are well written, or badly written. That is all."[38] Cave acknowledged the trigger of "the loss of my father created in my life a vacuum, a space in which my words began to float and collect and find their purpose."[39]

As if nodding in acknowledgment to the American poet John Berryman and his epic numbered sequence of poems *The Dream Songs*, Cave would adopt the name "Henry" for the eponymous *Henry's Dream* album.[40] *The Dream Songs* revolve around the perspective of Berryman's alter ego, "Henry," infusing Cave's widescreen dream of the fantastical nightmare of America, where reality is stretched to breaking point seeking the truth within the dream.[41]

The scourge of Berryman's sickness was also his inspirational drive: a loose libido mixed with alcoholism and as a child traumatized by suicide. In 1926 when Berryman was eleven years old, his father shot and killed himself. Amid rumors of foul play, Berryman's creative preoccupations became lived-through obsessions.[42] He seemed to inherit some internalized death drive, just as Cave was able to flaunt and play with these same characteristics, he went the same as Hemingway who shot himself with his shotgun in Ketchum, Idaho, suffering from deep depression after losing his home in the Cuban revolution and losing the ability to write after frequent ECT treatments.[43] Where Berryman struggled to escape the narrative spiral of his own life, Cave would avoid writing nakedly personal songs. His lyrics would arrive autobiographically, often influenced by Cave's current home city, and filtered through characters that more recently would become anonymous voices as expressions of spirit.[44]

Berryman's writing encouraged Cave to tap into the illogical subconscious wilderness beneath the veneer of civilization, the same evolutionary leap between Berryman the college lecturer and the electrically charged performer, drunk on his own words. Cave talks about creative work as a continual dreaming, all through normal life, residual ideas working their way through the subconscious, so when it comes to the time to write it becomes the act of working the dream, finding shape to meet the urgency behind the inchoate thought.

Noting the seriousness of his own work ethic, Cave also found that determined creative efforts could turn against you, particularly with the surprise desertion of the muse. Jesting and jousting with the false condition of writer's block, on "There She Goes My Beautiful World"[45] (2004) he predicts the autobiographical strain of "We Call Upon the Author." In an anarchic blend of high and low culture he lists all the authors who got shit done in spite of themselves—a synthesis of dedicated application and learning to let go and allowing ideas to bleed through the fog. Dorian Lynskey notes how Cave rhymes "Nabokov's socks" with "Chinese Rocks," elsewhere Cave casts outrageous rhymes of "hernia" / "Guernica" / "furniture" in the Dylan-esque sprawl of "Babe I'm On Fire" from 2003's *Nocturama* album. Connecting the eroticized heat of Gauguin's tropics to Philip Larkin's hermetic exile in Hull—suddenly here is nowhere—the artist's life is transposed from the heights of great art to domestic mundanity as its own kind of freedom.

From the more formal history of Berryman as a serious poet and academic, whom Cave has labeled as one of the best, there also stands the counterpoint of Charles Bukowski, "a jerk."[46] It's hard to hear of Bukowski's chosen role as the beaten down stay-at-home lush, who rolls from his bed to the typewriter to work at the post office as a sorting clerk, only to do it all again the next day, and not think of the dissipation of Cave's early career. Where Cave seemed to possess vampire-like romantic intensity and the tragic glamor of his itinerant junkie lifestyle; Bukowski was scruffy and gross, the self-described "dirty old man" to Cave's persona of dark, sensual threat. But in fairness the two authors tap into parallel veins of nightmare imagery, dissipation, and broken love; some of Bukowski's aging, lust-driven hump would not be out of place in the occasional bitter, but full-blooded, gutter living of Grinderman. Cave is never entirely above or below these points of tone and subject, perhaps having more in common than he might wish to admit, although delivered in very different styles. In the novel *Factotum* Bukowski fucks his partner, the long-term-ish middle-aged "Jean" (all of his women are transformed through various aliases until, ultimately, he is always chasing the same piece of skirt). Bukowski refers to his member as the "purple onion," noting that Jean: "took it like a knife." Bukowski would sprawl on his sofa unshaven and barely dressed, gut-flushed from beer and junk food, "showing his belly" in every sense and expecting, if not demanding, a rub from the critics sympathetic to his deepest groans. Even as Cave would later tap into the gentleman lifestyle of hand-cut suits and loquacious interviews, he too would sometimes struggle to be taken seriously by literary writers beyond rock journalists, in part because of his doom-laden subject matter.

Since *Push the Sky Away* Cave made a creative break from his earlier songwriting style of straight narratives delivered via a blood-and-honey dripping tongue, populated by characters who seemed to walk right out of the pages of a pulp novel. Larger than life they are known by name: people like Elisa Day echoed the tragedy of countless young women at the hands of the men who claimed to love them; or the nameless man of "Red Right Hand" standing in the shadow of figures like "Judge" Holden from *Blood Meridian*. Personifications of menace and tragedy, they would become iconic in The Bad Seeds' discography but also tied

Cave further to the weight of history, fixing him alongside a growing cast of antiheroes, villains, and victims; notorious figures of folk legend, such as "Stagger Lee" and "Jangling Jack"; or female figures become objects of obsessive desire, such as "Watching Alice" and "Deanna" who seem to hold sway over the singer.

Cave's recent lyrics have become more fragmented and impressionistic, reflecting an increasingly complex view of the world: "The idea that we live life in a straight line, like a story, seems to me to be increasingly absurd and, more than anything, a kind of intellectual convenience."[47] Where before Cave would spin out a chain of events, his songs now exist outside of a fixed time and place, wandering through a mapless place of the imagination. We stand with him on an eternal beach, a nameless wasteland, a nowhere room; we are made to feel the experience more vividly than having events played out in front of us.

Cave's songs evolve into a less linear style that retains his pitch-perfect eye and ear for surreal and challenging imagery, culminating in a search of wonder, horror, and beauty in the spaces in-between, where stranger things really happen. Though this isn't a postmodern contest of ideas, Cave opens up the songs to other possibilities, clashing meanings. Cave would note the birth of a song in the smallest of great beginnings: "You only need the tiniest of ideas for something beautiful to come out of it." From this the initial lines of lyric begin to spark off one another and together form a magical whole: "Without warning, you find you have taken one line of no consequence and attached it to another line of no consequence and a kind of reverberation begins between the two lines, a throbbing—or as I like to call it, a 'shimmering'—it is something you can actually see!"

In *Skeleton Tree*, Cave begins to incorporate more images orbiting patterns through his songs: circling animals, a ring of shadow, a deeper fear of slipping out of reach away from his center. By the time of *Ghosteen* Cave's lyrics would be pared down to a minimum of words, reducing considered verse to something more instinctual. This becomes a broader spiraling motion rising into light.

Increasingly Cave uses the line of a song lyric as a looping form, words chase one another, a renewed phrase straddling thoughts then

striding over into the next line. In "Magneto" Cave offers the image of the rat running in its wheel. The written lyrics reflect this disjointed state that fractures the poetic line, his lyric blurs "laugh/love/move" as the singer makes a feverish search for emotion and meaning, the song circles back around eating its own tail as Cave revises earlier lines—struck by the echo of an afterthought. In "Anthrocene" Cave blurs the attachment of love into repetition, finding the true depths of his yearning of love offered, lost, and regained, hands running over hands like water until the two bodies become indivisible. On "Mermaids" Cave flips lines, "distant waves" reaching into "waves of distant love," a switch that shifts the meaning but also takes the metaphor further with the pressing weight of the gathered sea. The rhythmic density of his relentless speech is intimate, almost smothering, a wandering line of frayed and broken thoughts left hanging.[48]

"Rings of Saturn" and "Girl in Amber" would further embed the imagery of spinning and spiraling motifs, where one remains in static motion (on the spot) the other continues trailing out from its center, with Cave finding theme in form. Where before, Cave would look through the third-person point of view of his characters, in later songs his gaze turns inward, a voyeur upon himself. What begins as cold-eyed detachment, a deadening of affect, comes a new empathy; Cave sees other people caught up in a similar emotional cycle, merging grief with recovery to the point that they are sometimes indistinguishable. Meeting with a sudden loss of gravity and swept up by events outside of our control, his characters seem to follow a path that is not entirely of their choosing.

On "Girl in Amber" Cave veers away from the earlier Greek chorus of The Bad Seeds as backing singers, exploiting the pure power of solo repetition, he adopts myriad voices to explore a mind lost in looping thoughts. Cave begins the song with the phone ringing off the hook, fearing more bad news or questions. He repeats the persistent echo of its calling until at the end of the verse it suddenly stops and rings "no more."[49] Cave shows us twinned perspectives of isolation, a deft lyrical inversion that suggests the cycling sound of the droning ringing—then its sudden absence—as if the line has been cut dead. On first hearing many listeners would imagine this as Cave's struggle with grief in the immediate aftermath of tragedy, but like so much of *Skeleton Tree* the song only seems to realize this meaning in hindsight.

Cave said the title of "Girl in Amber" came to him during initial *Skeleton Tree* recording sessions at Warren Ellis' garden studio in Paris. Seeing a tarantula on the table preserved in dried tree sap, it became the image of life in stasis, the body present but no longer living.[50] The girl in the song seems trapped herself, as if seeing the world from behind glass, watching her reflection captured in that frozen golden eye. The song's title inspired Cave's largely improvised vocal; its mantra-like flow was born from the closing chorus of "Push the Sky Away," a form Cave would continue to explore on *Ghosteen* and *Carnage*.

As his focus intensifies Cave subtly shifts phrases as he moves from room to room, the removed "she" turns into more intimate "you." Cave would explain that the "she" figure of the song would become embodied by the image of his wife, Susie. The song suggests a woman divided, caught between the painful, difficult present and a longing for a simpler time, trying to regain control in a universe of relentless chaotic motion. She moves almost without pause to seek escape velocity to catch a free breath among the pressing vertigo; the power of choice becomes the lionized dream like a burning heart. She keeps on turning toward the past, always out of reach, spinning further away from the center of her life. The more she turns the faster it disappears.

By the time Cave and The Bad Seeds returned to Paris' Le Frette Studios for three weeks in autumn 2015 Cave was struck by the prescient power of the lyrics. The album's closing sessions held in London in early 2016 were born out of equal parts frustration and pervasive melancholy that Cave described as a difficult and harrowing time, trying to see the record through without forcing it.[51] "Rings of Saturn"[52] casts a similar spell within its spiral of densely woven lyrics. Cave refers to himself, the author, as a black funnel-web spider, spinning lines like a rapper spitting bars; caught in his lyrical undertow, the listener is drawn deeper along with him. Cave watches himself from a distance, he is both "there and not there"—a kind of disassociated purgatory.[53] The deep seriousness of the song is peppered with wild sparks of the imagination that constantly jolt the listener into a stranger place, the carnid insectoid as alien on earth. Cave closes "Girl in Amber" with a ghostly croon: "Don't touch me." After so much isolation it becomes a plea for distance, the overwhelming noise is mirrored in a deafening silence and the continuing weight of an absence.

Cave explains how "Rings of Saturn" began as a story of a young woman exploring her sexuality; she is "preoccupied with her own promiscuity," caught up in its tangling web that leaves a hanging question of doubt and self-recrimination. Where on "Stranger Than Kindness" there was a clear map that leads from desire to intimacy, "Rings of Saturn" suggests the search for a deeper, lasting happiness of love. Cave's words stride over one another, vaulting from one line to the next, he cuts his breath short, becoming an endless stream of language outpacing thought. Tripping over herself, the young girl takes her first new steps toward becoming, urged on by Cave's determined piano chords and Warren Ellis' hesitant backing synths that slide up and down, a heartbeat unmoored from gravity. Time slurs until the girl—suddenly awake to the present—reaches out toward "a child's dream" like the promise of a star.[54]

Together the two songs offer haunting abstractions that gradually reveal an intimate pact of transmutation: a grieving woman retreats into herself, returning to a willful childlike state, while a young girl realizes an authentic moment and discovers herself as a woman and a mother, the person she was always meant to be. In spite of both songs' sure-footed melodic flow, a doomed waltz under ether, these unsettled feelings continue across *Skeleton Tree*. Captive to its own savage undertow, it remains a crystalline, fragile, and complex album realized under a black sun.

Cave is an artist who stands alongside his words as much as he believes in the affirmative and life-changing power of books as artifact. In the body of the text blood and ink merge, guiding us toward discovery of the world: to awaken the heart of memory—speak, life. In Red Hand Files #192 Cave acknowledged that his office with all of its paper and books was just another room. After packing off its contents for the global touring exhibition of *Stranger Than Kindness*[55] he no longer found the office or even the instrument of the typewriter necessary to songwriting: "My sacred space became the rolling fire of the imagination." He would explain to Mark Mordue in 2017 that he had shifted away from the fixed place of work to more domestic spaces, like the kitchen table: "I work differently these days. I have abandoned my office completely and am finding great pleasure sitting at the window in my bedroom, surrounded by my books and just thinking and writing words. I am not worrying too much about writing actual songs as such, rather just amassing a stockpile of lines and thoughts, images, and ideas."

Cave's collected lyrics have been published at several stages in his career, and were recently updated in a 1978–2022 edition. It has become normal practice for long-standing musicians to publish their lyrics in book format, as if reading them on the page adds the credence of serious poetry or Literature. But there are few artists like Cave whose lyrics stand up to the creative weight of Bob Dylan, Van Morrison, Kendrick Lamar, and David Bowie, who in particular remade the popular song as a reflection of culture back upon itself. Across Cave's discography we can see the influences from classical to modern literature, philosophy, and the Holy Bible making the volume reflect and refract Cave's wider reading, as opposed to lyrics printed between book covers.[56]

Lifting away the veil of nostalgia around the artist as sacred creature Cave's recent work in music and various forms of writing and art suggests a continued creative renaissance. He ditches the claustrophobic intensity of mythic fire, shadow, and brimstone to rediscover the weightless force of light in all its ferocious possibilities—his songs have never been more personal, exploding from introspection to universal resonance. Cave remains a romantic writer open to wonder, rich in imaginative detail and wordplay, he has fun with language but now seeks to further unsettle and disrupt it from old forms. Tracing the fault lines of a splintering Western culture, his words follow an equally jagged train of thought—interrupted, fragmented—becoming a text-in-progress where the ending is never certain.

A TEAR IN TIME

[COSMIC HECK JUNK FRANCHISE]

The heavens declare the glory of God;
And the firmament shows His handiwork.
Day unto day utters speech,
And night unto night reveals knowledge.
There is no speech nor language
Where their voice is not heard.
Their line has gone out through all the earth,
And their words to the end of the world.

—PSALM 19

In *Rings of Saturn* W. G. Sebald makes a powerful address to the slow revolution of the earth, nights and days colliding across the hemispheres into cycles of light and darkness. Looking out east from the Suffolk coast he scans what he calls the "German ocean" to the horizon and imagines people on the other side of the world waking into day as his skyline dips toward dusk: "The shadow of the night is drawn like a black veil across the earth, and since almost all creatures, from one meridian to the next, lie down after the sun has set, so, he continues, one might, in following just behind the setting sun, see nothing but prone bodies around the world, row upon row as if leveled by the scythe of Saturn—an endless

153

graveyard for a humanity struck by falling sickness." Sebald's thought ends with a determinist full stop, a reminder of our own insignificance on a small planet held within the schema of the universe, with all of its wonders. Witness the sparkling ice rings of Saturn slowly being eaten away by the planet's gravitational pull and radiation from the sun, each cycle brings destruction remade as creation returning to a new equilibrium with the dawn.[1]

From the start of *Push the Sky Away* Cave finds a sense of renewal carved up by the state of twilight, when the sun glows just below the horizon it can seem to be neither rising nor falling. This transitional state is marked by the appearance of the planet Venus as the "morning star"[2] just before sunrise in the east, and shortly after sunset, as the "evening star" in the west, before it slips out of alignment and into the night.[3] Twilight becomes the cosmic hinge between first light and the fall of darkness; as to become indivisible.[4]

Though images of moon, sun, stars, and tides enrich Cave's lyrics, they are defined by the vast darkness of space that threatens to overwhelm his music with its shade. From earth we often see the universe through the wrong end of the telescope, placing ourselves at the center of the story; the finite passage of human life against the span of the universe. This expands from earthly concerns toward mystical cosmology, like the universe contained within a grain of sand held by a human hand.[5] Just as the world can seem coldly indifferent in its random cruelty, the mysteries of the universe become the greater part of Cave's ongoing compact with brutality and tenderness.[6] As humankind is born to question and try to contain the vast infinity of space by understanding its impossibility, it becomes the void into which we throw all our hopes, dreams, and terror. Filled with so much heavy matter, space manages to seem both greater and lesser than our terrestrial troubles.[7]

Cave manages to suggest both awe and exhaustion at the scale of these infinite distances. It sends him reeling toward the threat of being swallowed up or spinning out into nothingness, a double anxiety of being "lost" and disappeared among so much space.[8] At the beginning of "We Real Cool" Cave sings of the distance of Sirius, the brightest star in the sky 8.6 light years from earth,[9] whereas Arcturus is almost

37 light years away, casting his voice out to the stars and the "far side of morning" the earth's orbit spirals back around.

Where science suggests to us the luxury of knowing, the night sky mirrors the great experiment of the imagination.[10] Marked by constellations of stars that Flannery O'Connor described as the scaffold of the sky (suggesting heavenly design), the stars give space distance, direction, and shape, just as songs attempt to give voice to our feelings, both becoming waymarkers to meaning.[11] There are also moments when Cave looks toward the universe with a spiritual eye full with the light of inexplicable glory and wonder that stand in for the richness of human emotions, in Cave's songs "space" manages to seem both mythical and real, bound up in both science and dreaming.

In "The Mercy Seat" Cave watches over his doomed narrator weighing the power of objects; the ragged mop and the distorted prison cup[12] radiate some kind of invisible field, felt rather than seen. This is the sensory overload of "witnessing" a holy presence, if not the glory, of God in all things, some mystical aura of energy or inner purpose. The weird hyperreality of "The Mercy Seat" masses into one searing shock that forces the song's narrator to feel horribly and intensely alive, as he moves one step closer to his imminent death. Facing down his final moments, life shrinks to a microcosm of experience , pushed into hypersensitivity, his mind is alive (too late) to all possibilities of the world as if the charge from the executioner is already coursing through his body, granting him a new second sight.

This depth of vision evokes the writing of religious poet Gerard Manley Hopkins and his concept of "inscape" the immutable presence of things or beings full with the energy of life, imbued with the holy spirit in action.[13] What Cave might refer to as the beauty all about the world, Hopkins sees as a glimmering wonder, the flash of light on shook foil. In his poem "As Kingfishers Catch Fire" (1877), Hopkins thrusts us into the extreme present, with the brightly colored birds swooping down from the sky like a dart into the water, living to the utmost of their being. These normal scenes of a kingfisher hunting fish become fantastical and otherworldly, souls fulfilling their

nature. The reader and viewer of the poem is brushed by the wingtips
of transcendence:

> *Christ plays in ten thousand places,*
> *Lovely in limbs, and lovely in eyes not his*
> *To the Father through the features of men's faces.*

The inmate of "The Mercy Seat" is brought down to earth with a bump
by the mundanity of squeaking meal trolley wheels moving along death
row.[14] Bringing sustenance to the doomed, it might as well be a hospital,
a restaurant, spinning on through all of our lives as time running away
from us—but now it becomes more sinister as it brings the last supper of
the convict ever closer.[15] Three decades later, on 2019's "Bright Horses,"
the second track from *Ghosteen*, Cave would already be overcome with
longing for a renewed sense of wonder; sick and tired of things in themselves, the world is reduced to hard concrete objects as a series of revolving scenes. The movie of his life is deadened dull, until the arrival of
the horses, like a deus ex machina, bringing with them a terrible and
enlightening flame; things are at once too real and crushed under the
leaden weight of grief.

The incommensurability of human experience under God, the shock
and awe that cannot be explained away or solved by science, a discipline
of both art and faith. Cave's lyrics would often absorb the challenge
of physics within his own coded language to become another form of
mysticism, playing up to the romanticism of astronomical symbols transcending the flatlands of earth. Flush with the yearning of "(Are You)
the One That I've Been Waiting For?" Cave reaches toward a sense of
magical wonder where he sings about stars exploding into brightness
against the dark sky. Like Jack Kerouac's high-flying visions, his voice
strains and cracks on "(Are You) the One . . ." and the image is broken
along with it, he flatly denies any lasting power of the fading dream.[16]
Cave defuses the emotive metaphor and instead grounds us against the
elevating traditions of lyrical verse: "Stars have their moment and then
they die." It is the apocalyptically messy fallout of love, blinking out one
by one, the scourge of fire as enlightenment.

Cave also paints the moon into his songs as the blank all-seeing eye, on the 1984 B side "Moon Is In The Gutter" a seeming nod to Oscar Wilde's claim that we are all of us in the gutter looking at the stars, it flips the order of things.[17] Perhaps taking its title from a 1983 French film where every night a man returns to the same spot where his sister committed suicide after being raped, with only the reflection of the moon to keep him company. What could seem like a "cosmic" connection is just a ghost image captured on the water's surface. The *Today's Lesson* podcast noted how the song offers a key to Cave's preoccupations of murder, disposing of a body and the guilt that follows after. The moon, like its brother sun, can suggest the final witness, a light that singles us out in the darkness.

In exploring the nature of space and the planets as the dance of the spheres,[18] Cave would observe a continued metaphor of shifting from connection to isolation in his songwriting. We see Cave combine multiple perspectives beyond the straight narrative of The Bad Seeds' earlier songs, an atomic center clashing themes. The cycling lyric and orbital piano motifs of "Girl in Amber" and "Rings of Saturn" develop into the swooning, swaying dance of "Magneto."[19] Cave's wordplay flows with the motion of the seesaw melody, his swooning voice turning to laughter, giving bloom to a sense of inner space and radical light. At once as incidental and meaningful as a splash of stars like in these songs Cave breaks away from the dirt and decay of gloomy corners toward a celestial force of making and breaking connections.[20]

Finding new momentum on *Skeleton Tree* and taking flight on *Ghosteen*, beginning with its "Spinning Song" Cave and Ellis continue their exploration into the hypnotic mantra of repetitive rhythms from "Push the Sky Away," revisiting the idea of the song as heartbeat, the very motion of the feather thrown up in the air, its bright white shape carving a path through the air. On *Ghosteen* Cave embraces the haunting shape of the spiral suggesting both a descent into sadness and a transcendent form of rising, the continued spinning gives motion to the experience of shifting through grief toward its aftermath. The pattern of the spiral is either to spin away from its center or to be drawn inward to its vanishing point. Across *Ghosteen* Cave returns to the image of children climbing into the sky spiraling up toward the sun returning to a spiritual state beyond imagination and reality.[21] The song ends, as if at the beginning, with the image of his wife sitting in the kitchen listening to the radio, Cave's song filtering through the static of cosmic airwaves.[22]

By the time of *Ghosteen* the sun has overtaken the moon to become both blinding fire and cleansing light. Like Philip Larkin's vision of a lion's pitiless stare, it exists independent of our noticing it.[23] *Ghosteen* presents the aura of spiritual connection felt as a kind of cosmic radiation, gesturing outward, suggesting a deeper meaning to space or a guiding hand at work. Cave would refer to sonic and lyrical ideas behind the *Skeleton Tree* album as being "received." There was a vision before a note was written or a word sung: "Something intervened: a cosmic radiation that rescued it from our own interference. I feel I had very little to do with it." He alludes to this in the shuffling static drum patterns alongside the warped hums and synthesizer parts played by Warren Ellis that occasionally sounds like feeding back lost signals seeking an open receiver. *Skeleton Tree* is an album that glows with an odd lumination, like stars on fire or a distant scourging ball of spiritual energy. Cave said, "Its conception was immaculate. Out of nothing, came something." Speaking in similar terms to the otherworldly inspirations behind *Ghosteen*, Cave suggests a shared energy or determination between the two records, though with different lyrical and sonic languages.

As if continuing the lyrical themes of 2016's "Jesus Alone," Cave finds the dying light of a star in the image of Jesus in his mother's arms on *Ghosteen*'s "Fireflies." It is a brilliance beyond the lyrical idea that is placed in front of us, a spare piece of light flush with meaning.[24] In the travel of light across space time, the star we now see in the sky might have already disappeared by the time its signal reaches us. We catch the secondary brilliance of events after the fact, seeing the past as the present. This suggests that although there is truth in witnessing, reality is often deferred from absolute knowledge: "I feel that the events in our lives are like a series of bells being struck and the vibrations spread outwards, affecting everything, our present, and our futures, of course, but our past as well. Everything is changing and vibrating and in flux."[25]

At the opening of "Carnage" Cave croons the listless feeling that he is always on the move again as if chasing something, forever saying good-bye, the trains and their stations become the marker of time lost and regained as if the journey of life never ends.[26] Both on "Bright Horses" and "Waiting for You" Cave stands, captive to waiting and the weight of expectation, looking for the great return. It is the unknowing of waiting without end that is only answered when we see, hold, and hear our loved ones again; until then we are mired in uncertainty and doubt.[27]

The two songs speak to one another: at first Cave is expecting his beloved to come back to him on the 5:30 train, embodied by Cave's wife, a feeling that reaches across to "Waiting for You." He plays with the idea of the passing Jesus freak announcing the resurrection, a stark contrast to the earlier pessimism of "Time Jesum Transeuntum Et Non Riverentum" where the stars and moon knocked off-kilter show the world spinning at the wrong angle, where everything is wrong. Cave can choose to believe him or ignore his calls; only God knows if he is right or wrong.

The suggestion of the resurrection from absence fuels the yearning and searching spirit that drives the beating heart of *Ghosteen*. Where moments of *Skeleton Tree* Cave suggest he is resigned to grief, he now seeks to accommodate a life beyond loss. The struggle of waiting for our loved ones to return, knowing they will never arrive but living alongside some other kind of hope beyond the limitless world of uncertainty—it becomes a divine force that carries him great distances—hope as something worth holding on to.[28]

Cave has always written from myth, legend, biblical scripture, poetry—on *Push the Sky Away* he connects with the twenty-first century as his theme. The shipwreck of popular culture that unmoored ideas from their foundations, fractured old certainties, where doubt becomes a wrecking ball. "Higgs Boson" stands as a testament to the album's major themes about the struggles of memory and forgetting. Recorded in one live band take, Cave improvises his sprawling lyrics on the mic, his vocal throwing its arms around the world, beyond apocalypse. A non-instrumental process he would continue with *Carnage*, being captive to the moment and holding the listener there with him in a high-wire trapeze act between flight and utter collapse.

Much like "Jubilee Street"[29] Warren Ellis' slow burn riff hammers on a note then slowly slides the same chord shape up the neck another octave; drawing upon Neil Young's "On the Beach," he escalates and builds the mood and groove of both songs toward inevitable explosion. From his more virtuoso familiarity with the violin, Ellis takes an almost minimalist approach to guitar playing, more about texture, raw sound and groove, using a four-string tenor electric guitar tuned CGDA, more like a mandolin or a cello.[30] A major progression from The Bad Seeds' "Six Strings That Drew Blood" toward the revolutionary autocannibalism of "Lyre of Orpheus" Ellis' deconstructed guitar style helps to overturn rock and roll heritage as Cave presents the birth of the instrument, adding a modern voice to Orpheus, the original singer.[31]

The grandiosity of the track affects the intense metaphorical weight of the thesis behind the CERN experiment's Large Hadron Collider, the reactor designed to reach back toward a scientific reenactment of the creation of the universe, seeking out the original "God particle," a process that Professor Nick Groom sees as a thwarted ambition to "replace celestial creation with theoretical physics." The lurching chaos and restraint of "Higgs Boson Blues" trawls pop culture iconography meeting with a car crash of postmillennial comedown; it becomes his latest anthem to the next apocalypse, all set against the burning world of twentieth-century atrocity—the listener is abandoned to a landscape not knowing if they are alive or dead.

Cave drives to Geneva, toward the mystical epicenter of this great (re)happening, where in the fierce rush toward scientific advances where humanity might be left behind, or as suggested by Mark Mordue, be rushing toward its own ending. The explosive reckoning of the "God particle" realized in the information overload of "Higgs Boson Blues" becomes the interruption of static, decaying information—Cave grapples with the blind will of this wild, untamable energy.

He sings of the missionary who comes at you with a smile, presenting the false gift of smallpox-infected blankets, the conquering of the Wild West by germ warfare with thousands of Native Americans succumbing to European diseases as the invention of the cracked atom becomes the new bigger bomb, an inventory of murder and tyranny performed in God's name, to kill with the ruthless kindness of assumed moral authority.[32]

After the birth of the universe's heart, humanity becomes its throbbing beat—where there were no answers, only questions—so it remains. "Higgs Boson" presents the mixed equation that science is unequal parts faith, beauty, and trial and error. John Mulvey hears the "eliding barriers between truth and lie," where Robert Johnson, Martin Luther King Jr., Miley Cyrus, and the devil himself breach the limits of the personal, the political, and the universal. These hot spots of cosmic energy become tipping points of history where Professor Nick Groom would note, "Human culture collapses into the idiocy of popular culture, and like an eternal and unrelenting cycle at the very end we return to our beginning," where Cave restates the song's opening line: "I can't remember anything at all."

The desire to reach back into the creation of the universe and discover some essential truth would haunt the reflections of *Push the Sky Away*, the modern world confronting Cave with the death of knowledge, drowning in information: the more we know the less we understand. The songs of the album were written over the course of a year, appropriately jotted down in a little black notebook. On "We Real Cool" Cave heralds the bulletproof thrill of cocky young youth, set against the new determinism of Wikipedia as heaven.[33] The 1959 poem "We Real Cool" by Gwendolyn Brooks offers Cave the sharp slang phrase of young African American men hanging out in a 1950s pool hall. The short three-word lines that describe their simple but joyful lives full of pleasure soon becomes a rhythmic chant, but ending with the abrupt line "We die soon." It suggests the young lives run short, either burning out into middle age or premature death; all their bravado and self-knowledge will not save them.[34]

Shivering strings and descending piano chords plot the way toward deeper uncertainty beyond the immediate now, where the stark simplicity of black-and-white conceptions of good and evil become mired in shades of gray. The wandering thoughts Cave accumulated were a sign of his trawling the internet, drifting through the shifting sands of knowledge, and jotting points down "whether they're true or not." as scraps coalesced to form the emergent post-truth world.[35] Cave exposed the new order of disposable knowledge and shifting facts. History seems static but is constantly rewritten, embracing the fresh hell of the online universe's mass content posing as information becomes a data overload, and Cave accepts the risk of balancing out the internet's "societal dissonance" alienating and lonely, where people retreat into narrow viewpoints, desperate to attack and to defend for fear of making a mistake, getting stuck and hung up on other people's opinions: "These songs convey how on the internet profoundly significant events, momentary fads and mystically-tinged absurdities sit side-by-side and question how we might recognize and assign weight to what's genuinely important." As the poet Antony Owen wrote, "I have googled the earth / And I'm tired of paradise,"[36] suggesting the search for knowledge has outgrown our world, but also the idea that the internet could somehow map reality while leaving the human perspective behind.[37] The fear of modernity in the age of surveillance is announced on "We No Who U R," a track driven by gentle paranoia as self-checking that meets with "Jubilee Street," a girl with no name but the letter "B" followed by secret police with her little black notebooks of oblique secrets. The song is cloaked in the shadow of betrayal, Cave swaps brute text-speak for florid scenes of devastation set among shards of chiming organ and synth notes as the lyrics turn upon themselves like burnt edges of paper curling in toward their center. We feel the rising heat of being watched.

Cave's song shows modern man feeling blindly around the body of the elephantine system, constantly shifting, growing, changing, a false constellation. For Professor Nick Groom "We Real Cool" lays out the crisis "of the virtual universe of the internet and the infinity of Wikipedia, which like Jorge-Luis Borges's 'Library of Babel' has the potential to contain all knowledge, but in which it is impossible to distinguish truth from illusion."

The scourge of the internet is to suffer its own restless drive to remain alive and up to date, shuffling knowledge like a deck of cards, we see glimpses but never the whole. This grab bag of discovery is displayed in

Cave's wild listing of beliefs and shaken certainties in "Mermaids" and "Higgs Boson Blues." They become instantly dated, a heritage act, what the ten-year anniversary press release for the album stated as "the contemporary settings of myths, and the cultural references that have time-stamped Nick's songs of the twenty-first century mist." Cave affirms the relentless tides of time where the past is "here to stay."

Sometimes it feels like the further we go on, the less we know, a manifestation of the uncertainty principle.[38] Cave allows that human life often seems to continue outside of space (and time), we simply happen to coexist in the same universe, as if by coincidence, piling on impressions overlaid like waves eroding the shoreline into fresh uncertainty. What limited design there is appears stripped of direction or intent, as unswayed as the Unmoved Mover. We are collections of raw energy, buoyed by native curiosity, from which a little wonder can go a long way. The nature of art is to move beyond the surface of things, rebounding and sparking from one idea to another, the magical wonder that emerges from the chaos of life becomes its own spiral of energy, a light that never goes out.

Remain true to yourself, but move ever upward toward greater consciousness and greater love! At the summit you will find yourselves united with all those who, from every direction, have made the same ascent. For everything that rises must converge.

—PIERRE TEILHARD DE CHARDIN, *OMEGA POINT*[39]

HERE COMETH THE MAN

They meet with darkness in the daytime, and
grope in the noonday as in the night.
—JOB 5:14

All is darkness. A human form crouches down huddled, held by its own arms, hands reach about its bare shoulders, like an animal curled up into the warmth of its own body.[1] As the world turns night upon the day, light into shadow, the universe turns its cold shoulder against the naked figure of the human. There is nowhere to hide but in the shelter of memory—a cluster of rocks, the hollow body of a dying tree, flowers wilting without light—the remains of a forgotten world. Desperate eyes scan the arid flatlands, looking far and long into the great blankness that surrounds them. It sniffs, stares, sees other forms in the gloom, silhouettes break away from the landscape. In the darkness we are never entirely alone, both hunted and haunted, imagination takes over, waiting for the unknown.

The setting for the *Skeleton Tree* song "Anthrocene" finds Cave lost deep in his own grief and self-doubt. Like the German philosopher Friedrich Nietzsche's metaphor of the abyss, he is confronted by a dark distance that also feels like a close and immediate threat. In this black mirror Nietzsche argued we see something of ourselves—the longer we stare the deeper it looks back into you. So often on *Skeleton Tree* we see

Cave brought low by the persistent weight of grief, now lost in a state of permanent night; he is not simply alone but captive to his loneliness.

The song's atmosphere begins at the pain of waking, another day, a fresh reminder of all that we have lived through and must yet begin again. Philip Larkin's poem "Aubade" speaks to the same fright of the very early morning that could also be nighttime, the deathly hour when no one else is around, so you might be the only human being alive and awake in the world. Cave breaks down his misanthropy to expose the impact of sudden disconnect from the earth. The often-intense isolation of grief becomes manifest in the song, where Cave's self-alienation is turned outward, casting a gloom of wasteland all about him.

To create the track's title Cave drops the "po" from the term "Anthropocene," a unit of geologic time that marks the point at which humanity's presence on earth started to have a significant impact on its ecosystems where harmony shifts to discord and balance is upended. Cave's altered term "Anthrocene" suggests the final state of this process: man's footprint is everywhere and has ground down all other life to the point of extinction standing still. In part the Anthropocene places humanity at the top of the food chain.

Cave sarcastically intones the rise of the Anthrocene as something of quiet and terrifying magnificence, "behold, behold!" His words echo the biblical announcement of Jesus "*ecce homo*" (here cometh the man), a tone dense and foreboding as the darkness that surrounds him. Perhaps he is calling into the shadow of humanity cast upon the earth. Protected and insulated by our cities and sustained by technology and production, we can defy scarcity, while breeding poverty among others. The place of man within the earth is not unlike a god, both generous and cruel in uneven measures. On "Anthrocene," Cave has overturned the dominant dynamic, imagining an almost posthuman world realized by our destructive impulses, perhaps the result of nuclear war or environmental collapse, a point of no return where humanity is yet to become the next great extinction.

As an exploration of emptiness Cave lets the song's subtle but lush orchestration circle its way around him, slivers of tremolo guitar edging back and forth like a breeze, fuzzy synth and skittish snare drum tapping bloom into washes of cymbals before rolling off the tom-tom drums. Cave picks away at plaintive piano chords struck with both hesitation and a lingering sense of purpose. The loose form of the track lands like improvisations following off-beat rhythms, charged with a constant hum of background static. The Bad Seeds use these dissonant sonics to establish an oppressive tension that isolates Cave's voice adrift in the ambient hush of gloaming half-light, drawing our attention to his words. Like the fading signals of a dying star haunting long after its last gleaming, Cave's vocal breaks through the haze a pathway that might guide us back toward the light.

The track "Magneto" is built largely out of synth static and the throb of looming bass slides. "Anthrocene" uses jazzy skittish snare and tom fills typical of Thomas Wydler's ability to drum loose "around" a track rather than trying to dictate its flow. This merges into the web of humming harmonies and deft piano chords. You feel like Cave (with The Bad Seeds largely in the background) is almost playing solo.[2]

"Anthrocene" becomes Cave's black hole fever dream, the waking nightmare of a ruined planet that finds him out in the deepest desert of the lunar cycle where reflection becomes reckoning. When we might feel ourselves truly alone, we are no longer forced to bear witness or to be seen under the harsh light of day. Our presence extinguished by the night we might find a new kind of clarity. But the underlying menace of the song's mechanics and Cave's lyrics soon capsize any hope of peaceful contemplation.

Across *Skeleton Tree*, we find Cave chained to the weight of consciousness, struck by wave after wave of emotion that at once draws him back into memory and thrusts him forward to the bleeding edge of the present. On *Ghosteen* these feelings build into relentless self-examination, echoes of the past "and its savage undertow" threatening to suck him under. "Anthrocene" exposes Cave held painfully awake to everything, captive to the present looking over his shoulder toward a better past as he tries to deny the inevitability of the future. The downbeat mood of the record finds him frozen in supermarket queues or stuck behind the wheel of his stationary car; he steps outside of himself to observe his own life. Cave is stalled before the crushing inevitability of time passing by, with or without him. In racing thoughts, he wanders, out of place and time, across an alien landscape. Under the dawn of the long night, he reflects upon the future of the earth and his (our) place upon it, finding himself caught between the dawn of man and postapocalyptic emptiness.[3]

Cave's mood of isolation smothers the track, echoing in the form of a nocturne. Drawn from classical music, such as Chopin's and Satie's often spare and haunting piano pieces, it is representative of the album's minimalist approach. Cave's song speaks to the same mournful tones of the nocturne and its use of fleeting runs of piano or violin that build toward a crescendo that never comes, using the rise and fall of volume, intensity, and attack to create restrained dramatic force. Nocturnes tended to be composed with the theme of night in mind, where the hour meets the mood. The nocturne has its roots in the traditional canonical hour *nocturns* in the practice of Christian worship, the Liturgy of Hours. Inspired by the Bible Psalm 118/119:62 ("At midnight I rise to praise you"), referring to times of night worship that crossover between sleep, dream, and waking life. The exact hour has changed in contemporary practice, but traditionally the night offices were delivered at midnight or Matins at 2:00 a.m. to mark the quietest hours in which to give praise through the reading of psalms, hymns, and prayer.

Setting "Anthrocene" in the nocturne aftermath, between the day's ending and the new hope of dawn, Cave edges the ritual practice of night worship further into the darkness. He turns to face imagined enemies, half-hidden furies in the long night of the soul, a time of personal searching in a sea of doubt and uncertainty. He realizes a nowhere place where our prayers yield no guidance or deliverance from our struggles and we are left to beg the question of a silent God as a figurehead of power and authority ambivalent to our concerns, and so to doubt his very existence.

The song speaks to an emotional disconnect, not recognizing the person looking back at you in the mirror, physically the same but with an aura drastically altered. Where there is nowhere left to turn, the temptation is to withdraw and retreat (into silence). Accordingly, Cave's vocals are set quiet and spare behind a vast flattened soundscape of reverb; he treads gently, tiptoeing into the broken glass of his phrases, as if waiting for a sharp and sudden shock that seems imminent but also endlessly deferred.

At one point in "Anthrocene" Cave offers up a prayer "to the air that we breathe." This lyric works as a form of worship toward the earth as an ecosystem that sustains all human life, a brutal reality delicately balanced and fleeting as breath itself, but also as a reflection on the immateriality of prayer as a conscious act. We reach out in the hope that the words passing from our lips might cast our struggle, pain, and regrets beyond the concrete world to connect with something greater than ourselves—the spirit of the earth as the prime force of nature, or a higher power such as the Christian God. In David Bowie's "Word on a Wing," he uses the same language of breathless exhaustion to plead for holy intervention to rescue him from the depths of his cocaine addiction. All he has to offer are his words as an address to the "void of unknowing," that deeper kind of darkness. It becomes a cry for help that was never meant to be answered, but we say the words all the same.[4]

In the wake of much disaster movie–style imagery, the Bible offers a representation of God as formless but powerful wind that tears mountains in half, and within it a calmer sound that can only be heard through an open and ready heart: "And after the earthquake a fire; but the Lord was not in the fire: and after the fire a still small voice."[5]

In other translations the voice arrives as a soft murmuring, a gentle whisper, these qualities suggesting that we might hear God best in stillness and contemplation, in a place of quiet, close and near as when we become awake to our own breathing or hear the pulse of our blood in the ear. Suiting the temper of the song and reconnecting with expressions of terror in the earlier Bad Seeds sound, "Anthrocene" underlines something of the new minimalist phase in Cave's music, in full voice but with the lights low.

But "Anthrocene" reaches into a deeper, more primal fear than spiritual abandonment. In the emptiness of the night sound carries farther, bringing every small noise closer, a heartbeat pulsing within the ear, lodged in your throat, an unutterable word. Even in the city, drunk-loud voices, swirling sirens, and footsteps bouncing off the street, a bottle spinning off into broken glass seem louder and more intrusive than in the day. It is only with the clear light of morning when we see the subterranean world clouded in darkness made normal and whole again.

Cave's central image of the "last man" surrounded by a dying world suggests a return to the atmosphere of "The Good Son" where Cave evokes a smothering blanket of night that in shrouding the naked body also emphasizes its very separateness from the dark space that closes around it. The night is both familiar and alien, a cold comfort that swallows up distance, bringing our fears forward into a position of intimate threat. We withdraw into the need for retreat, but there is nowhere left to go as the very "realness" of the world becomes too much to bear, the horrific intensity of "seeing things as they are," like a dark mirror, we witness the muted glow from a screen that overwhelms the image it tries to show.

In *Darkly*, Leila Taylor's brief history of Black lives and the gothic imagination, she uses the images of a door left ajar, the edge of the woods, or stairs leading into a dark basement to present the tipping point between curiosity and uncertainty that marks the edge of the unknown. This is a liminal place of strangers where some of Cave's darkest songs are not simply heard, they happen *to* us. "Anthrocene" draws upon our more primal fears: the shapeless mystery dancing in the dark, a movement we can feel but are unable to define. We go forward into the night in both wonder and terror.

Within the environmental framing of the track the world is cast into a great coldness; like Adam and Eve banished from paradise they finally see themselves as naked, adopting shame and the fig leaf. They feel the sudden chill of spiritual abandonment, being exiled from God's grace, haunted by a sense of desertion that follows them like a shadow. Cave would return to the lost promise of Eden (as a state of mind) that is regained with *Ghosteen*.

The ghostly approach of "Anthrocene" evokes the premise of William Golding's 1955 novel *The Inheritors* and the coming of a new age. Set

toward the end of the prehistoric era, a time well before our most ancient civilizations, the novel features the lesser creature of Neanderthal man confronted by the new breed of humanoid being, Homo sapiens. The "cave man" is forced out of existence by evolution and the survival imperative of the selfish gene, humans driven to thrive and to overcome: veni, vidi, vici. With the rise of the first Homo sapiens the extremes of man's needs come to the surface. Cave sings with the wounded heart that at once seeks someone to love but also something to set on fire, laying bare the dual aspects of our nature.

Modern man arrives like an army marching over the horizon of history; in their nascent sophistication of using fire, animal skins, and flint tools the humans bring with them a new day and a new faith in technology, after which the world will never be the same again. Cave sings of the human being as he was and the Homo superior he wishes to become, drawn tall, rising into its hubris. This modern species readies itself for a fall. In their coming they bring with them an aggressive new attitude to life, eradicating their forebears as a potential threat, erasing their past. They see themselves as the future.

Following the song's through line, the people living in contemporary society are set to become "the last man," accelerating toward their fate as a species of individuals splintered across tribal divides of class, wealth, and status. Where *The Inheritors* shows the "cave men" in a primal but more benign position of needs and means, the last man now lives beyond them. The neoliberal single-minded vision of culture often polarized between the ideologies of neoliberal Western capitalist democracies or nonsecular authoritarian states is driven by desires for wealth, progress, and individual freedom, so the environment becomes a lesser consideration. This is the new (modern) world Cave started to confront on *Push the Sky Away*. The globalizing reach of technology has made the world more connected but also shrunk smaller with individuals more atomized from one another.[6] But the world is not only "I," the universe revolves within itself, not individual or collective human concerns, and with the growth of the family many people begin to speak and think not only of their children's future on the planet, but of all children's place on earth.

"Anthrocene" reaches back to the casual nihilism and wider misanthropy of Cave's earlier music; humanity is an abortion of failed promise. As hinted at on "People Ain't No Good," people are not inherently bad or evil, but they are often found wanting where the person who believes in nothing finds nothing in the world worth saving. Perhaps Cave sees humans as the symbiotic parasite that degrades and damages the planet, with our climate change crisis a prime example of neglect and self-inflicted harm to our global ecosystem where the realest threat to the human race is humanity itself: the constant undercurrent of violence and greed, alongside the damage caused to the planet, manifesting as extreme shifts of climate, destroying ecosystems, and diminishing natural resources.

This scenario carries echoes of *The Road* where the earth is changed beyond recognition. Washed-out CGI would be used to flatten the sky into an endless dirge as lifeless forests stand petrified beneath dead air. After much struggle the boy and his father arrive at the West Coast of America, and the father apologizes to his son that the Pacific Ocean is not blue, the constant oppression of faded color like a body drained of blood provides the hopeless canvas of the film.

Philosophical theories of environmental ethics[7] place humanity's role and responsibility for the well-being of the earth at various levels of deep and shallow ecology, with one argument aligning to Christian theology claiming that the God-given status of the human on earth is as caretakers of the garden, charged to live for and within the natural world, enriching and sustaining the wider ecosystem. In looking at the planet as an external life-form separate from our wants and desires, "Anthrocene" suggests a relatively benign albeit indifferent system that supports the possibility of all life and natural flourishing. This enables us to step back from the indulgence of pure nihilism and put his healthy skepticism to one side.

But elsewhere Cave's level head is upended by the gut punch of brute reality, which is always there in the background, threatening to erase the good we are capable of with a sweeping gesture of blinding fire. On the 2004 songs "Breathless" and "There She Goes My Beautiful World,"

Cave at once praises the divinity of nature but also laments its verdant wonder, and human potential might yet be thwarted if we lose our way, after which all we will have left is the "sad music of humanity." Even then, knowing that such brilliant growth must give way to decay and with the brilliance of the creative human spirit, our best work is sometimes carried out at the ignorance and expense of others and the world around us—writing great words of art while the house we live in burns down around us. This is not strictly an argument for environmentalism but simply an acknowledgment that the imaginative handprint of the human also demands the impact of its footprint. In the race to outdo one another, to colonize the blank space of the moon for its own sake, to exploit and shape nonhuman life comes to dominate our worldview, like a false god, we preach both survival and extinction, from which "Anthrocene" reaches forward as the blind future echo.

In the modern world the most real threat to humanity is humanity itself: we are our own worst enemy. Self-inflicted wounds of pollution, deforestation, waste all damage the ecosystem and diminish the natural resources we depend upon. In a wasteland that suggests both imaginative and environmental collapse "Anthrocene" finds Cave examining the situation of the last man, standing at the center of a great nothing, showing the human animal as alien invader and native destroyer, suddenly foreign and detached from its place in the world, the universe, and beyond.

"Anthrocene" comes from a place of personal grief but becomes a requiem for the human race but also as a warning to veer away from the precipice of no return. As the pain of wider destruction overwhelms the last man in the song, Cave comes to appreciate the closing of one age and the beginning of another, after which everything has changed, and nothing will ever be the same again.

> Feel how your breathing makes more space around you.
> Let this darkness be a bell tower
> and you the bell. As you ring,
> —RILKE

BOOK III
DAWN

ROCK AND ROLL SUICIDE

"Only in art will the lion lie down with the
lamb, and the rose grow without thorn."
—MARTIN AMIS

On the single cover for "Tupelo" we see Nick Cave sitting with a resonator acoustic guitar across his lap. Set against a couple of spare American stars, he is looking off to the side, as if into a far distance and the continued dream of America.[1] Taking it all back home again, Cave and The Bad Seeds would consistently mine the mythic power of rock and roll but almost immediately broke out from its monoculture of English and American twelve-bar blues, pushing toward a more frayed alternative sound that went beyond rock music, just as it threatened to roll back against itself.

Much like the irreverence of pop music, the spirit of rock and roll chases real feelings toward deeper meaning but does so through an attitude where everything amounts to something and nothing at once. For Cave rock music was his childhood inspiration—between the holy trinity of gospel, blues, and emergent punk rock emerged the one true king of modern music: Elvis Presley. Within his own persona Cave fulfilled some of this maligned promise of the outsider rebel, which began to precede him in the myth of murderer, poet, victim, lover, loner—embroiled in a self-fulfilling romanticism. Cave identified with familiar iconoclasts such as Iggy Pop, Mark E. Smith, Tom Waits, Leonard Cohen, Shane

McGowan, and Johnny Cash who all followed a crooked line, praising and overturning musical traditions along with outright rebellion against societal norms and anticonformist conceptions of spirituality and atheism. But Elvis would still stand as the one true model for Cave, the prism through which all his future music would be filtered to become emancipatory, life-changing, universal.

Along with Presley's own religiosity Cave would go full tilt into heroic God-fearing/praising rhetoric with "Get Ready for Love," a punk-ridden glam rock stomp that offers both the promise and threat of holy power.[2] In an often cruel world there is not enough praise to meet the demands of God, as infinite as his love are the expressions of religious devotion made various.[3]

While The Bad Seeds came together in the final ebb of postpunk, they remained a defiantly non-80s band, as if they simultaneously reached backward and forward, embracing the old sounds of twanging edgy guitar strings, bottle slides, and wild harmonica.[4] Although the screed of "Tupelo" (1985) seemed to put a final nail into the coffin of white blues for Cave while invoking its spirit within a ghost dance of lost futures,[5] already by 1986 The Bad Seeds were reaching far beyond the strictures of guitar-based music, often ricocheting at odd angles from Cave's piano chords to find new creative directions. With each album they sought to reinvent the idea of the "Bad Seeds sound," skipping Echo and The Bunnymen, Teardrop Explodes, and Psychedelic Furs at the more indie-psych end of the postpunk spectrum turning into new wave. Rowland S. Howard pointed out the major flaw of those bands was not to take sufficient artistic risks, afraid to make a mistake or embarrass themselves. He complained that in live gigs they just went through the motions—as in their music—bands who did everything expected of them.[6] Cave noted more of an affinity to the acerbic edge of The Pop Group, Gang of Four, and The Fall, weird and wonderful indefinable tangents of music that sought to escape the cliches of their musical roots.[7]

Greil Marcus notes that after a string of bad movies and with less time spent in the studio by the mid-1960s Elvis had "disappeared into an oblivion of security and respectability," a man lost from himself spun into his own noose. Ground down by mass-produced "hits" with diminishing returns and forced musical numbers, the electrical force of the king had short-fused; he now wore his legend as thin just as others held it cheaply.[8]

Perhaps the original Second Coming of Elvis was his 1968 comeback show—a victory lap of his powers reasserted his larger than life presence, from which there could only be a long comedown, struggling to hold on to a relevance long since past. Greil Marcus sees the performance of a victory, but not the winning of it. Elvis cannot transcend himself therefore he must spiral downward. In the 1970s, where others saw a zombie king forced back into life, Cave saw the performances of Elvis as a kind of slow crucifixion: "a deeply suffering individual going on stage and just doing it anyway. He was literally pressed up against eternity."[9]

Cave was looking with twinned vision at both the peak years and the lax-luxe glamor of the jaded and faded comedown, a broken lion chained to the classics of an endless Vegas rerun. There was a lesson here for Cave: American lives had no second acts, only quicker endings. To beware falling into his own cliché, he had to evolve or die. As his own songs became classics he had to create new music or be crushed under the weight of nostalgia. Elvis cornered himself into becoming the Jesus of rock and roll music. His great fall seemed to cast an arc over the death of a more innocent and optimistic America—without hope the dream dies.

With suitable perversity of song choice, Cave's solo career started with a cover of Elvis' "In the Ghetto" drawn from Cave's favorite era of the king's career downswing, as if in homage to the damaged hero he wished to become.[10] "In the Ghetto" has the same mawkishness of "Do They Know It's Christmas?," a glancing drive-by social observation. Having grown up in the poorer black neighborhood of Tupelo Elvis would hit on familiar territory of the need for a gun or a car as an escape to get out of town. This also exposed him to more gospel music, and when his father was released from jail the family moved to a nascent housing project in Alabama.[11] The phrase "ghetto" would come to describe the "wrong" side of town, ostracized, persecuted, and undermined, so the housing projects would become a gentrified form of this. As a later song in the Elvis canon it's hard to see "In the Ghetto" as anything but another ballad, albeit one with attempted social conscience, though the song tells the story of a defeated would-be criminal reduced to poverty, prejudice, and alienation from society.[12]

Cave found that his own tribute to the blues wrestled with an (unresolved) internal tension where the original black American music became absorbed and assimilated into white rock and roll via pastoral country music and hillbilly, with Elvis following soon after. Presley's first-generation skyrocket success came from his ability to merge white and black musics, or more accurately to bring the soul of the blues to white audiences and to break through to some black audiences that he was not just another hillbilly—he could be strange, exciting, and scary. The blues gave rock music its core structure and an attitude of expression—from guitar scale patterns like the twelve-bar blues to pushing boundaries of free expression. Where the blues players were physically and metaphorically restricted, the white rock and rollers were free and welcome to roam, where other musicians were not.

Cave's journey was fragmented and iconoclastic, like Elvis, a self-contained ball of energy, there was need to shape or sculpt himself into something else—he simply needed a stage. "Tupelo" in particular expressed Cave's exaggerated approach at a hyperreal Deep South vernacular, and its internal clash of opposing voices. The Bad Seeds' original Bassist Barry Adamson, a mixed-race man, born and raised in the Moss Side area of Manchester where he grew up among systemic racism, found aspects of Cave's tenor in "Tupelo" disconcerting: "I felt quite challenged by the viewpoint of black people as demons."[13] Though he was keen to find a way to exist within Cave's white approach to a "fractured blues world,"[14] Adamson was concerned with the appropriation of a black American vernacular seen through a white man's prism, Cave's use of "a big black cloud come" perhaps too readily aping the vernacular of Leadbelly: "Nick listened to blues a lot and all his obsessions seemed to reach a boiling point. And the further he got with his novel, the more closed he became."[15] Cave biographer Mark Mordue would note that Cave made it his own: "John Lee Hooker in particular gave Cave an atmosphere to explore violence and loss and isolation, the unspoken thing to be on your own, Nick found that space in the blues."[16]

Speaking in a 1994 interview almost ten years after *The Firstborn Is Dead*, Cave sited himself as a white middle-class Australian, using the mythology of its culture as a jumping-off point to create a new Bad Seeds sound.[17] Cave would admit that his open-ended adaptations of blues music sometimes "gnawed at my conscience." Admitting that he never suggested he shared the same authority or experiences as the blues musicians or even Elvis, he also acknowledged that within the wider ecology of musical inspiration and influence the blues could never remain the sole preserve of black musicians from whom it originated. Cave shared something of Presley's country background, growing up in close proximity to the infinite landscape around Wangaratta, though in very different racial climates. Elvis was first labeled the "Hillbilly Cat," a white negro figure who was "hip" enough to appreciate the bigger picture of American musics. Many white listeners heard a black voice splitting their racial loyalties down the middle, but Presley couldn't entirely escape his impoverished background, and while he began as an everyman truck driver, he might otherwise have been the white trash rube destined to fall between the cracks of popular culture and be forgotten.[18]

The creation of rock and roll that early Bad Seeds tracks cling to is mired in the atmospheres of the Deep South, a torrid damp heat of blood driven into sweat all suggesting a permanent sense of ruin and decline. It is from here that Cave began to explore the psychopathology of people through landscape, shifting from swamp and lakes and clashing with the more traditional biblical visions of mountains, prairies, and forest, a land of plenty: the lifeblood of the Mississippi Delta region, a site of great natural fecundity reaching toward a crunch point of salvation and ruin, another crossroads of myth making and survivalism, evoking ecstatic loves and fraught endings.[19] In *The Mind of the South* W. J. Cash wrote, "Even the southern physical world was a kind of cosmic conspiracy against reality in favor of romance." He depicts the summer sun of August coalescing in the breath of the southerner to become a thunderstorm explosion, "a violent outburst of emotion," the human being in the natural world turned against itself. On "Tupelo" Cave brought it all

home, the mystique and the crushing realities of the American South, arriving at a fantastical place where the truth is stranger than fiction.[20]

Americana influences dominate much of Cave's early discography, reaching for the gothic aura of the Deep South but also anchored in the equally mythic Wild West. Cave would mine the Australian outback, a burning land of searing heat and desert drought through to scenes of endless rain and flooding as the inverted mirror of an equally borderless landscape sustained by myth and legend.[21] For The Bad Seeds' 1992 album *Henry's Dream* Cave looks west, beyond the pale of the civilized world toward an emerging society where laws are bent or broken in the interest of survival and progress, where everyone makes their own way and morality becomes a fluid concept. *Henry's Dream* is shot through with warped visions spotted from a speeding car blurred along a lost highway—a Gonzoid road movie seeing the cliches of the American West ahead of him foreshadowed by the echo of the outback in the rearview mirror. Speaking of his upbringing in the small rural towns of Warracknabeal and later Wangaratta, Cave said, "I wasn't particularly interested in my own culture in Australia, which was quite normal for Australians at that time because, on some level, we didn't have our own culture."[22]

Cave-as-Henry rolls on through the songs as The Bad Seeds chant their way farther on down the road[23] along a journey to nowhere. Within the album's kaleidoscopic vision Cave finds a crisscrossing cast of settlers, preachers, cowboys, sheriffs, hustlers, and outlaws, all fighting for their slice of the American Dream that could just as easily turn into a nightmare. But it was the implicit lawlessness of a seemingly untamable environment that most attracted Cave as a songwriter where his tall tales span the vast and rich landscape from mountain, canyon, and plain where endless vistas outrun the eye. Denis Diderot would argue that poetry should be "barbaric vast & wild," which accurately would describe the lived poetry of the American West in Cave's songs.

Similar tensions would be reflected in the 1971 Australian film *Walkabout*,[24] telling the story of two children who become stranded and lost in the outback and are helped home by a native Australian aboriginal. Made famous by a film version, it became a seminal text in the fractured colonial history of Australia in its ongoing cultural clash and struggle with national identity and addressing the racist government policies of the past, which reflects America's own social disunity.

Cave alludes to Cormac McCarthy's early novel *Child of God* (1968) following the depraved debaucheries of Lester Ballard, a sexually repressed outcast whose endless road is merely a pilgrimage of the lost.[25] A recurring theme for both McCarthy and Cave is the metaphorical journey—to meet with the gallows, go deeper into the wild, leaving town for the final, last time—overpowering the distance traveled, becoming repetition walking toward some final destination, imagined or impossible, that is really no place at all, whether it be spiritual realization, death, or somewhere to run to (not simply running away from).

In Cave's songs loners and outcasts bring narrative to the land's emptiness, America's dream becomes their own inverted fantasy, though they are often painted as the enemy of community by virtue of their extreme differences. "When I First Came Town" presents the drifter once welcomed by new friends who bought them drinks; now isolated and alone they find their bottle has run dry. Almost a rewrite of Karen Dalton's version of the traditional song "Katie Cruel" it is the wandering disquiet behind her eyes that must decide her fate.[26] Interviewed for the 2020 documentary *In My Own Time* Cave speaks of Dalton as a "fellow traveler," perhaps noting a shared melancholy.[27] Cave would mention the roots of the song originating from his time in São Paulo: "When I first came to Brazil I was treated as something like a hero. And having lived there for a while the tables turned, particularly in the press." This is expressed through the musical spirit of Ennio Morricone, with gently soaring strings in the outro of the song. Elsewhere they rise and fall across *Henry's Dream*, as the album continues to reveal itself like pages turned across a book. In each twisted tale it becomes a lovelorn story of struggle and defeat, subverting the tradition of finding glory out west just as it pays tribute to it: all the brutality of Sam Peckinpah going hand in hand with the romanticism of Sergio Leone.[28]

Cave's close collaborator, the director John Hillcoat, would find Australia's relationship to the landscape more complex than it might first appear, tinged with a knowing and wary respect for an earth culture that can never be truly understood, only negotiated with. Hillcoat was keen to point to the origination of the Australian bushranger, arriving well before the cult figures of the American Western movie genre: "The bushrangers were outlaws who went into all the remote areas: outback Australia was a final frontier full of people trying to escape their past, very extreme and harsh and brutal."[29] The clash was between the outlaw Irish-convict generation, British colonizers, and the indigenous aboriginal population native to Australia who bore a unique relationship to the land, all caught in a triangulated conflict.[30] Warren Ellis would admit that natural spaces would be a major factor in the soundtrack work with Cave, exploring the tensions of people created within those environments. His and Cave's experimentation in making music would "live and die" in the moment. Sometimes working without footage or the script to hand, they would find a mood that would neatly slot into the final edit. "Gun Thing" from *The Proposition* soundtrack gives a vision of morning sun and endless riding, searching through the Western genre's cycles of revenge and redemption, but as in so many of Cave's songs, there are no real heroes, merely survivors with longer stories to tell.

Compared to the innate chauvinism of America's expansionism and tapping into natural resources of gold and oil, land was a route to riches and a kind of mad freedom. In Australia it was an excuse for moral self-emptying, free of the demands of history and the deep cultural history of Europe. As in *Walkabout* the untamed empty stillness of the glowing sun-scorched dust of the burning color of the land expresses both space and a closeness of oppressive heat as the canvas to portray spiritual desolation of the colonial trying to make sense of a place where he does not belong or that he does not understand. The character Captain Stanley played by Ray Winstone is suggested as a *conflicted* moral center within *The Proposition*. Seeing Australia as another country to be conquered, his first impression is one of shock where Cave borrows from Dorothy Parker's razor-sharp quip "what fresh hell is this?" He presents an embittered and disillusioned attitude, the whole continent reduced to "this Godforsaken hole." He takes comfort in a mantra of quiet resolve, repeated to himself, "I will civilize this place." Interchanging "land" for "place" his little lie manifests as the overbearing metaphor of colonial chauvinism, pushing against the grain of nature in an attempt to "tame" the native population and forcing some alien society onto a country seen as having no culture or identity of its own. Within this Stanley lives alongside his wife in the quiet desperation of his squared-off, picket-fenced ideal of home. He tries to build the dream of the traditional green English garden, including fake snow to replicate Christmas "back home" compared to the pressed swelter and smothering infinite of the outback.[31] There is the interesting note of the aboriginal servant who tends the family home and takes off his shoes when he leaves the house at the end of his shift, back to the earth.

The 1971 film *Wake in Fright* tells the story of John Grant, a Sydney city boy who ends up stranded in the wayward outback community of Bundanyabba or "the Yabba." Alienated from his own country he is the new colonial crash-landed into the wild.[32] Described as a "peculiarly Australian kind of hell," *Wake in Fright* makes landscape its key character in the raw, red earth of the largely desert continent suffused with fierce heat and isolation.[33]

Ryan Anderson notes the sense in which the disorientation of environment, heat, and emptiness, like Kurtz going farther down the river, could turn a person against their true nature: Cave would redeploy these aspects in his music. Cave described it as "the best and most terrifying Australian movie in existence"; its influence is profound in how he transmuted aspects of the Australian cliches into the America of his early songs. With *And the Ass Saw the Angel*, Cave would admit to a profound ignorance of the native flora and fauna of America, and that his own Deep South would actually be distinctly shaped by his rough and ready childhood in rural Australia. Explaining to Mark Mordue that, like "Red Right Hand," the book's true spiritual home was in the town of Wangaratta, the formless desperation and tight-knit solidarity of the small farming community.[34]

In 2020, Cave listed Cormac McCarthy's 1985 novel *Blood Meridian (or The Evening Redness in the West)* as one of his favorite books. A modern lyrical Western set in the mid-nineteenth century, it sets the stage for Cave's understanding of a unique and rare time where a civilization was trying to birth itself from a state of near-lawless destruction, the wide wastes of America as a living hell. The title of the book uses the creeping horizon to mark the dim blood tide of carnage and mayhem wreaked all across the frontier land of America, as if the age of unnatural destruction was seeping up into the skyline, held by the birth and death of the sun. From the mid-1970s McCarthy put years of research into the book, basing himself in El Paso, Texas, visiting archives, following traditional trails, and learning Spanish.[35] In the novel he maps out scattered histories and broken lives to discover the psychopathology of landscape in a nation with no hard lines to its borders menaced by roving packs of men: Rough Riders, scalp hunters, the Mexican army, Native American tribes, and free-range militias, moving as wave upon wave of "drunken djinn" crisscrossing amorphous territories scarred by endless conflict always held beneath the sun's red shadow at the horizon's edge.

The book's protagonist "the Kid" is a young man who oversees all of these bloody horrors set against his nemesis, a huge hairless albino of cold-blooded calm, relentless violence, and ruthless intellect, Judge Holden. They fight alongside one another, and the Kid learns much from this epic figure who, like a god, always seems to evade death even as it follows in his shadow.[36] The relationship ends in acrimony. Fated together the Judge is both the Kid's keeper and his undoing, the Kid's life was ever in his hands. The *Today's Lesson* podcast questions whether this submissive-dominant dynamic is also explored on Cave's "Up Jumped the Devil" where the accused man is hounded by the devil. A perpetual ne'er-do-well taunted by his own inferiority, the devil keeps him close—always there to trip him up and remind him of his lowly station. Where Satan was bound to hell with chains, the devil leads man astray by temptation and subterfuge, such that some are born forever under his shadow. There are further connections between the song and the novel. "The Kid" is also a doubly unlucky bastard, born out of wedlock and losing his mother in the process; he experiences the horrifying vision of watching hanged men and seeing himself in their place, foreshadowing doom through an out-of-body experience of the gallows tree shook by the devil, echoes reverberate across McCarthy's text and

Cave's lyrics Where his books make a gradual turn toward neo-Westerns as the emergent future is one of slow decline of the old ways, a trajectory that would be fulfilled in The Bad Seeds' music and in particular Cave's lyrics.[37]

Cave's outlandish visions of the American West would feed on more surreal outlandish material. When filming *Ghosts of the Civil Dead*, director and future collaborator John Hillcoat passed on to Cave a copy of Michael Ondaatje's 1977 book *The Collected Works of Billy the Kid (Left-Handed Poems)*. A hybrid Western well ahead of its time, the book blends prose poetry, newspaper clippings, archive interviews, and photographs to blur the facts and myth into a new form of creative (non)fiction cut through with poems. We get impressionistic flashes of a real-life figure overexposed into hyperlegend by film, folk song, and tall tales. We also see glimpses of the polite and precocious teenager who was as beloved as he was notorious and despite his many escapades and close escapes was dead by the age of twenty-one, claiming to have killed twenty-one people "one for every year of my life." The real figure is thought to have been closer to nine, and included men, women, and children. In Ondaatje's version everything is slightly twisted. Billy the Kid's close friend and later nemesis, Pat Garrett is noted as having a mean disposition but also being remarkably handsome, despite a crooked smile and crooked face, his good looks somehow off-kilter. Garrett is the very inverse of Billy, the sweet-natured, cool-blooded, boyish murderer, as with so many of Cave's songs the opposing characters each suffer from a disproportion of the bad mixed in with the good, and through this strange new creatures are made.

There is mutual appreciation between the works of Cave and Ondaatje. After an accidental meeting in Iceland Ondaatje said he particularly enjoyed the Cave-scripted movie *The Proposition* (2005), itself an extension of the Western genre into the Australian outback. As an alternative Western, *Billy the Kid* is less about action than meditative and brooding psychology of men set against one another in empty deserted reaches of scrubland plains, taking on psychic proportions of each man meeting his own nemesis. *Billy the Kid* contains some horrific imagery of bullet wounds and high-sun fevers; after he is captured and tied to a horse for a six-day march in the blazing desert heat Billy leaves his own body to see his dick grow hypererect and drive through his skull. Such examples of psychosexual fantasy, brutal and vivid as if to become fact, must have fired the young Cave's imagination and inspired many of his own Western-style characters that brought the weird and the eerie of the West home to the range of madness, his own subgenre of wild gothic.[38]

Equally scenes of extreme violence play out in Cave's songs across the mid-1990s. This is often the outlaw murderer killing everyone in his path of "Stagger Lee" and the gentle love song guarding against the harshness of the landscape in "Loom of the Land." These themes would reach forward to the restrained and meditative *The Assassination of Jesse James by the Coward Robert Ford*, filmed by future Cave collaborator Andrew Dominik in 2007, with a soundtrack crafted by Cave and Warren Ellis. This film goes the other way from more overt Westerns; using the intimated threat of violence over explicit scenes, action happens in parentheses off-screen to meet the brooding of Jesse James living beyond his overbearing legend set against the ticking clock of his would-be assassin who he knowingly brings closer to him, adding a layer of inevitability that hints at an allegory of Jesus and Judas.

The promise of the West in the early years of America was its restless waking dream for a new heaven on earth (that can never be fully realized) that created the new imperialist vision of Manifest Destiny. The wilderness of the country and its native populations demanded the rugged individualism of the outlaw as an agent of necessary chaos to tame and overcome the landscape while working within and beyond the confines of the law and all proportional forms of moral sense. These were men who could get done what needed to be done, no matter the human cost. This figure is embodied in slave bounty hunter character Arnold Ridgeway from Colson Whitehead's novel *The Underground Railroad*, who in his mantra of "the American Imperative" preaches the noble mission "to conquer, build and civilize" while at the same time to "lift-up, subjugate, exterminate and eliminate" the "lesser races." To allow slaves to break away from their masters and white control was to admit a flaw in this imperative.[39] This would culminate in following a "divine prescription" to overcome the Western territory of the North American continent, involving seizure of Native American lands and the breaking up of the northern half of Mexico to become California, with God-given right to make the nation one whole and for each to take his own share.[40]

The novel *Blood Meridian* ends with a brief epilogue of men making holes in the ground with a posthole digger ready to build a barbed wire fence across the land. The author and English literature professor Aaron Gwyn finds a deeper meaning where this passage predicts the rise of a new Prometheus that will overtake even Judge Holden, who in his God-like extremes admits to a world created in no image but his own, and where none shall rise above him. Gwyn remarks that with the invention of barbed wire five years before the ending of the novel in 1878 it marks the death of the Wild West as it was known, cattle fenced in, the roaming rangers and cowboys no longer needed. Mexico is defeated and reshaped into California while native Americans are forced onto reservations—the new man is born in the figure of the oil baron, carving up land and swallowing up oil from it, sparking up the dark satire of *There Will Be Blood*, the new outlaw was the rogue businessman turned oligarch. Gwyn calls it "a kind of technological Entropy at work. Heat Death. An American tragedy, if you ask me." The antiheroes are absorbed into the new carved-up landscape to become misfits suddenly belonging to a different age.[41]

For Cave the great promise of America was really a sour dream; he loved the idea of it but balked at the reality. Despite playing many early gigs there, he found he hated New York, a city where so many rock stars would find a new life. Cave did not need to be reborn under the aegis of the American metropolis. The city was creative fuel to chewed on, burn up, and spit out again.

Cave clashed head-to-head with the long-term fallout of the imperialist, consuming, and all-consuming tradition of America's rampant capitalism. It would devolve into the scathing critique of "Jangling Jack," Americana exposed in its worst light of plastic fantasy, The Bad Seeds push the limits of rock's banality with the "doot'n, doo, doot'n, dooo" chorus but also pay homage to an undeniably catchy rhythm.

"Saint Huck" also mocks the "civilization" of the big city with its sexy cash, randy cars, and the two-dollar fucks, eroticized slick and shiny. It is all fleeting and edging out of reach, reflecting Cave's growing recalcitrant disposition toward the brave new nation.

The Cadillac, an American symbol of freedom and prosperity, shunts its way into "Up Jumped the Devil." To the childhood of anglophone singers like Cave and David Bowie, their imagined America was coined in the image of key icons such as the big, powerful expensive car, becoming America's self-image. On Cave's holy bluesman tribute "Blind Lemon Jefferson" he rejects the car as a symbol of wealth finding value in music. The charming stranger of "Red Right Hand" promises a car and money to whoever might want it, though doesn't ever mention the true cost of this transaction. Elsewhere, dirt-poor Euchrid Eucrow is born in the back of a Chevrolet; literally the family seat, it sits immobile in their yard. The car, the vehicle of the future meant to fly and bring us to the moon with its tail fins and chrome, is a grounded vessel, a monument to the ruin of impossible ambition.

Contrasted with the claustrophobic fever dream of the South, the widescreen West lent itself to a different kind of hyperbole, blown up in explosion of scale. The rampaging road trip on the *DIG!!!LAZARUSDIG!!!* album swaps New York for LA and San Francisco; the cities become interchangeable aspects of the escapist dream, shuffling the hollow sunshine dream the city of angels wears its toxic halo, eclipsed by the glare of the sun, stars are mad pale and all celestial lights are exiled from the city.

"Albert Goes West" adopts the venturing spirit of the cowboy to stride out into the land in search of his own myth but becomes a cliché; after crossing "vast indifferent deserts" he overdoses on psychotropics on a dude ranch, overimmersing himself in the real West gone off-piste tourism. Henry returns to the city a lovesick shadow of himself; while bland Bobby steps into an average faceless dive bar and disappears in the shadowy corners, he fades into the furniture and forgets himself. These are fragments of wasted energies thrown into the pursuit of something, passion, desire, addiction, or even love; their short-term actions wear them out fast, and the dream state remains only that.

Where Cave used America to explore freedom and its limitations, it was only to discover the reflection of rock and roll's rebel power of emotional extremes and wild narratives to alter and remake reality. Cave said, "The songs that I like are the ones that you can't visualize, that are just cries from the heart—those very straight, direct songs that make rock & roll music so wonderful." The philosopher Michel de Montaigne said, "To philosophize is to learn how to die"; perhaps by contrast rock music is learning to live and to feel to the fullest extent of our being—existing in spite of death in fleet minutes and pure moments that we can revisit in the songs we know and love.[42] Cave's music has long banged its head bloody against the destruction of body and soul and more recently grown alongside it; to accommodate loss is to face up to our own mortality. Where before we might say the music is morbid and gloomy, it has become doubly life-affirming without veering off into pure sentimentality.

Cave has become, if not a guardian, then at least a keeper of the rock and roll spirit, not only its more limited expressions of music as volume and sonic aggression to force a reaction but also to explore the limits of creative and emotional expression. In the earliest part of his career Cave personified the primal force of youth as doomed deity, fated to age and become truly adult, writhing against its own condition. The power and poise of The Bad Seeds' songs is sustained by an innate swagger and use of restrained attack, an attitude absorbed into their last-gang-in-town approach. Certainly the early days of the band as musical outlaws working beyond genre limitations and set against conventional ideas of morality and good taste. Cave would still praise this outsider element of the artist, particularly within rock and roll and its natural rebelliousness with Cave's most extreme lyrics adding an extra streak of deviance. So The Bad Seeds remained bound to the electric tension cast between overturning heritage and driving forward in musical evolution. With his most recent albums Cave has shown how there is sometimes greater power and depth of expression in looking into the abyss of pain and deep, wounded love than there is in simply dancing around the edge of it. In this regard albums such as *Skeleton Tree* can seem far more frightening and challenging to listen to, not because of inevitable autobiographical traits but because they confront us with the beauty in terror.

Cave would acknowledge the power and mystery by which music seems to appear before the artist, with one note played alone generating only "idiot noise" when another is played next to it. This becomes music imbued with some emotional resonance, with the potential to "turn into something that could change your life." He said, "It got through to me, the only thing to get through to me of all the things that were happening when I was 15. Rock and roll then was real, everything else was unreal."

Speaking about *Carnage*, Cave observed, "Allowing our music to do its thing, advancing us toward our better selves. At least, it seemed that way. Music can do that. Make you better." Even at its most scabrous and wild, music carries emotional resonance; uplifting and regenerative, it connects to the deeper, more vital part of our natures. He acknowledges a creative spirit, unique to each person, "a good and essential force." Allowing it to guide and take shape helps steer us toward our artistic passions as we apply ourselves: "The more dedication you show to the process, the better the work, and the greater your gift to the world."[43] Cave would continue to acknowledge the gift of Warren Ellis' contributions as a songwriting partner, noting his "uncynical, unironic view of music" bearing a naturalist approach that frees up Cave to work more flexibly and openly than he had done so before.

Cave notes that for lots of people rock music seems to fill a "god-shaped hole," a vacuum formed by yearning for something transcendent, what he calls a sacred space—as much as it offers escapism Cave offers that music can change us. On "Push the Sky Away" Cave at first brushes it off as only rock and roll, but for all its knowing plasticity of artifice an authentic force of feeling that cannot be contained dwells within it, as Cave invokes salvation in music: "it gets you right down to your soul."[44] Giving a voice to the brilliant and terrible sensations of human life, it becomes a medium toward something higher than ourselves, where for every listener rock and roll creates a new reality.

PRAYERS ON FIRE

Nick Cave started life as a true believer. Beginning as an eight-year-old choirboy singing in Wangaratta cathedral on Sundays, this grew and blossomed even into a more serious and devout Christian faith. But as Cave discovered the new religion of rock and roll his own music would be more concerned with dancing with the devil, a more urgent faith half-absorbed, half-preached, and lived to the limit. Grappling with the spiritual uncertainty of religion the teachings of the original rebel son of Jesus Christ were far more alluring to the young Nick Cave of The Birthday Party than the fixed entity of God. He grew into sinner and saint combined in turbulent and brilliant communion.

Touched by the metaphorical weight of the Bible as a work of literature, Cave began to read it seriously around the age of twenty-two, searching for the original true stories, fables, and myth to inform his songwriting, leaning upon the passions of good and evil. By the time of the early Bad Seeds' records many of his lyrics took their cue from the ornate flowing verse of the King James edition such that it became a kind of second language indivisible from his persona.

Cave's use of biblical allegory drew upon a psychic shorthand for extremes of human behavior: the seven deadly sins, all stories hardwired into the Judeo-Christian structure of many Western democratic nations. The muscle memory of the Bible's conception of good and evil is inherited and established the commonplace moral compass across

Western democracies and provided something for Cave to interrogate and occasionally to kick against, overturning the values of his elders masquerading as his betters.

Cave being well versed in the Bible was something of an understatement, knowing much of it by heart, his songs and titles borrow whole lines, phrases, and expressions. Early Cave biographer Ian Johnston records Cave meeting a group of Jehovah's Witnesses at the airport. Stood up in what seemed his entire worldly possessions, a single dark suit and small briefcase containing only his syringe and cooking kit and a night-black Bible, Cave was better read in the scripture that the strangers who were trying to convert him. With or without the absolutism of ritualized belief Cave found something there and peopled his earliest songs with reimaginings of the characters and moral lessons. The Bible became a space of creative antagonism inverting its cliches to drag sin and redemption into a modern context and make the old tales new.

Certainly Cave absorbed the narrative storytelling power of the Bible built into its verse structure. Born of the oral tradition it is memorable to the reader or the listener, sounding out strong whether spoken, or even sung, a style familiar also to the poet and seer William Blake. While Cave at first presents as the man who cuts his fingers on the gilt edge of its pages, the Bible's word of the Lord carries much pain, but it is balanced across inspiration, retribution, revenge, and regeneration, myriad forces casting a long shadow across his difficult path walked in zigzags of art as life.

Early on in his career Cave embraced the vitality and urgency of the Old Testament, a force more literal than metaphorical and allusive, much of its storytelling hidden behind the strength of its bloody and salacious imagery. It often presented too narrow a worldview of violence and inevitable doom, which threatened to restrict Cave's songwriting toward melancholy.

Cave noted a conscious shift in his songwriting around *The Boatman's Call* from rereading the gospels, falling in love again with the language of the heart and the noble idea that spiritual goodness is possible in everyone, arresting and reversing the view that the collapse of milk and honey into blood and sorrow was the only inevitable truth. Cave actively disrupted this with the love, hope, and optimism of the New Testament, the "seduction of Christianity," and the abiding power of faith, but turned this inward as creative inspiration to practice his own version of faith without Christian dogma.[1]

The New Testament also introduced a more personal revelation for Cave, an awakening to the possibilities of self-transformation, and how this offered the true realization of an open and spiritually aware path: the state of constant becoming, working toward being a good Christian and more importantly an empathetic human engaged in the world. For Cave this would mean creating art that even in profanity, anger, and nihilism worked toward the glory of God, to become an enervating, enriching force.

At one time Cave fully confirmed this transition from the Old Testament to the New, and his writing accordingly shifted from darkness into light, admitting that his work began to "labor" under the relentless pain and suffering of the darker first half of the Holy Bible. More recently he argues against his past self, claiming that the burning seeds of creation, merged with destruction, had always been there in his music, as they are in the Bible. Life shows us punishment and redemption as two sides of the same coin, embracing the gray area of necessary evils. Cave's songs remove the expectation of people as being wholly good or ungood; though his songs veer to these extremes, it is the dynamic push and pull that also gives the Bible its visceral tension, reflecting the challenges of real people.

After the Bible, the book that most confirmed the religious disposition of young Nick Cave was his close reading of Flannery O'Connor's 1952 novel *Wise Blood*. Alongside John Huston's near frame-for-frame movie adaptation it is one of his favorite books. The sardonic gallows humor of serious intent offers a fable-like story he keeps returning to. A stinging rebuke of the long distance traveled between faith, heresy, and false prophets, a kind of pilgrim's progress for her acerbic antihero, Hazel Motes, a character who would not seem out of place in many early Bad Seeds songs, just as Cave himself might have stepped out from the pages of *Wise Blood*.

The book opens with Motes staring down an old lady on a train, returning to his hometown from military service. He suddenly barks at her, calling out her hollow faith like an accusation and a question: "you think you been redeemed." Immediately after arriving at the station he visits an unattractive, aging prostitute, driving himself sick with self-loathing. In several darkly comic turns Motes finds himself played and let down by everyone he meets from shady car dealers, "blind" lay preachers, and lazy-eyed disciples. He echoes the lament of Cave's protagonist Euchrid Eucrow: "Too many Christs and not enough crosses." Cave ridicules the role of the anointed preacher, as misguided as those he tries to lead, in "Papa Won't Leave You, Henry." A histrionic reverend waxes lyrical about life beyond death (in heaven) presenting the losing edge of faith as a kind of fervent insanity.

Adopting the stance of an outsider to religious orthodoxy, Motes continues a further shift away from society. He recognizes a body of faith without attachment to an overarching figurehead, harboring the desire to establish his own "church of Christ without Christ." This echoes something of the young Cave's belief in a God without the chains of Christianity, for spirituality over the rules and conformity of the systems in which organized religion is founded. This is echoed in a statement from Cave: "I believe in God in spite of religion, not because of it."[2] Like Nietzsche Cave despises a closed, systematic philosophy and a deeply organized religion of moral censure, as Euchrid Eucrow says, "Too many Christs and not enough crosses."[3]

As with so many of O'Connor's characters, Motes' flaws are laid bare in the dynamic of his personality, battling with self-contradiction and his naive self-righteousness of the spiritual calling, whether real or imagined. He is, as Yeats might say, overcome with passionate intensity. O'Connor exploited similar grotesques as Cave: emotionally damaged, bearing visible or psychic limps as with the ensemble of "the Carny," the masochism of physical aberration of the hunchback in Leonard Cohen's "Avalanche," and the blinded apostate of Hazel Motes, he becomes his own martyr having lost faith in God, humanity, and himself. He can no longer bear witness to continued human corruption that so reflects his own shortcomings. This nihilistic reach overshadows Cave's songs of people condemned to fate to fulfill their natures, the crooked man struggles to walk the straight and narrow path.

O'Connor experienced her own form of physical purgatory, suffering from lupus, an autoimmune disease that mistakenly attacks healthy tissue, as in Cave's songs: physical mutilation, psychological flaws, the trauma of victims, the abuse and scarring of innocence, the struggle to live within the body turned against itself—this is life as trial. Cave's gallery of disaffected and wonderful freaks must undergo the acid test of life in a cruel and sometimes savage world. O'Connor practiced what she preached in her writing, finding that it is both sinners and the maligned that are most tested and therefore most beloved by God, causing them to have the greatest need of faith: "Grace changes us and the change is painful."[4]

Wise Blood is driven by O'Connor's disdainful attitude for lesser forms of Christianity beneath her own Roman Catholic devotion, casting her own schism between naive commonplace preachers in the shallow waters of Protestantism to the elevated high-minded realm of Catholic traditions affirming flame with its extremes of behavior met with pomp and circumstance of heavy ritual bound to the Pope as God's representative on earth. Cave would assert his own carnivalesque street preacher vibes as shown on his incantatory performances of "Tupelo" in a whorl of broken-tongue ranting, inciting and inviting the flood as much as he condemns its devastation.

Not unlike the doomed figure of Motes, Cave would readily adapt and exploit the singular characters of Christianity's many saints, instant icons tied to fabled origin stories, the superheroes of an era aligned to God but were elevated beyond normal men and women. Finding the saints as various and colorful as the characters in his songs, he pored over Butler's *Lives of the Saints*, extracting tales of sinners redeemed into spiritual awakening, such as the poet John Donne and St. Augustine's notorious revelation, "Please God, make me good, but not just yet," a line of dark-winged humor that might have been written by Cave. In "Christina the Astonishing" Cave's voice soars far and wide alongside a humbled church organ, telling the tale of a young woman about to be buried who suddenly returns to life just after the recital of the Agnus

Dei. She rises up to the ceiling clinging to rafters; no one is sure if she is possessed by a demon or an avenging angel. Driven to near madness by the earthly sin she sees everywhere that so disgusts her Christina is transformed into a religious force both shocking and enlightening. From her elevated state she looks down and casts judgment upon the gathered mourners who should be seeking penitence, not praying for her. Their lack of moral character is turned back onto them. Initially an undead folk hero she was later recognized as a saint and became part of the ongoing tradition—an expression of the will of God through a mortal form.

Cave exploits the powerful hold of the sacred and profane in his songs, where the rising into sainthood is counterbalanced by the measure of sin and deviance in the world.[5] Trading base metals of raw experience he joins a pagan celebration of bodily ecstasy with the contrived temperance of the forbidden. As sex inevitably meets with the demands of falling in and out of love, the forces of lust are delivered as temptation and rejection to become emotional suffering and revenge. While Cave willfully scratched out a dirty niche of high and low culture in the Bad Seeds' music, many of his lyrics aspire to touch upon metaphysical concerns and the spiritually sacrosanct.

Susie Bick cites the implicit sensuality of the Catholic imagination as an influence in her The Vampire's Wife fashion line, claiming *The Black Narcissus* and its tale of a nun's spiritual corruption by forbidden love as her favorite film. It maintains a religious attitude of dogma and austere glamor, the romantic allure of a heritage built upon the solemnity of ritual, inferring dominance and submission toward a higher power and authority. The strict confines of Catholic law and teachings are compounded by abstinence and denial, fasting to feasting. Though Cave himself would reject most formal religious systems, his music takes great zest in interrogating the wielding of faith and the struggle by which we might yield—or not—to it, cycling within most sects of the Christian church, by turns conformist and controlling.[6]

Across Christianity the saints performed extreme acts of masochism as worship, carried out in self-harm and sacrifice, as protest and defiance against evil, and to highlight the deeper moral and spiritual flaws of

humanity—their outrages a scream at the devil within. In Cave's songs we feel the same ebb and flow in the "issue" of blood along with the spatter and solar of abject gore. Like the saints, he exploits the energy of erotic charge as much as harrowing body horror.[7] In "Mercy" Cave uses the examples of John the Baptist, executed by beheading for his beliefs; the licentious image of Saint Sebastian, bound naked to a tree and stuck full of arrows; and of course Jesus nailed to the cross, wearing a crown of thorns and penetrated in the side with the spear of destiny. Doomed to a brand of thwarted heroism and good deeds, the saints are people elevated to a higher calling, the tension and struggle of the physical against the ephemeral. And in our moments of transcending the body humans come to enact a similar extension of the soul, where orgasm, exquisite melancholy, and death might be combined in the grand elevating idea of the *petit mort*.[8]

As if in tribute to sacred embodiment of human flesh the song "Brompton Oratory"[9] shows Cave attending church service with scripture reading from Luke 24.[10] Based in the Knightsbridge area of West London close to where he was living in 1996 Cave would often wander past and sometimes slip into afternoon Mass shortly before going to score heroin. The church would stand as a symbol of abiding faith and worship, a safe harbor in the storm of multiple breakups, and a psychic refuge from the overbearing reality of everyday life.[11] Cave speaks to sipping the holy wine as blood of Christ from the cup; taking the sacrament in his hands he is met with the smell of his lover still wreathed around his fingers, the touch of her lips haunting his. The metaphorical issue of blood becomes a visceral reminder of sexual intimacy: kissing, fellatio, fucking—grounded by the raw fact of experience. Cave's lyrics also carry the universal nature of the body as both a holy vessel for human spirituality and the form of intimate connection, at once sinful and sacred, the word 'love' is made flesh.[12]

The schism of love, sex, and death would be given shape in the visual interpretations of the Bible in statues, artwork, and iconography that so inspired Cave's music. Gian Lorenzo Bernini's famous marble statue *The Ecstasy of Saint Teresa* (1652) shows the saint experiencing the divine light of God as a golden spear, held by an angel, to be thrust into her real and metaphorical heart. Touched by the arrow of God, she is shocked into radical affirmation of belief. Like Saint Sebastian's masochistic pose, it is suggestive of both sexual penetration and sacred revelation—Teresa is spiritually pierced by her vision, and we see this in her gaze. As St. Teresa of Ávila recounted in her autobiography, "all on fire with a great love of God. The pain was so great, that it made me moan; and yet so surpassing was the sweetness of this excessive pain, that I could not wish to be rid of it." Cave would praise the ecstatic, eroticized language in her collected writings, as her words convey religious union with God, the statue depicting her face again reminds us of the transcendent state of orgasm.[13]

Cave would mark his own unholy transgressions within the artifacts of his early notebooks; half scrawled with song lyrics and bloody junk-sick graffiti, Cave included pasted-in icons of saints and pornographic postcards. In the *Straight to You* documentary he flicks through the pages of camp erotica such as a woman who is observed urinating. On the facing page Jesus stands at the well with St. Genevieve, then St. Therese de Carmelite next to women being tickled—reveling in the disjunct of shock and awe—with Cave's creative imagination meeting somewhere in the middle. Much later the photographer Wim Van De Hulst would show Cave the sadomasochistic Catholic aesthetic–inspired work of Joel-Peter Witkin: "I do remember his eyes fell from their sockets."[14]

Where so many of his songs bear the hallmark of original sin, Cave makes great use of Adam and Eve's loss of innocence and repeats it as both metaphor for the evil of the world and as humanity's wider fate under God, born to be tried and tested. On "Saint Huck" (1984) Cave shifts the narrative a hundred years into the future and anoints his own noble idiot as a young man ruined by the big city.[15] A sarcastically thwarted believer of the common garden variety the song offers a reimagining of Mark Twain's bildungsroman[16] *The Adventures of Huckleberry Finn* (1884). Cave pushes him toward heavy autobiographical tones of his own descent into the netherworld of Berlin. The shadow figure of Huck is the scapegoat buffoon, both blessed and blighted. Having lost all his money he wanders the streets, from bar to cathouse, starved for food, spiritual

BERNINI.

guidance, and the milk of human kindness. Huck offers a paradigm for Elvis who became a victim of his own appetites, given over to excess and twinned need between adoring audience and waning star, the idly righteous saint soon capsizes into full-blown sinner.

When asked about the incongruity of writing a song about the Deep South while living in Berlin Cave would note something of Huck's downward spiral trajectory driving through a long Hamburg street, the notorious Reeperbahn "or *ripperbahn*, as I prefer to call it."[17] Full with the shallow glimmer of bars, brothels, and cabaret sex shows Cave suggests that this seedy part of town that so appealed to his own dissolute needs reflected the crisis faced by young Huck, delivered there by the River Elbe before drowning with its filthy undertow.[18] The song would feature electrifying guitar from Hugo Race: "With Saint Huck, the bass work was already there when I joined the band, then we added things. The lyrics were rewritten a lot, too. That process of elimination was key to the way we worked." The song's irrepressible beat of drums and hammering guitars[19] marks the relentless flow down the dark and increasingly dirty Mississippi River, for poor Huck too mired in self-corruption he must inevitably meet with his own heart of darkness.[20]

Trawling along the river as conduit of struggle and shame, Cave makes Euchrid Eucrow bear all the psychic scars of the saint, a thwarted individual seeking redemption through faith, though he presents more as a twisted self-proclaimed prophet extolling the wonder of sin and obedience. Cave drew some further inspiration from the photographs of Julia Margaret Cameron, a Victorian photographer, from a book given to him by Bronwyn Adams of Crime and the City Solution.[21] He noted that Cameron was one of the first people to do "portraits" of biblical figures and events. Imbued with a hazy sense of the past and dressing up her models with costumes and props, the photographs resemble relics from an earlier time.[22]

In spite of their wholesome subject matter and their dreamy, sepia soft focus, a knowingly vintage aesthetic, Cameron's photographs offer discomforting saccharine visions. She invites a fantasy view that straddles the preeminent reality of sacred truths that to others are mere fiction.[23] Many of the naked child models are visibly frustrated, bored, and indignant at being made to pose, more human than the allegorical figures of perfection they were meant to represent. They become crooked angels with faces made clean, kicking back against the artist's desire to capture the idealized shot of beauty.[24]

Cave used one of Cameron's images for the book cover of *And the Ass Saw the Angel*, a book full of broken communities, religious hypocrisy, and mutual self-loathing. Cave throws the cover image at us like a sarcastic parody on the benevolence of a mother's love. The photograph *Venus Chiding Cupid and Depriving Him of His Wings* (1872) incidentally satirizes familial comfort and emotional warmth never experienced by Euchrid Eucrow himself. Resembling a cliched cherubic angel Cupid, normally a Roman or Greek god, is grounded just as Eucrow is born mute, outside of good grace they are forever falling.[25]

After carrying his small black King James pocket Bible over his heart for so long, it would seem inevitable that the Old Testament's revenge dramas would become transmuted into Cave's murder ballads of love and loss. His early songs would steadily bend to the perspective that humanity is "pitiful" under God: weak, naturally inferior to his glory, and born to sin. Accepting that in the name of faith and sacrifice God's hand is as red as any other, Cave was struck by the native cruelty of his love: "What occurred to me was how severely and despotically the God from the Old Testament acts. How he almost curses those people. And it seemed that I adopted that cursing voice in my singing."[26] This spirit is reignited on "Hand of God" with a healthy dose of terror and awe, the image of the sky split like a burning, living wound, God's will expressing itself by reaching down to the earth, bringing apocalypse in his wake.

In Revelations 1:8 God proclaims: "I am the Alpha and the Omega."[27] He declares himself the last word on the confluence of our existence and destruction: "I am the beginning and the end." We live, and survive, only under his forgiveness, or he is simply the force at play whose power and intent is beyond our comprehension. In its place we accept the withering vagueness of "omnipotence."[28]

In many religious doctrines God becomes a hidden hand, invisibly moving pieces on a board. Cave seems to reject this starkly fatalist view

of the "unmoved mover" on "Into My Arms," denying any belief in an "interventionist god" who holds direct sway over us. Elbow frontman Guy Garvey hears much humor in this line, referring to Cave's performance as "pure Elvis Presley theology," his voice falling heavily on the "dah-ling" at the line's end. It's a jarring juxtaposition of romance and faith delivered as a half-hearted apology.

Yet in the same lyrical breath, Cave invokes the power of God to deliver his loved one to safety in his own arms, not God's. A temporary suspension of disbelief, he offers to kneel in worship, a form of spiritual sacrifice, bringing himself low. The song moves upon an "I-Thou" orientation that "invites the listener into its posture of transcendent relation."[29] Cave is in awe of God's influence, though he never bends to it himself. Compare this to the sly wink of "Brompton Oratory" from the same album, where with some small arrogance Cave declares that neither the devil nor God could bring him to his knees as quickly as his forsaken lover.

Equally Cave is not arguing for absolute free will. After the fall from grace, humans were fated by God to become sinners; on a more determinist reading the maligned gears of God seem to chew people up and spit them out as a matter of destiny. For his part the devil is humanity's true metaphor reflecting each other's capacity for wrongdoing and the temptation to make and break laws, thus there is a little devil in all of us. "Up Jumped the Devil" offers the provocative tale of a young man, apple-seed dumb and plum unlucky, he is cajoled along like a puppet with the hand of Satan working him over from within. But even with the sufferance of undue influence Cave demands we accept responsibility for our own agency—hence the sticky endings for so many of his sinners. As Milton allowed it in *Paradise Lost*, "The mind is its own place, and in itself can make a Heav'n of Hell, a Hell of Heav'n."[30]

Cave suggests that by its nature faith trips you up. We commit to being tested by God, but in doing so he presents us with the challenge to live, and to live well. In the story of Job the good and true believer is subjected to increased suffering, losing his wealth, his children, and his health—his faith pushed to the breaking point, though Job still refuses to curse God. In the common eye he is a righteous person who in spite of himself becomes a poor man put to task: whether he should continue to be observant and patient of the burdens God places upon him or that he is simply not faithful enough, he must prove himself worthy of God's love.[31]

Further reaching into the fallout of God's shadow image, Cave closes the 2013 song "Mermaids" by reeling off a seemingly demented shopping list of twenty-first-century anxieties. He alludes to the terrible deception of ideas splintering into fixed ideals, equally daft and deep. He points to troubling dangers that lie submerged ahead. The journalist Tom Doyle notes it as an inversion of the litany that makes up the central spine of Lennon's "God" where he climbs down from a position of preaching, finding a ladder that is all broken bones of ideas and hopes that could never be fully realized in the real world.

Drawn from the *Plastic Ono Band*, an influential album for Cave, John Lennon declares, "God is a concept / By which we measure our pain." He repeats the lines, doubling down on his doubts, at once both crippling and enabling him to shore up his ruins into a simpler life of just *being*. Now a spokesperson for himself alone, Lennon is freed from the chains of what the public or his fans wish him to be and the entrapment of fame. The ex-Beatle rejects his old band, all forms of spirituality, and twentieth-century icons, dead and alive.[32] Through a half-grin Lennon he declares love between him and Yoko as the final, infinite thing that will outlast their own lives and while declaring the "dream is over" he closes the door on the imagination.

But Cave's belief goes deeper. He affirms positive belief in the threat of the next rapture. Cave nods to seventy-two virgins on a chain[33]—to Lennon's infinite cynicism and self-regard, Cave repeats the mantra of "why not?" admitting a natural mysticism of life. Why should he deny them, demand evidence in return of faith? The enlightened place of suspending disbelief becomes its own new form of magical thinking, the place where creativity is allowed to happen. As if in response to Lennon's cri de coeur, on Red Hand File #196 Cave offers the rhetorical question: "Why does it take a devastation for the world to reveal its true spiritual nature?" This suggests we cannot feel the love of God without also being tried, tested, and sometimes found wanting. So much of the Bible contains stories of faith affirmed through pain. Cave's perspective is that trauma can act as "purifying fire" from the scorched earth; we might find something stronger and everlasting to believe in.

A devout man, imbued with healthy skepticism rather than the dogmatic, unthinking mode of Christianity that Cave rejects, C. S. Lewis quotes Lucretius (De rerum natura, 5.198–199) as one of the strongest arguments for atheism: "Had God designed the world, it would not be a world so frail and faulty as we see." Witnessing the brutal and cruel acts of humanity, it does not seem to be the work of a truly benevolent God. However, Lewis' claim rests upon the moral authority of the divine power that fashioned the world, God as a being with a fixed, wholly benevolent nature, something that Cave routinely argues against.

On the 1988 track "Mercy" Cave draws inspiration from a favored painting, *The Beheading of St John the Baptist* by Pierre Puvis de Chavannes (c. 1869), to express man's plea for clemency from God, calling out "mercy on me" as he gets down on his knees for execution but also in the pose of prayer. Housed in London's National Gallery Cave mentions he would spend hours staring at the large-scale canvas that shows John kneeling before his executioner, having already foreseen his death in a series of visions. Now a real sword is raised over him as to make death inevitable. Only divine intervention can save him but it never comes. All his suffering becomes sacrifice. Cave would present John's kneeling posture as that of prayer alongside the gesture of sacrifice in the name of an idea and belief in the possibility of something beyond oneself.

The living of a Christian life is difficult and plagued with doubt and uncertainty. As a pessimist who spent much of his early career invested in the teachings of the Bible as a form of poetry Cave seemed to throw up his hands at the impossibility of it all, seemingly in thrall to the devil, a relentless foil battering against faith. In his sonnet 14 John Donne is immured against God. Not unlike Cave's many transgressions of sin, he has built his defenses high, though he remains bound to a yearning hope for faith he could not erase, even if he wanted to. He calls on God as a servant: "Your force to break, blow, burn, and make me new." Through which God might "ravish" his heart and affirm faith, a sentiment that is echoed in Cave's "I Let Love In."

Nor does Cave lean upon the oblique symbol of God, in all of his unassailable infinities that we cannot fully conceive of. The real hero of his songs would be Jesus, the counterpoint to Satan's crooked interlocutor, revealing Christianity to bound up in his example as a guide for how we might live more fully engaged lives: "I find that using the word 'Christ' as the actualising symbol of the eternal goodness in all things extremely useful."[34]

On "Sun Forest" Cave sings about Jesus as a man only, all too human. His great promise was to deliver us a word, *the* word of God, a light that would banish the darkness of night that had been held over Cave across *Skeleton Tree* as the sudden masking of God. Where on "Push the Sky Away" God's hand is neither guiding nor vengeful, the heavens are an agnostic abstraction that drives Cave to take a bigger picture view on global issues, recognizing more in the human condition that indirectly affects him. The more egotistical and amoral solipsism of earlier Bad Seeds records is gradually worn away and replaced by a sense of universal selves.[35]

By the time of *Ghosteen* Cave has rediscovered a deep and enduring form of love born out of empathy for Jesus Christ. We feel his pain, coming to know his suffering as we do suffer. Where David Bowie in 1976 "found" the original rock star in the megalomania of Adolf Hitler, Cave recognizes the compromised passage of Jesus, leading by virtue and kindness in spite of the world—after Cain—he represents the first true rebel: "Jesus roamed the land expressing what were, at the time, considered dangerous and heretical ideas. He was literally the embodiment of the terrifying idea."[36] Seeing the wrong in others and reflecting it back upon himself, Jesus becomes a martyr to humanity's redemption, exposing the ease by which we can all make bad choices at the wrong moment.

Cave would explore the tragedy of Jesus' crucifixion on The Bad Seeds' B side "Time Jesum Transeuntum Et Non Riverentum."[37] Setting the scene of a forest where "the wind blows 'eloquent' and meaning abides throughout this hallucinatory land" demons are captured, tied to trees, and tortured, eventually giving over a small scrap of paper that recounts the song's title: "Dread the passage of Jesus for He will not return." The absolute death of Christ presents the denial of the Second

Coming; this is the demon's silent and bitter revenge that will eventually cast quietude over their captors. Cave's spoken-word reading shifts from the enlightenment of Christ's love to the loss of spiritual understanding. This becomes the life settled in seeming tranquility where the car, the house, and the normal life are all stripped of meaning, everything is wrong. Caged birds sing but the people have "run right out of words" as if the loss of the good or holy idea has rendered all future talk useless. Perhaps the greatest tragedy is that they do not understand why this has happened, for Nick Groom their accidental apostasy becomes the erosion of deeper spiritual meaning.

On "Hallelujah" Ellis delivers another hard-swerving violin performance, playing toward the tipping point of stillness, holding a note then letting it fall away deeper into a melancholy swan dive. This is the sound of a lost man trying to return to his senses. Across the aching bridge Ellis drags him further over the rocks, employing the slow-build power developed with The Dirty Three but with unyielding restraint. When his fierce bowing finishes it is heavy with the exhaustion of a character returned home still to his reeling thoughts. Crushed by the endless vision of the snow speaking to the later mid-album piece of "Fifteen Feet of Pure White Snow," for Cave the obfuscation of blinding light is returning horror and revelation.

On the title track of the superlative *DIG!LAZARUS!DIG!* Cave offers a different perspective on Jesus brought closer toward mortality. The biblical figure of Lazarus who was raised from the dead is here rechristened as Larry, perhaps in a nod to Cave's raconteur writer friend Larry "Ratso" Sloman. Cave said, "Ever since I can remember hearing the Lazarus story, when I was a kid, you know, back in church, I was disturbed and worried by it. Traumatized, actually. We are all, of course, in awe of the greatest of Christ's miracles—raising a man from the dead—but I couldn't help but wonder how Lazarus felt about it. As a child it gave me the creeps, to be honest."[38] In the Bible Lazarus emerges in his burial clothes, strips of linen, like an Egyptian mummy. These are removed and he is sent on his way into the world. The universal playground of constant good times' dissipation soon becomes a prison, the torture of mirrors endlessly reflecting Lazarus' anxieties/inadequacies back at him. He is a silver thin mercurial glimmer, a flash of stardom, and then nothing more.

More of a zombie, an unholy creature that should not exist, Derrida noted that he is neither one thing nor the other. This is its own purgatory. "Larry" lurches between waking life and the afterlife. By his actions and self-regard/ego Larry is too high on his own legend, and so seems to digs his own grave. And as much as he goes out of his mind and fucks his way mindlessly across the country he is denied the final release of death. The lyric states that he forsakes his dreams, a canny suggestion that Lazarus is denied gift of dreaming in eternal rest, immortality on earth is perhaps a curse.[39]

In his 1996 lecture *The Flesh Made Word* Cave notes, "Jesus said, 'Wherever two or more are gathered together, I am in their midst.' God is a product of a creative imagination, and God is that imagination taken flight."[40] Cave noted the power of religious and artistic communion where people gather together within a shared experience. The church is not simply a building but the souls and voices united under an idea, like the meeting of its arches, one resting against the other. As each person can be said to have a specific relationship to God, or their own version of him, there is a bridging of spiritual understanding. In *Faith, Hope and Carnage* Cave suggests that the lost ideals of religious community, essentially an enlarged family, offer new forms of connection. While this might suggest a monoculture, it also presents the challenge of exchanging ideas, potentially encouraging a more open and engaged society.

Cave would retain an enduring fascination and twist-turning engagement with religion, continuing to test boundaries of his own belief (or not) in God as the active tension demanded of true spiritual faith. In keeping with his restless perspective on religious affirmation in 2010 Cave stated his position to the *LA Times*: "I am not religious, and I'm not a Christian, but I do reserve the right to believe in the possibility of a god." In Red Hand File #194 Cave admits that a (false) belief in God as a real existent being can be a good and healthy thing, though it is not for everyone. In 1998 Cave more firmly attests that doubt is a necessary component of faith: it demands questioning and in this way spiritual affirmation continues to live. Speaking in 1998, Cave confirmed: "I would distrust anybody who didn't doubt." In a recent interview Sam Leith compares Cave's ongoing religious struggle with a line from the screenwriter Dennis Potter that religion "isn't the bandage, it's the wound," never meant to heal, nor should it ossify into a scar of absolute resolve. This enduring tension leaves the believer more flexible to thought; it is there in the middle of experience that revelations can occur and there can be glimpses of God's power and his grace.

Elsewhere, he is more accepting toward the outright existence of God and the possibility of a better place or way of being beyond the physical realm. "There Is a Kingdom"[41] suggests surefire deliverance. God the "king" himself is both without and within us, his love is the disembodied, inchoate aliveness we connect with, but not something we can possess or hold outright. Where on "Hand of God" from 2020's *Carnage* Cave seems to critique this notion, arguing against the idea of a fixed heaven we can all earn backstage passes to simply by being faithful and loyal to God expecting reward: "There are some people who aren't trying to find anything / But that kingdom in the sky, in the sky."

In Red Hand File #136 Cave argues that we are often held back and kept separate from the divine by our personal hangups and barrier defenses. Instead he prefers to see "The Christ in everything." Cave prefers an inchoate view of God's presence. We only glimpse (little) everyday miracles, coincidences and oddities, the brilliantly inexplicable. God in his mirror—for a man to appreciate God in the mind of God—the confusion of seeing himself there.[42] Cave alludes more to a free-range Christianity that allows people to wander and to return by their own will and choosing, outside of a deterministic framework, the offering of God that shifts by various interpretations.[43]

To appreciate the true fear and trembling of God's grace the philosopher Soren Kierkegaard suggested we must all make the "leap of faith" demanded of us to bridge the gap between a knowing sense of doubt and willingly give ourselves over to God, or even just to trust in faith itself. This struggle is articulated in Sylvia Plath's listless line "I speak to God but he does not answer," to do away with some of the human chauvinism that God is here to serve us.[44]

Our prayers are not necessarily made to be answered but to live in hope enough to pass from one day to the next. Cave takes issue with the notion of pure deliverance: "It seems to me that people look at God in the wrong way. They think that God is there to serve them, but it's the other way around. God isn't some kind of cosmic bell-boy to be called upon to sort things out for us. It's important for us to realize that God has given us the potential to sort things out on our own."[45]

Looking back to *Wise Blood*, Cave embraces his "free" church of the spirit. Open to belief it is not contingent upon the existence and actions of God, instead embracing the teachings of Jesus. In Red Hand File #196 Cave realizes this compromise as a form of righteous consolation: "Each day I pray into the silence." Investing himself in these prayers, they become filled with the potential of hope, the striving toward the possibility of better things yet to come. The philosopher Richard Kearney suggests that while this silence might seem atheistic it offers a return to "god after god—where there remains a lingering question of God, a faith beyond faith."

Ghosteen frequently returns to the image of the sun forest where light penetrates the shadows of the boughs and in brief seconds that become moments there is a piercing glimpse of a godly presence, the harbinger of a holy fire, equal parts destruction and regeneration. "Bright Horses" carries the tone of Chopin's nocturnes, steady and brooding, in which Cave "articulates the uneasy necessity of faith,"[46] embracing a willingness to believe, while admitting to a great unknowing and allowing a benign illumination of feeling and ideas. Cave is unafraid to face down irony with authentic feeling where spirituality can manifest as the negative capability that the artist requires to make the world new in his eyes. Embracing the freedom of his individualist heretical take on Christianity free from dogma Cave's songs cast out more challenges and questions to the faithful than righteous affirmations. But in continuing to test the waters of belief without giving in to the submerged threat of blind abiding faith, Cave finds it safe enough to drink from its edge and each time for hope to be renewed.

IN BLOOM

The book of Genesis states in the beginning there was God and the power of creation from which all life flowed. Cave has long used classical imagery of plants as metaphors in his songs, from flowers and trees to a bestiary of birds, bees, and hounds from hell. So much of Cave's work feeds on inspiration of the natural world as totemic symbols of beauty taken at face value. Celebrating bucolic scenes as hymns to wonder and design is also to admit to the cyclical forces of growth and erosion, decay and regeneration. Grounded in the brute fact of life Cave's songs are still mired in the blood and dirt of paganist realism, where the beauty found on earth that is given praise through art and love must also be bound over to new life merging with old death.[1]

Artists sometimes speak to the mother of invention as a generic term for the "source" of ideas, as naturally occurring appearance or awakening to each truly powerful and lasting idea Cave refers to, but even in *Paradise Lost* this high-minded concept of creation is brought to ground. With the "mortal taste" of the forbidden fruit eaten by Eve the fruit itself bears all the metaphor of bloom, fade, and seasonal change, returning to the earthy message of the flowers: "For now we are beautiful, tomorrow we will be worm food."

Cave's 2004 song "Breathless" embodies the lightness of nature in the spirit of love at full flight: birds tweet, tunes springing into bloom, and the sun burns through the haze—everything the eye alights upon is spurred on by life. The whole things rides on a breezy, carefree bossa-nova rhythm of acoustic guitars, brushed drums all twirling about Warren Ellis' flute, like centaurs set loose in a holy garden drunk on nectar of the gods.[2]

Rich with the largesse of spring the song is an ode to love delivered through the infinite and returning force of nature, bringing a sunshine blush to the heart. It suggests the image of St. Francis of Assisi, the patron saint of animals, who is often represented as being surrounded by animals and garlanded by birds, as he speaks to them or reasons with the wolf. In St. Francis' song *Laudes Creaturarum* (Praise of the Creatures) we see his vision of "varied fruits with coloured flowers and herbs" as a gift from God on "Sister Mother Earth," perceiving a new unity between animals and man as fellow creatures (great and small).

Birds appear in many of Cave's songs; their ability to fly hints at some kind of transcendence, but they are often depicted as darkly symbolic, watching patiently, or circling high above.[3] He returns to the carrion birds of the crow, the vulture, and the raven, the beat of their dark wings. A crooked bird shadow passes over the voice of "Your Funeral, My Trial," a harbinger of doom suggesting metaphorical power of clashing shadows as the expression of souls meeting by overlapping fates. Elsewhere they just sit and watch.[4]

On "Breathless" the birds are spiraling heralds to the dawn and its good omen of love. Cave presents himself as the earnest robin, full with the gift of song but standing trembling and humbled before his beloved, so in awe of her he suddenly fears he has lost his voice. Cave would explore further images of birds as creatures of seeming innocence: on "Henry Lee" the bird "lit down" upon the edge of the well as a mark of guilt over the girl who has slain her lover. Later on "Idiot Prayer" Cave would deliver the throwaway comment that love is "strictly for the birds." He rejects it as a hopelessly naive exercise.[5]

Elsewhere birds become less-ominous symbols of unrest. On "People Ain't No Good" blank-eyed pigeons stand in for cooing doves. Flying rats that divebomb with their corrosive shit onto cars and monuments are the tombstone bullets to their brighter brother, the dove, heavenly darts of passion.[6] The comparison presents romance defused by normality—exposing the heart of the song's theme. On "Babe, You Turn Me On" Cave observes the butcher-bird following its namesake with "pointless savagery," a plain-eyed pessimism from which love rescues us.[7]

Through Cave's reflections on different birds we realize that in flying all express an everyday miracle. There is a poetic through line in "The Spinning Song" where Cave's lyrics wrap around the melody as a string of cadences that tie visions of home, family, flight, and transcendence caught in the breeze: "Spin the feather and sing the wind."

Cave presents a lasting image of animals as creatures hardwired into wild nature, their instincts coming to the fore when our worlds overlap. In "Where Do We Go Now (From Nowhere)" (1997) the kitten in his lap suddenly swipes at his cheek; transmuted into the power of a bear, the lovely creature he is fascinated with still harbors its private aggression. He returns to this image on "As I Sat Sadly By Her Side" (2001): the kitten is totemic, passed back and forth, and ignorant to the storm of emotions passing overhead in the debate above. She is the vulnerable body to be protected, but equally threatened by the godlike indecision of the humans caring for her, clinging to the anchor of her body as they become lost in their own musings about life and the universe.

At first glance the flowers in Cave's songs are simply pretty things, but in their forms of symmetry and variation they become a representation of pure beauty, a further expression of godly design. For Cave flowers suggest a deeper sensuality as metaphor for erotic desire. In *And the Ass Saw the Angel* he again merges the sacred and profane in the vision of lilies like nuns' hats; the blooming of a flower becomes a metaphor for sexual maturity. In "Nobody's Baby Now" Cave notes the blue violets embroidered on his lover's dress, "the one that I like best." Undeserving of their delicate beauty, he is almost afraid to touch for fear of destroying her seeming innocence. Beyond this plant imagery remains suggestive of human genitalia and sexual pleasure, particularly the confluence of petals and female labia in lilies, with physical love merging toward the figure of motherhood and the healthy blooming of new life.[8]

In the bittersweet song "The Sorrowful Wife" (2001) Cave marks his marriage to Susie Bick on August 11, 1999, the day of a solar eclipse, returning to the loaded melancholy of "Sorrow's Child," reflecting that his wife had always carried a certain sadness about her that he found deeply attractive from the start.[9] Cave would draw upon the memory that inspired the song's third verse of a visit to Kew Gardens with his wife Susie in the spring of 2000, lying under a yew tree and noticing the fecundity of the gardens. Cave contrasts the emergent life of babies waiting to be born and the deep age of the ancient tree, while pointing to the pervasive melancholy of the "momentary bluebells."[10] At the end of each verse Cave finds his wife is pushing back against time, counting off days on her fingers like petals from the flowers that surround them before a great surge of guitar hits. Cave cries out for help and all hell breaks loose.[11] The happy moment is, like the flowers, hinged upon the future progression of all living things, where the flowers are to be admired and enjoyed today, for tomorrow they may be gone

The songs of *No More Shall We Part* (2001) are full of yearning love and aching melancholy. Its album cover shows a dense oil painting of funereal flowers, beautiful besides death they will inevitably go to seed. In contrast the flower and bird artwork of the 2004 album *Abattoir Blues/The Lyre of Orpheus* and its singles would evoke its bright blue sky feeling of openness toward nature, away from darkness and dirge. It would represent The Bad Seeds' renewed way of working—full of immediacy, freshness, and vitality.[12]

Cave would keep returning to the framing device of gardens: "The Willow Garden," "Lime Tree Arbor," and "Gates to the Garden," formalized spaces cut off from the wild—a perfect world in miniature.[13] On "Darker with the Day" Cave passes by three flowers in a garden—camellias, magnolias, and azaleas—with a woman standing among them. Cave briefly loses himself in the harmony of colors and the beauty of the woman standing still amid the chaos of the world, the way we might be stopped in our tracks by a sunset, then he walks on, back into the darkness.[14]

Employing various forms of tree and flower, Cave professes to some knowledge of plants on "There She Goes My Beautiful World," mentioning wintergreen, juniper, cornflower, chicory, elm, ash, and the linden tree, as if reciting their names would preserve them in his mind beyond the blank slate land of natural devastation.[15] These touchstones of color and shape garland the exultant mood of the song's music, while standing tall against its mood of ideas and inspiration slipping away. The trees announce themselves as near permanent things worth saving in the world, rooting memory to a place and time, the names of trees and plants that Cave admires, hum alive with meaning. Providing the great escape and reset from more formal concerns of life, in his notebooks Walt Whitman provides the perfect reflection on the enervating force of plants: "Nature remains; to bring out from their torpid recesses, the affinities of a man or woman with the open air, the trees, fields, the changes of seasons—the sun by day and the stars of heaven by night."

One of The Bad Seeds' biggest hits, Cave's 1996 duet with Kylie Minogue "Where the Wild Roses Grow" would make the album *Murder Ballads* an unlikely bestseller. Where the rose is the classical flower of love, its thorns and petals combine to express the dual nature of romance and violence that Cave had begun to explore on the 1994 album *Let Love In* and would further lament on *The Boatman's Call* in 1997.

The song tells the story of a doomed romance, where a young woman Elisa Day recounts her own murder, reaffirming her own name above the nickname of the "Wild Rose" by which she is branded by her lover/murderer.[16] As with "Henry Lee," also from *Murder Ballads*, we see the world with her female eyes, while Cave's male voice of the duet lends itself to her testimony, which slowly becomes a confession after he smashes her head in with a rock.[17]

In the song's video we see Kylie, a singing corpse looking more like a sex doll, set adrift into the river by the sorrowful Cave, crowned by scattered roses floating on the water, a conscious echo of John Everett Millais' famous painting of Ophelia from *Hamlet*.[18] Kneeling down he plants a rose between her teeth marking the mouth as an orifice of pleasure and violence. Cave anoints her bloodred lips with a final kiss goodbye and whispers, "All beauty must die," a hymn to the vitality of love that must inevitably come to an end. Perhaps a more selfless romantic gesture would be for the young man to end his own life by suicide as an act of love, but this is consistent with so many of Cave's songs and the self-serving life of the murderer. Like the bloody stain dripping from the rock the flowers of her namesake have shed their petals to become the deathbed of Elisa Day; with their red tears they are weeping for her.

The more benign images of flowers are often set against the heavier symbolism of trees. In Cave's songs, they present the unimpeachable security of age, counting down the rings toward deep time. Where in Robert Frost's famous poem the woods offer mystery, perhaps even the release of a melancholy comfort, in many of Cave's songs they are the anonymous, isolated place where bad things happen, a scenario first coined by Cave in the ritual murder of The Birthday Party's "Deep in the Woods"

Taking the idea further, Cave would present trees as symbols of sadness on 1986's "Sad Waters." Cave shows the willow tree bent like the body of a kneeling woman growing into the posture of sorrow; it sheds leaves as tears into water. Trees would also become silent sentinels marking the aftermath of disaster on "We No Who U R," the first track of *Push the Sky Away* (2013). Cave wanders past the Brighton palm trees that in his dreams are ignited in flame to fade off into smoke, a vision that reaches forward to the flame trees laid down to die then rising up again as ghosts in the album closer "Higgs Boson Blues."[19] Cave flips the cliché of ink-black night into the jagged shadow that follows the crooked man grown wrong. With blood rising high into the sky there is the sense of things being turned upside down.[20]

An unlikely first single from *Push the Sky Away* the album opener "We No Who U R" is a subtle, moody track that speaks to emergence and concealment within the context of nature. An official music video was directed by Gaspar Noé (the director of *Irreversible* [2002]). Recorded in one take, it follows "the silhouette of a human form through a wood at night." Like "Anthrocene" it returns as a song about air and breath. Within the scheme of nature that is all around us the flaming trees reach skyward with their pleading hands now burned black, with nowhere safe for the birds to land.

When asked if the track was meant as an "environmental hymn" Cave said, "to me it is a huge song. It was not actually supposed to be an environmental song, but I'm quite happy for it to just be what it wants to be. It is a concern of mine. We've treated nature abominably and it's getting back at us with a vengeance."

With no forgiveness offered, it could be an attack upon people destroying nature who deserve no pity or absolution or as a metaphor for the trees as massed humanity against the voice of the lone bird. Either way it presents a forbidding and haunting vision of veiled threat and disquiet; the lyric video ends with the spare lines "And we want you to burn / And we want you to burn."

Where the willow overhanging water has become the shadow of a memory, in "Say Goodbye to the Little Girl Tree" Cave calls out to the "gallows tree." It becomes the deathly image cast before the event.[21] The song trades in surreal imagery of the tree casting an eye that reaches over its limbs that stand in for a young girl's body. As he considers strangling her, he imagines his body moving over hers, moving through her boughs as limbs, the nascent pubescent "bumps" of the female form, their bodies entangled in forced intimacy. This is Cohen's fevered imagination of the song "Suzanne" where the eyes trace the body as touch becomes real in the mind. "Sad Waters" uses the same musculature of naked root and creeping ivy, hinting at tenderness of clinging and being clung to. There is also the further bondage of roots tied to the earth, a captive home, her plaiting willow fronds is a childish game, becoming a folk act of reverence toward nature.[22]

"The Little Girl Tree" becomes a highly sexualized object, to be bound about the mainstem of her body with glimmering silver wire, an insidious blinking light. Like a chastity belt or the wrapping of feet, this is the man's older voice expressing his desire to trap, shape, and control her body. He wishes to keep her young and small, though he knows one day the little girl must outgrow him. The belt image suggests entrapment of the girl in the burgeoning growth of her youth but also the inevitable noose looming from the shadowy gallows by which the man might eventually hang himself. Cave borrows some of the macabre atmosphere of the protest song "Strange Fruit." Most well known for the versions sung by Billie Holiday and Nina Simone, it protests the death of black people murdered by white lynch mobs, swaying in the hollow breath of the passing breeze.[23] Cave presents a similar echo of death with the "rhythm of the orchard," which becomes the passage of young lives flowering into bloom's promise and the descent into death and decay.[24] Cave leans heavily on the arboreal imagery to find a way through the song, an almost murder ballad that reveals itself an obsessive hymn to forbidden passion and suppressed lust—perhaps the even forbidden temptation of incest—the almost ruin of the beautiful young thing the man cares for but also desires in the most unseemly and cruel way.

On "Do You Love Me (Part Two)" Cave's reprise of the album opener draws from a short story "The Juniper Tree" by Peter Straub,[25] concerned with a young boy repeatedly sexually abused in a cinema by an unnamed man. The child later becomes an author, writing about his own experiences in a meta-fictional tangle. Cave teases out a finely wrought line using the vernacular of the original fiction: "The clock of my boyhood was wound down and stopped." The young boy is preoccupied with the image of being dead, buried under a juniper tree, inspired by an old folk story, where the dismembered corpse of a child calls out for the parts of his body to be made whole again.

Cave would refuse to be drawn on the exact meaning of the song, but in his lyrics he tries to evoke the subtlety of the story's play with words. It soon becomes clear that in keeping with the tenor of the album's discussions of love as sometimes abusive and controlling, the story contains sections where the thoughts are presented verbatim as isolated lines on the page suggesting internal monologue of the adult abuser, or being heard as memory echoing in the child victim's mind—also appearing projected out from radios, comic books, and in nightmares, offering intimations of love: "I love you" and "I love you, yes, I do." Isolated lines on the page we find the abuser mired in self-doubt: "Don't I love you? . . . And you love me too, don't you? . . . Don't I show you, can't I tell you that I love you?"[26] Cave borrows from the vernacular of the short story to express the conflicted nature of love and lust in all its complexities, where love is not always reciprocated, mutually understood, or even consensual.[27] The author Peter Straub would argue that he aimed for a clarity of hard prose meant to transparently show the painful events at hand, unmediated and without decoration: "I was caught by the odd ambiguous, ambivalent ratio of power between the abuser and the abused."[28] Of course in drawing upon a short story about pedophilia, the song alludes to deeper emotional trauma caused by a corrupted form of love that casts a long shadow over life.

In "People Ain't No Good" Cave describes being married under cherry trees and their falling blossoms. It is a joyful image tinged with melancholy. The falling blossom might signal the death knell of hammering rain or sweeping wind that rips trees out at the roots, bending their bodies to the ground—this is nature turned back against itself, swept up in the shifting curve of the earth.

Any romance around the sky is soon subverted by the disastrous power of rain. In John Lee Hooker's "Tupelo" rain arrives as a slow drip of memory where in Cave's version it gathers and surges into a malevolent tide. In their own way both songs speak to the flood's threatened aftermath of death and devastation: the skeletal frames of houses stripped of their flesh, collapsed roofs turned upside down, like the belly of a sunken ship; becoming a surreal world where everything is wrong. In *And the Ass Saw the Angel* rain falls for five years straight, beating people down like a peg into the dirt, washing away the Ukelite's prosperity, everything reduced to the primordial squalor of mud that sticks like being mired in the sin of hypocrisy. In "The Carny" rainfall makes a mockery of the attempted burial of Sorrow the horse. Misery begets misery as the corpse is spat back out of the earth, a grisly remainder, unwilling to yield to death.[29]

In Cave's reading of Homer such as *The Iliad* and *The Odyssey* there is the returning image of "wine dark seas," a peculiar mix of water as bringer and destroyer of life, an image that is further explored in Christian religious motifs of wine representing the blood of Christ—all merging into one blood-dimmed tide. Mixing with the dirt of soil the erosion of bodies returned back into the earth, an inheritance from which new life grows, the echo of "Ashes to ashes / Dust to dust."

On "Sad Waters" the play of blood into water and darkness is ambiguous: perhaps the girl "Mary" is drowned or murdered, or the song signals the breaking of the hymen at first sex; it becomes an issue of blood blooming in the water. Perhaps it is this image that surprises or shocks the girl in the song, or we are simply seeing her shadow cast across the pool toward Cave. An adroit lyrical touch from Cave he presents an image both normal and metaphysical where her shadow touches from a distance as it reaches over his heart. In a song slowly burning with the desperation of nostalgia, it is perhaps the first feelings of love as desire shift from innocence into maturity for "Mary." Dead or disappeared, she remains as she was in the nascent adulthood of her teenage years, again the memory that water holds endures long after she has gone.[30]

Elsewhere, when Cave sings about water it is the force of life raised up into a holy light that mingles with recollections of the past overlapping his earliest and most recent songs. Biographer Mark Mordue observed that when Cave speaks of water in his music, he always seems to be revisiting the same river and watering hole of his childhood town of Wangaratta. Becoming the extended metaphor of a constantly evolving song-world water is often present as the force of memory:[31] "In my memory Wangaratta is a magical place, where only good things ever happened . . . if a song has a river in it, it's that spot in Wangaratta just under the train tracks where we used to go as kids."[32]

Cave would also remember tall tales of jumping off the railway bridge into the same pool,[33] the rural idyll of bliss-ignorant young, happy just being and being free. "Sad Waters" becomes the watering hole hemmed in by willow fronds and jutting roots; the bucolic imagery is seductive in its entrapment and close feeling of familiarity and childhood's uneasy certainties in a world full of dangers and rich with risk that he nonetheless felt safe and at home in. Cave rarely finds time to be openly nostalgic in his music; the progressive force of The Bad Seeds has always retained a strong modernizing feel upon classic themes and musical styles. He would admit to writing escapist songs, spanning real and imaginary times and places to make something other, creation moving beyond his own autobiography: "To get into one of my records, you have to enter my world, an alien, romantic, extreme world of my making. You don't drag one of my records into your world."[34]

Deeper into the strange shapes thrown by the universe, on "Carnage" Cave forges a vision of nonlinear time that does not travel strictly forward or backward but moves all around the way memories fade and coalesce. He completes the song's first verse and then, returning to the opening chord, he shifts from a vision of his childhood to the present-day narrator, Cave himself, sitting on the balcony rereading a Flannery O'Connor book during lockdown, some time before the song was composed—beginning and ending are conjoined. He has traveled nowhere and everywhere, it is a deeply personal and internal visitation that comes to new life in the body of the song.

It is often written that authors tend to spend their whole creative life writing and rewriting the same novel. They are distinct works but always trying to resolve some inner tension from their very first work, particularly in the often unrealized ambition of a sprawling roman à clef that later becomes a symbol of opposition to be overcome and bested by future works. Cave continues to revisit the broad elemental themes of art: love, death, sex, God, and in the end even rock and roll itself—a tension that can never be resolved. And while this becomes a constellation of tropes and moments across the discography, with each album and every song they are realized in new and strange forms. Alongside his work of writing scripts, novels, and film soundtracks, more recently Cave has reconnected with his art school past and begun working on sculptures.

On the 2016 song "Girl in Amber" Cave reflects that his little world has been spinning since 1984, perhaps an allusion to the point at which The Birthday Party ended and he became Nick Cave and The Bad Seeds. Toward the end of the song Cave trails off the line at "nineteen," leaving the year open; it becomes the idea that he has been spinning the same plates in a different way for a lifetime, a whirling dervish of reinvention. On the 2020 title track "Carnage" Cave sees a ghostly image of himself standing barefoot watching his uncle decapitating chickens in little fountains of blood. Watching his younger self bear witness, Cave is both the child and the man, stepping in the song and out again. It becomes a living memory that now endures within the song itself.

On the 2004 track "Nature Boy" Cave offers a lasting confirmation of love entwined with the settings of nature, a companion song to the outright declaration of love in "Breathless." The song introduces Cave's future wife, the model Susie Bick, who he meets at a fashion show in 1998 standing beside his favorite fossilized dinosaur, Dippy the Diplodocus, at London's Natural History Museum.[35] The song is a tongue-in-cheek play upon the rituals of flirting, full with wordplay and double entendres built around Cave's "unrighteous intentions" that meet with Bick's mocking address to Cave as the nature boy, staring miles away into nothing then suddenly noticing her. Cave would recount the intensity by which he was struck at the sight of Susie Bick in the Red Hand Files: "I was swept helplessly into the slipstream of her beauty, exterior and interior. I have been happily flailing about there ever since."[36]

Set against the deep-dead fossilized reptile the song is full with life, humming along to the tune of Steve Harley and Cockney Rebel's "Come Up and See Me (Make Me Smile)." Cave throws out the surreal image of being thrust into a deep-sea diver's suit, suggesting a condom, and manages to rhyme wisteria with hysteria, implying entangling bodies. Perhaps it is all the love-blushed fantasy at first sight, and his mind runs away with him, crowded by a chorus of flowers springing into bloom. It returns to Cave's hope of beauty being a force that might save the world rather than simply make it appear pretty; by association love might rescue Cave from himself.

Again Cave finds renewed positivity in the force of green-space states of feeling. In 2001's "Gates to the Garden" Cave meets his lover at the threshold of the gate that seems to divide them. Reaching over to kiss enables them to cross the limits of paradise, suggesting a better place in life where happiness is a door neither fully open or closed. This private Eden hints toward the better place envisioned in *Ghosteen* where the garden can become an expression of hope and wonder renewed. Here Cave creates a place where nature flourishes wherever he and his wife meet and come together, suggesting the endurance of a love that springs eternal.

FIRE IN THE LIGHT

In 2019 Nick Cave and The Bad Seeds would return with their new album *Ghosteen*. The album was released three years after *Skeleton Tree* to almost universal acclaim. Cave would move away from the private abyss of doubt and sadness that had come to overshadow his last record—although turning back toward the still raw sensations of loss. *Ghosteen* would become an openhearted reckoning with grief, and life beyond it.

Ghosteen lays bare its hurt but is also rich with visions of seemingly divine experience, as Cave realizes a kind of ghost Eden offering escapism but also a confrontation with death.[1] Rather than an operation of mourning, the reality of the record is more complex. Moving beyond the factuality of loss Cave overrides the daydreaming nightmare of *Skeleton Tree* and anchors us back to the living present. Gradually, Cave embraces his pain toward an affirmation of faith and a new openness toward postlife states, bound to feeling and memory, from which the recent past crashes into the future to realize a burning and brilliant present, bearing witness in the light of an open wound.

Cave would choose to make *Ghosteen* a double album, stating, "the songs on the first part are the children" while "the songs on the second part are the parents." Where part I is built more from verse-chorus structured songs, part II is built around two longer tracks joined by a short spoken-word piece, highlighting the shift from acts in memoriam

231

to the emotional aftermath of grief. There is a cyclical aspect to the two parts of the record as when children later become parents themselves. Cave acknowledges the lost and those who are left behind to mourn and remember them. Though Andrew Dominik would also note that within this the album remains a hymn to the enduring power of love, particularly for Cave's wife, Susie: "Every song is about her. She's there through the whole thing. It's like a gift to her. Arthur is there—but I think it's for Susie."[2]

Ghosteen might seem sentimental, nostalgic even in its tone, a series of sad, slow songs that fade in and out of one another, but its patient unfurling sound can be misleading. Across the album Cave and Ellis temper emotional fragility with sonic force and a firm artistic resolve, at different times shocking and confrontational.[3] As Cave has explained *Ghosteen*'s power as a record is not wholly benevolent: the record's pained beauty is in part about evoking the quiet threat of annihilating grief, which can sometimes prove overwhelming in its intensity. Overturning the perception that the album might contain a series of mournful ballads, the songs offer bursts of light—cutting through shade or burning away behind a veil of trees—a searing kind of truth at once warm and illuminating but also threatening blindness. The album's unassuming, slow-burn instrumentation rewards patience, for example where the title track's synth patterns "rise and fall in heartbeat time" like waves raking over the world anew.[4]

Since "The Carny" (1986) and "The Mercy Seat" (1988) The Bad Seeds have always maintained an abrasive, industrial edge of *musique concrète*[5]—using the raw physicality of beaten metal and broken-down instruments, a brutality of fact that returns in the raw electronica of *Ghosteen*.[6] The song "Gun Thing" from *The Proposition* soundtrack uses muscular sonics, the gears and grind of human operations of the heart cut through with the squall of guitar noise and feedback, while "The Rider #2" present a sonic vision of mental chaos; the confusion between music and noise straddles the divided mind.[7]

These more abrasive styles would later become suffused with equally striking and ambient sounds on *Ghosteen*. Advancing from their soundtrack work Ellis would highlight a growing roster of instruments: "We've opened out more into electronics, choral stuff. Nick adds a lot on vibes, harmonium, celeste. It's allowed us this sort of freedom."[8] Equally there remains a profound a digital primitivism in Ellis' use of synthesizers, with a sound more commonly associated with 1980s synth-pop pioneers, turning between featherlight trembling and monstrous expressions of volume, a process begun in Cave and Ellis' soundtrack work that would bleed into *Push the Sky Away*: "I had a synthesizer that had been waiting around. I bought that in Japan in the early '00s. I remember trying to get it on Grinderman and every time I tried to start up there was just this deafening silence or confusion. I didn't know what I was doing with it either. When we did *West Of Memphis*, I just took that synthesizer to Nick's house and he was like, 'Where's the violin?' I was like, 'I'm not playing the violin, I'm playing this.'"[9] Repeating his studio performances onstage, Ellis rocks back and forth in his chair with the same intensity as his violin playing, pushing harder on the keys, wavering on pitch, adding a physical impact and lightness of touch in keeping with The Bad Seeds' dynamics.

The metallic clang that introduces "Waiting for You" and "Galleon Ship" draw upon loops of sound constructed by Warren Ellis. Cave remembers the industrial groove that opens "Waiting for You" as being more visceral and aggressive, high in the mix and recurring throughout the song. On the advice of Coldplay's Chris Martin, it was thought to be too jarring and counterproductive to the main melody of the song; it became merged with other layers, allowing the ballad atmosphere to breathe, letting Cave's lyrics rise up, pure and distinct.[10]

As if to offset the fierce undercurrent of noise at its heart, "Galleon Ship" begins with a handful of words softly spoken. Using a heavily processed vocal sample to introduce the song, Cave and Ellis chose to use these unknowable phrases to bury a feeling or sensation within a song already full of yearning and the revelation of learning to let go of something beautiful. I heard "you can run (look?) beyond / you can see it," holding to my private interpretation of what that might mean; where music is not necessarily about the right answers but the feelings it brings out in you, this would be the song's ability to encompass a powerful vision of loss but also in the same moment be willing to say goodbye to it.[11]

In spite of its experimental arc the album remains rooted in a deeper sense of empathy. Cave expresses the conflicting sensations that mourning demands, shot through with sudden rushes of memory; we are reminded of how grief can suddenly rise up out of nowhere, threatening to capsize us. Cave would argue that music finds a new life and meaning with each listener; once it is released into the world it becomes theirs. In this spirit *Ghosteen* becomes an offering toward what Cave calls our "universal selves," encouraging the listener to reflect upon our common experiences of loss, while highlighting the fact there is no typical experience of grief. Many listeners have noted that the intensely personal nature of the record made them feel uncomfortable, too close to Cave's own life, but this is also the album's great strength. Its power is in its ability to soothe and unsettle at the same time. In contrast to the more inward-looking black mirror of *Skeleton Tree*, *Ghosteen* presents a more empathetic connection with the listener. It manifests as a more vital and urgent record than as a continued lament of sadness; instead, it becomes a source of resilience, helping trace a path to live both alongside and within loss, an attempt to reconcile a rupture in time returning to life's endless flow.

Alongside the *Carnage* album completed by Cave and Warren Ellis in 2021 when The Bad Seeds were kept in forced hiatus, *Ghosteen* suggests an extension of the new ground first broken by *Push the Sky Away*'s deconstruction of The Bad Seeds' musical DNA with its use of "atmospheric, weightless sound." Freed from the lock in of a straight rhythm section Cave noted the lightness of the music counterpointed by the direct intensity of the album's lyrics, cutting and biting through to Cave's inner feelings. This established a haunting template almost unrecognizable from the band who produced "From Her to Eternity" and "Tupelo," but no less of a creative risk as an attempt to tame inner chaos—but slowed to a more considered and practiced form, as shocking and powerful as anything by August Strindberg or the highly controversial volte-face of Stravinsky's *Rites of Spring*.[12] Keith Cameron would note the looped bass of the album's closing track "Hollywood," the returning ripples from *Skeleton Tree* that would continue to build into a coolly menacing groove toward its sweeping, monstrous transition, which Keith Cameron called "the album in 14-minute macrocosm."[13]

In a review of *Ghosteen* by the Quietus, Patrick Clarke notes the album's projected "wonderland" in part expressed through the finely wrought, near saccharin album cover. Adapted from *Breath of Life*, a work by the artist Tom Dubois, influenced by his own Christianity, he draws upon the book of Genesis and the miracle of creation.[14] His work depicts the Garden of Eden, made more fantastical by Cave, devoid of humans; it features an array of animals beatified as mythical creatures, with a lamb at its center. Together they embody the imaginative space of new possibilities. The artist states that he is trying to capture a moment of divine essence, a subtle magnificence in the whispered shout of glory, an aspect in which God can become manifest through nature and revelation.[15]

At first sight the image presents a willful haze glossing over deeper trauma, its warmth becomes an invitation to enter into the album with a certain naivete toward an openhearted suite of music and to allow for the power of imagination to stride over the brute reality of facts and assumptions. Offering a return to a kind of honest innocence, the album's mode becomes the sincere expression of humanity's capacity for joy in creative affirmation.[16]

Cave alluded to the idea of the "ghosteen" itself as a "migrating spirit," someone we have lost whose memory is alive inside of us, but also a kind of good ghost that seems to persist within and without our mortal human world, meeting with Cave's description of the album as "a kind of free-floating conversation with the spirit world."[17] In the book *Faith, Hope and Carnage* Cave notes that it is both Arthur's presence and his absence that dominates the atmosphere of *Ghosteen*, describing the need to accommodate something of this spirit into his life going forward, suggesting the album as a place in which a part of him would always reside as a kind of living memory.[18]

Cave would refer to the priest and religious writer Cynthia Bourgeault, who talks about "the imaginal realm," a place of impossibility between imagination and dream: "It is an 'impossible realm' where glimpses of the preternatural essence of things find their voice. Arthur lives there. Inside that space, it feels a relief to trust in certain glimpses of something else, something other, something beyond."[19]

While Cave has been extremely candid talking about the album through interviews, in person and on the Red Hand Files, he would excuse himself from trying to too closely define the exact nature of the "ghosteen" relationship, for fear of damaging the inchoate idea or using the wrong words that might be easily confused. Beginning as something deeply personal for Cave, *Ghosteen* becomes a collection of songs that finds another specific meaning for the individual listener. There is an underlying tension between respectful distancing and our own interpretations, often mediated through memory, which evokes loss and grief but also occasionally warmth and joy, which adds to the power of the work.

Speaking in 2003 about the sudden loss of his father as his first experience of death, Cave mentions that he sometimes felt his father to be "present" as an influence over his songwriting.[20] Cave would variously confirm or brush away the importance of this. Certainly, from the beginning of his challenging teacher and pupil relationship with his father, and the echo of his spirit, this could be seen, felt even, as the knowing hand on the shoulder, a larger-than-life figure casting a shadow equally approving and critical.[21]

Across *Ghosteen* Cave's lyrics repeatedly allude to the sensation of a spiritual closeness, particularly on "Ghosteen Speaks," as if the absent person is standing right beside him. Cave takes the spatial interactions of being and knowing as feeling, an experience he would also note from the process of recording the album. Like being watched or "touched" by an invisible presence,[22] feeling the electrified hum of another soul in some quiet communion with our own, where a spiritual form of body heat creates a charged metaphysical space, their quiet fire feeding us a strange, rare energy. It does not have to be supernatural, but it is hard to define beyond a sensual brush with spirituality, transcending the divides between reality and the imagination.[23]

Cave employs various images of connection—and disunion—in his music focusing on love and loss, the combined sensation of holding and being held in return. On "Lime Tree Arbor" Cave takes the bride's hand in his, and seals this connection with his other hand over them both, a twinned experience that presents the romantic allusion to being tied to someone by the invisible force of love.[24] The song seems to harken back to Cave's marriage to Viviane Carneiro in 1990 as the communion of love that offers protection and expresses deeper connection. Though the song is written after their divorce in 1996, the shadow of the boatman still lingers years later, a present tense memory of flesh and blood that wills him back to that past moment. On "Old Time" from *Carnage* Cave repeats the idea of this marriage pledge to his future wife Susie Bick, singing that he is only ever a few steps behind her.[25]

Cave would also use the more symbolic language of the three Christian virtues of faith, hope, and charity, with "hope" traditionally represented by an anchor. On "Waiting for You" Cave sings in the first verse "your body is an anchor / Never asked to be free" and in the second verse flips the object to "your soul is my anchor / I never asked to be freed," an escape beyond the body that can be both a burden and the necessary form through which we directly connect with other people. On "Sun Forest" he offers a vision where "a spiral of children climbs up to the sun," transcending the physical toward a place beyond pain, sadness, and uncertainty.[26]

Looking back to the *Skeleton Tree* track "Girl in Amber" we stand alongside Cave watching "the girl" moving through a hallway, as if sinking with the slow time of memory. This transmutes into the image of Cave's son having his shoes tied as he too leaves, dancing down the hall spinning out into an indefinable shape. Later on, "Bright Horses" Ellis' sonorous backing vocals, filtering through delay and echo, become an ascending choral voice full of yearning, looking back to the same child of "Girl in Amber." Cave sings the line "Your little blue-eyed boy," reaching out toward the infinite mystery of loss heralded by an impossible wish that time can neither erase nor resolve. Cave added this deeply moving line into the song following his son's death; it emphasizes the teaching of children as the role to which parents are beholden, an act of loving stewardship to guide them on their own path. The image of feet and shoes speaks to each emergent step in becoming the person they were meant to be. Following the through line from "Girl in Amber" Cave sounds out the fragile thread of remembrance that ties us to the reality of loss. Through his whispered voice and the brittle synths haunted by strings on "I Need You" he admits to the impossibility of trying to hold on to something without physical form, but nonetheless speaks to this familiar feeling.

Both *Skeleton Tree* and *Ghosteen* would draw behind them echoes of Brighton's returning waves, rushing in and sliding off sifting pebbles into virgin territory to be erased again toward the next day.[27] In the summer of 2017 Cave found himself rising just before dawn in the deep mood of the "blue hour," venturing down to the sea while the rest of the world was still asleep. Cave would submerge himself until he was alone and loses his body in the water, held in the breath of tides closing the gap between the gravity of being and the weightlessness of forgetting, just being there.[28]

From these brief moments of isolation Cave would connect the dreams of his sleep to daytime visions that would gradually feed into the songs of *Ghosteen*. After initial recording sessions at Retreat Studios in Brighton during the spring of 2018 Cave would travel to Malibu in September. During that time Susie Cave would note on her The Vampire's Wife blog that she had come down with the flu and felt his absence more keenly: "Unfortunately, he is not here. He is in LA making a new record. Some of his songs reveal themselves at night in his fever dreams. They are his Fever Songs." Alluding to the half-madness of broken sleep and emotional trauma, the album would bring Cave's experiences into hyperreal focus.[29]

Perhaps more than any previous Bad Seeds record, *Ghosteen* would become an extremely personal album for Cave to the extent that the songs were happening *to* him, where the recording process of studio work was suddenly uprooted into a place without maps, describing the album as existing in a separate plane all of its own: "It lived in the jubilant and hopeful beyond."[30] Cave and Ellis found themselves channeling sounds and feelings that arrived in the long days and far into the night at the isolated Woodshed recording studio near Malibu owned by Coldplay singer Chris Martin. Over a fortnight they built dense loops and repetitive piano patterns and synth structures without the formal demands of Bad Seeds band structure making them freer to move into ever more experimental, abstract directions. They sidestepped guitars, then added and removed drums after they grounded the songs with too much gravity, as Cave and Ellis discover a falsetto lightness in their voices, continuing the minimalist reduction of *Push the Sky Away*. Ellis said, "It felt like there was something—or someone—else directing it."[31] Cave too has spoken of a sense of cosmic radiation charging the record with a second life all of its own. Cave is often afraid to speak to it, as if a spell might be broken.

Ellis would find himself caught in the continuing cycle of music steadily unfurling into the shapes of songs: "I'd get the mixes at four in the morning and I'd just listen to them in my pajamas on the veranda and sort of pass out, hearing these little ideas that went on to somewhere else."[32] The open-ended creative process became an invitation to more magical thinking, to supplant the ego and overcome the fixed thinking of more rigid song structures. *Ghosteen* presents an in-between state in which Cave and Ellis continued to take bolder steps outside of their creative comfort zones, to stand aside and simply let the music appear through them. Ellis remembered, "For me, it's the only time I've felt that if there was every anything else in the room, it was on that record. There was something going on making that record, the two weeks making it in Malibu. They were the two best weeks of my life."[33]

Cave's lyrics would embrace vivid fever dreams and stark visions that Cave had experienced as lived memories: burning forests, dancing horses, sunlight glancing off a beach's watery edge, halfway between drowning and rising, elsewhere everyday images turned into symbols of departure—the wildness of sun and stars as exit wounds all watched over by the pale grace of the moon.

Strange signs appeared in the hills—spare embers drifted in from houses, trees, or burning corpses appearing like the fireflies that float in and out through *Ghosteen*—bodies atomized as mistral light turning to ash. What began as little fires soon swept into a natural disaster, each tree went up like a ninety-foot stick of kindling—the imminent danger would seem distant but always edging closer. In November 2018, a forest fire tore through the area around Malibu, destroying the residential annex of the studio where Cave and Ellis had been staying just two weeks earlier recording *Ghosteen*.[34] Ellis referred to his and Cave's performance of their fifteen years of collected soundtrack work fronting a one-hundred-piece orchestra and forty-person choir at the Sydney Opera House in 2019 that took place during the bush fires that ripped through the eastern coast of Australia: "It was apocalyptic. Sirens going off. Smoke everywhere. Everyone in masks. Your instincts said 'run.'" They would play sections of music alongside projected images from the 2009 postapocalyptic thriller *The Road*: "it looked like the world outside. It was bizarre." This would soon be followed by the global COVID-19 outbreak, from fire to plague, the weight of biblical themes brought to bear against the world.[35]

There is a heavy air of inevitability to *Ghosteen* with both Cave and Ellis describing the songs as "arriving" more than they were consciously created. Peter Watts too noted the eerie prescience in Cave's lyrics, particularly across *Ghosteen*. Where Cave's songs are generally full of fatalism, leaning on apocalyptic readings of the Bible, the imagery of fleeing animals, rushing winds, the flight of birds away from the fierce heat of reddening skies seemed to confirm the album as some kind of augury for the coming disaster, a prediction of the future visible in natural phenomena. *Ghosteen* too would appear like a premonition that could only be fully understood once the album was completed.[36]

"Bright Horses" carries the imagery of fire toward a transcendental power, shuffling between layers of religious certainty through to "Hollywood," the first fires burning like a bloodred dusk across the skyline long through the night and into the following days. Director Andrew Dominik, present throughout the Malibu *Ghosteen* sessions, noted the "prophetic" quality in the new songs, seemingly loaded with metaphorical inquiry. It became harder to differentiate between allusions to fate and the gravity of the real.[37] In 2021 Ellis told the *Observer*, "It felt like the record I had always wanted to make." Though he feared it might also be a kind of peak, an ending to his creative relationship with Cave. For Ellis *Ghosteen* seemed to mark an almost overwhelming point of departure that would continue into the future: "I'll never get an overview of Ghosteen. But I know where it lives."

On an album that seems haunted by the imagery of fire as an illuminating, destructive, and sometimes cleansing holy light Cave's visions on *Ghosteen* seem to chime with Cormac McCarthy's two expressions of fire divided across the endings in two of the most well-known film adaptations of his books. In *The Road* (2009) fire is at first the sudden sign of destruction glimpsed through a window that introduces the story's state of apocalypse. Later it becomes a bright, healing sense of righteousness and hope in a crooked embittered world. In *No Country for Old Men*,[38] older police officer facing retirement Ed Tom Bell, played by Tommy Lee Jones, feels powerless to assert the law and stem the tide of meaningless deaths. He thinks back to travelers moving across the Old West, with one horse rider going on ahead cradling a ball of glowing embers, the heart of a fire, ready to establish a place of warmth and safety when the group made camp—he becomes the light for everyone to follow. In *The Road*, good people are seen to be "carrying the fire"[39]—doing the best they can to stay on the right side of a moral code that no longer seems to apply. The fire survives as a metaphor for the regenerative power of undying hope and goodness. After the death of his father on a gray beach "the boy" character asks a stranger if he is one of the good guys; as much as he can be, he invites the boy to join him and his family. The idea of fire as light, call it a faith or hope, is a feeling more powerful than the reality that surrounds it; it is something to dream on and to believe in.[40]

At the beginning of the track "Ghosteen" Cave chants of the beauty in love, trying to remind himself that good things still exist in world, then swiftly undercuts this sentiment, whispering "no, no, no"—so small a word but too easy an answer—struggling to convince himself in the perdurance of better things.[41] On "Brompton Oratory" he would find himself literally floored, sitting upon the stone steps, overwhelmed by the inchoate sensation of a beauty beyond words, expressing the conjoined wonder between spirituality and romance, so great it overwhelms his own brittle sense of belief.[42]

Performing with The Bad Seeds at the All Points East festival at London's Victoria Park in the summer of 2022, Cave plays "I Need You" solo on the piano. In full voice for the entire show, he seems to falter in repeating the song's final mantra, "just breathe," as the words seem to fall away from him collapsing into the expression of both love and loss. The crowd takes up the chant alongside him, drawing the song back toward life; it is a singular and powerful moment shared between artist and audience.[43]

Speaking in 2017, a year after the release of *Skeleton Tree* Cave would admit to the toxic force of loss: "The whole grief thing, there's nothing good about it whatsoever. People will tell you other things, but it's like a fucking disease. A contagion that not only affects you but everybody around you."[44] This perspective would be dramatically altered in the coming years. By the time of *Ghosteen* Cave would argue the album was ultimately a positive record, not an indulgence of "grief porn." Among its sometimes-unforgiving examinations of the aftermath of loss, it is steeped in the necessary rediscovery of joy; by refusing to look away or to suppress our feelings this confrontation allows for a new beginning. Cave intimates toward a sense of wonder in the creative act, a form of giving back to life, even if it means disruption and confrontation— rather than a return to more of the same—putting the comfortable at unease and comforting the disturbed.

Looking beyond the abstractions of beauty and truth, Cave's response to the first Red Hand Files question in 2018 would make the case for hope in a seemingly hopeless world: "In an artist's case (and perhaps it is the same for everybody) I would say it is a sense of wonder. Creative people in general have an acute propensity for wonder. Great trauma can rob us of this, the ability to be awed by things. . . . So how do we return to our lives—to the awe of existence—and reclaim a sense of wonder?"[45]

Though Cave often takes a hard real-world view of pain he warns against negativity and cynicism. Instead hope becomes armor to do what we can to counteract cruelty and ignorance. Music can make people better, improve and enrich our lives, even if the music is dark, challenging, or haunting, wherever it engages us through feeling it remains powerful, with its own unique aliveness.

A few years after the release of *Skeleton Tree* the doors and windows of Cave's Brighton home would be locked and shuttered closed, white sheets cast over the furniture, as if the house were sleeping. It would remain a place in the mind where Cave would revisit sometimes, perhaps in the songs, finding himself there as if waking from a dream. Cave would take his family to the unquestioning ubiquity of LA, where a freak can exist in isolation, the stray wolves and circling of hyenas kept at the gates under their steady gaze. There was the fear that wonder might fade. He and Susie would travel back and forth to Brighton as Cave recorded parts of *Ghosteen* in London and at a nearby studio in Hove throughout 2018. They would sell the Brighton house in 2022, settling in a small secret house in London.

It seems fitting that "Push the Sky Away" continues to endure as a Nick Cave and The Bad Seeds' song to say goodbye. Where Cave would sometimes pull one, fifty, or a hundred people onto the stage, joining hands, singing together united in a moment rising on the ascending elegy of the chorus line repeated like a mantra. Like "The Mercy Seat" before it, the song is often played at the end of every Bad Seeds show, revealing a point of closure and acceptance where nothing in life is ever fully resolved but that does not mean we should give up on it.

"Push the Sky Away" emerges fully formed, like a dream, its shining chords chiming with the voices of Cave, his fellow Bad Seeds, and the school choir, that at once manages to sound like a haunting mantra and a gently consoling force of awakening. The rising music invokes at once the glimmering promise of Venus, given to the darkness and light of the morning and evening star, seen just before dawn and after sunset as the world edges into night. For his part, Warren Ellis remembers the song as the beginning of a new creative era that would continue through

Skeleton Tree and *Ghosteen*: "I remember when we did the song 'Push The Sky Away' felt like it was throwing down a challenge. There was something about it that seemed to be very bold. The sound, what was going on with it, the whole thing. It felt like where to launch off from, and it always felt like there were three records in this."[46]

Speaking about the "Push the Sky Away" in 2013 Cave would explain, "We all have this feeling of the world folding in on us. Whether it's environmental, the economy, nuclear or whatever, I don't think there's anyone on the planet who's walking around thinking things are okay. So, to me, there's this idea that we need to carry on and do what we do. The song is optimistic in that respect. Of course, it's impossible to push the sky away but we need to try."

The French poet Yves Bonnefoy claims the horizon exists as a temptation, drawing us away from the here and now toward an imagined country—Bonnefoy calls it *thearriere-pays* (translated imperfectly into English as the "hinterlands"). It becomes the promise of a better future withheld, caught at a distance beyond endless mutability we never reach, but within the creative act of hope we can reimagine the boundaries of possibility.

Nick Cave and The Bad Seeds' songs of life, love, and death often reveal us to be flawed, vulnerable beings, and though we are diminished by death, the opportunity of life gives us the chance to experience and create great things in works of art and acts of love and kindness. In doing so we escape the limits of our mortality, forever moving against the tides in the hope that each of us will find a new day beyond the horizon.

> Where faces of the elder years,
> High souls absolved from grief and sin,
> Leaning from out ancestral spheres
> Beckon the wounded spirit in.
> —*THE HOUR OF TWILIGHT*, GEORGE WILLIAM RUSSELL

EPILOGUE

I took it as a kind of sign, a reminder that there was some purpose behind the project, not just to listen and rewrite the meaning of the songs, but to trace the creative path of a musician and artist whose work is bound up in their personal experience, but also exists independently of biography.

As I edited my proposal for this book toward the end of the weird and terrible year of 2020, I brought our Christmas tree in from its spot in the garden. Researching backward I had just read Nick Cave's Red Hand Files entry of August 2019 where he is asked whether he believes in signs and if he ever feels the presence of those he has lost. He mentions the odd appearance of a ladybird landing on Susie's hand in the period following Arthur's death: "Since then Susie and I see ladybirds everywhere." He also mentions the sudden appearance of ladybirds while recording: "When Warren and I were working on the last album [*Ghosteen*] a plague of ladybirds came into the studio."

My two-year-old daughter found a less common golden, white-spotted ladybird that must have traveled in with the tree. She decided to let it go back to the tree, then a red ladybird crawled over the desk where I had been working, moving across the keyboard and onto my hand. We watched it together as she sat on my lap then returned it to the garden.

As Cave said, the randomness of cruelty or benevolence of coincidence are rarely without substance. It reminded me that the rare oddity of pure chance can seem to denature the true meaning of our experiences, only if we allow ourselves to question it too much.

It is a strange echo of someone else's memory, an odd fluctuation that requires no explanation, except to note that pure chance can become an invitation to spark our native passion to wonder, as Cave would affirm through *Ghosteen*, an album that means a lot to me. Even through the looked-for thing of coincidence in action, we can find something from nothing that suddenly comes to mean everything.

ACKNOWLEDGMENTS

Edie, Maja, Gonzo! And Diesel the Cat

Matt Lakin: friendship, scholarly interest, books, reading, and rereading

Professor Nick Groom

Andrea Mbarushimana

Pod Like a Hole podcast

Ruth Stacy

Raef Boylan

Mark Mordue

Helen Kralova

Professor Aaron Gwyn

Ioanna Paunas

Hans at www.fromthearchives.org for the fifty one-act plays

Lynne Troughton

Today's Lesson podcast

Gavin Richard Hopps

Robert Montgomery

Rod Higginson

Danny Schwarz

Tony DuShane

Mat Snow

Since then—'tis Centuries—and yet
Feels shorter than the Day
I first surmised the Horses' Heads
Were toward Eternity—

— EMILY DICKINSON 479
BECAUSE I DID NOT STOP FOR DEATH . . .

NOTES

Chapter 1

1. Chris Heath, "The Love and Terror of Nick Cave," *GQ Magazine*, April 27, 2017.

2. Cave is still an alien (Australian) in a foreign land that was as much home there as anywhere, as he would explain in 2018: "I live in Brighton. It's at the very bottom of England, about as close to the edge of England as you can get before falling into the sea. I'm an Australian, and Australians always kind of cling to the edge."

3. Nick Cave, *Push the Sky Away*, ten-year anniversary press release, 2023.

4. Cave would praise Bargeld as his own experience guitar antihero, the inverse of the Marr-Morrisey alliance, the song and dance of Richards and Jagger, or the new "Jeff Beck" virtuoso combo of Mick Ronson and David Bowie. Bargeld's ability to "not play" as either standard musician or nonconformist meant he cut right through The Bad Seeds' songs.

5. Andrew Male, "The Bad & The Beautiful: 50 Greatest Songs of Nick Cave" / "Something Monstrous," *Mojo*, no. 319 (June 2020).

6. Writing in *Overland Journal* in 2009 music critic Anwen Crawford would lament Cave's emergent position as a growing "Monarch of Middlebrow," making alternative music from the very epicenter of the traditional music industry, grown into an increasingly narrow furrow of subject matter.

7. Speaking to Luke Turner for the *Quietus Radio* podcast in 2017 Ellis explains that he was first a fan of The Birthday Party, and later became a bandmate of The Bad Seeds as a session musician for *Let Love In*. He compares the shock of first hearing "From Her to Eternity" to Bowie's *Low* album or *Heroes*: "What is this, where did it come from?"

8. It's an interesting thing to note that The Bad Seeds rarely used power chords, overbearing distortion pedals, or guitar solos; this already marked them out as different in the thick soup of rock band cliches.

9. See her fourth album from 1971 *Journey in Satchidananda*, about as alive as music gets.

10. Although for Cave the communal living setup resembled the intensity of a stay in rehab: "I don't think anybody of our age, settled in our ways, wants to go and live with a bunch of other guys like that for three weeks in a place where you can't even leave the grounds."
Alexis Petridis, "Nick Cave's Greatest Feat," *The Guardian*, 2013.

11. Petridis, "Nick Cave's Greatest Feat."

12. Though *Push The Sky Away* would arrive months before *Yeezus*, it contains returning future echoes of the abrasive, experimental beat making that also straddled Kanye West's 2016 album *The Life of Pablo* both by turns brash, tender, and outspokenly confrontational, with the necessary braggadocio of hip-hop and its casual misogyny also present in much of Cave's earlier sonic universe. Both Ellis and Cave would continue to acknowledge West's sonics as an influence.

13. Described by Cave in the album's press release.

14. The Bad Seeds press release, November 27, 2012.

15. A trio consisting of Warren Ellis (violin and bass guitar), Mick Turner (electric and bass guitars), and Jim White (drums), formed in 1992. Check out their 1998 album *Ocean Songs*. Ellis got started on violin at age nine by learning "Orange Blossom Special" from watching *The Johnny Cash Show*, much like Cave who after seeing Cash on screen realized how music could be a "beautiful, evil thing."

16. Ellis would find his own sound through a mixture of accident and fate. After finding success with Dirty Three, Ellis' brother added a guitar pickup to his violin with a rubber band and a distortion pedal. From there he never looked back: "I just plugged it into a pedal, turned it up to 10. The louder and more out of control that it was, the better it felt for me." Ryan Leas, "Warren Ellis on the Past, Present, & Future of Nick Cave & The Bad Seeds," *Stereogum*, November 17, 2021.

17. ABC interview Jason Di Rosso, January 2015.

18. Drawing on their atmospheric soundtrack work from films such as *The Assassination of Jesse James by the Coward Robert Ford*, Cave employs rarer instruments such as the celeste, a light-touch glowing sound suggestive more of cosmic interference than rock dramatics or classical organs.

19. Writing in 2020 for *Uncut*, Peter Watts would refer to an unpublished interview from 2013, where even after the critical success of *Push the Sky Away*

Cave still had struggles of artistic conscience and self-doubt, "feeling washed-up and you were never any good anyway."

20. Male, "The Bad & The Beautiful."

21. A surreal day-in-the-life road movie where Cave appears in a shot-for-shot scripted film of organic improvised discussions between Cave and people from his life—family, band members, and collaborators—offering myriad glimpses of the Nick Cave we think we know, the man, his persona, and multitudes of past lives.

Chapter 2

1. The storm sound effects add an ironic cinematic flourish that perhaps takes away more than it adds to the atmosphere, like The Doors' "Riders on the Storm." This stock footage moment is knowingly plastic; it is the shock and awe of the music that brings the terror of the storm.

2. The bassline is actually played by Mick Harvey with Barry Adamson switching to drums, giving his own interpretation of the hammering thunder dragging the sky down to earth—subverting the bass riff of "Saint Huck." *Do You Love Me Like I Love You* (2011), series of 14 short films by Iain Forsyth & Jane Pollard.

3. Cave evokes both the biblical doom of Revelations and W. B. Yeats' poem *The Second Coming*: "something terrible slouches towards Bethlehem to be born."

4. The "looky, looky yonder" refrain that features in the song is derived from a three-part medley song first recorded by Leadbelly, released on his 1939 album *Negro Sinful Songs*. The song is an adaptation of a nineteenth-century American work gang song and an even earlier eighteenth-century marching cadence. Cave himself would later cover the song under the title "Black Betty."

5. This is very much Cave's view of the rock star who would later be scrutinized over the fact that he and his future wife Priscilla met when she was fourteen and Elvis was twenty-four. They started dating a year later, and even though they didn't marry until she was twenty-one, there has been reconsideration in recent years on the nature of their relationship.

6. Memphis Minnie and Kansas Joe McCoy would also write about these events in the 1929 song "When the Levee Breaks," which was famously covered by Led Zeppelin in 1971.

7. "Black refugees were forced to perform the heavy labor and were barred from leaving by National Guard members who oversaw their work with guns at the ready. Whereas white refugees were placed in indoor facilities, black refugees were detained in outdoor camps on the levee and systematically denied adequate food and shelter, with little promise of their homes ever being rebuilt." McMurchy, Myles. "The Red Cross Is Not All Right: Herbert Hoover's Concentration Camp Cover-Up in the 1927 Mississippi Flood." *Race, Ethnicity, and Immigration in U.S. History*. 2004.

8. Hooker's "Tupelo" is sometimes referred to as "Tupelo Blues" with the same spoken word delivery; the two songs have slightly altered lyrics, but given the looser, interpretive playing of the blues, I will let both versions stand as one.

9. Amid the floods and sinking mud, Cave offers a vision of the new king elevated beyond the destruction and mayhem of Tupelo, as if performing the miracle of walking on water.

10. Greil Marcus, *Mystery Train: Images of America in Rock 'N' Roll Music* (New York: Plume, 1975; 2015 edition).

11. Preaching outrage and defiance in the face of annihilation, Cave's lyric is a prayer *against* God, delivered as a mad rant; though cited in the real historical events, it remains rooted in an alternate reality.

12. Elvis had become the hero of his own imagination and would show what was possible for those who might wish to follow his path, but also the hubris of stardom merging into Greek tragedy serving as a story of caution: "I grew up believing in a dream. Now I've lived it out. That's all a man can ask for."

13. As noted by the podcast *Today's Lesson* (2021), they quote from Genesis 25. Jacob and Esau are twins, the sons of Issac, begat by Abraham. There is normally an interval between the birth of twins; Jacob is presented as trying to overcome the righteous birth order—Jacob is later wounded and walks with a limp, an echo of his earlier wrongdoing.

14. Elvis bore a deep and enduring relationship with his mother as protector, cook, and counsel, to the extent that when he married it was not a wife he was seeking but a surrogate parent to take her place.

15. The book's title comes from the Bible's Book of Numbers, Chapter 22, Verses 23–31: A man called Balaam is forbidden by God to travel, an angel with a sword appears and blocks his path: "And the ass saw the angel of the Lord standing in the way." The ass is struck three times by its master, who threatens to kill it. The angel speaks through the animal, opening Balaam's eyes: "Am not I thine ass, upon which thou hast ridden ever since I was thine unto this day? was I ever wont to do so unto thee?" The angel explains that the ass had saved Balaam's life. In his *Beyond Good and Evil*, Nietzsche makes a reference to the ass as having the power of its most conviction, a lowly creature who in spirit becomes "beautiful and most brave." Perhaps this becomes the affirmation of Euchrid Eucrow?

16. Cave started writing the book around 1984 and spent several years working on it until it was eventually published in 1989. As such it is hard to say where one work began and the other ended with ideas bleeding in and out between novel and album.

17. Joanna Babicka, "Genre and Language in Nick Cave's 'And the Ass Saw the Angel,'" 2011.

18. On "Up Jumped the Devil" the young man was delivered by macabre cesarean section performed with a Stanley knife, suggesting a messy murder more than a medical procedure, in which the mother dies but her baby lives. In "And the Ass Saw the Angel" a broken bottle is wrested away from the alcoholic mother and used to remove her child after she drunkenly falls unconscious.

19. Marcus, *Mystery Train.*

20. "Hear That Long Snake Moan," Michael Ventura.

21. Cave loses himself in the role of preacher turned prophet chewing through his lyrics, drenched in sweat. His spirited incantation stands alongside the ghost of Jerry Lee Lewis, who beyond Elvis really was a man possessed with the redneck mythology of the Deep South: "lynch-mob blood lust, populist frenzies, even incest." Marcus, *Mystery Train.*

22. Greil Marcus, *Dead Elvis: A Chronicle of a Cultural Obsession* (Cambridge, MA: Harvard University Press, 1991), 121.

23. For his part Moby, who found fame with the album *Play*, built from gospel and blues samples, claimed that in the past fifty years all great music stemmed from that tradition.

24. Born Thomas Lanier Williams III, even he was subsumed by the South's mythic allure, renaming himself to escape from under the namesake of his abusive father's shadow, but also using the birth state of Cornelius Coffin Williams.

25. Before a 1980s live performance of "Tupelo" Hooker would pay tribute to Elvis as "one of the greatest entertainers." Despite himself being an influence on Presley's music, Hooker would in fact outlive Presley by several decades.

26. In its continued struggle to assert itself above the North and the Union following the American Civil War, parts of the Deep South would remain trapped in the past of internalized conflict, alongside Christian conservatism that spawned masochistic tension between self-denial and self-indulgence, informing a hypocritical decadence and baseless self-destruction.

27. Sometimes spirituals are also referred to as "traditionals," a much broader term covering old songs handed down and adapted through performance and word of mouth, with the original songwriter remaining unknown and handed on from person to person.

28. Before the gospel songs of the church and its ritual hymns, spirituals were the songs of the slaves working the land of the plantation from first light to darkness, sometimes even under the full moon. Jermain Longuen, a freed man who later became an ordained minister and underground agent helping 1,500 slaves escape said, "No day dawns for the slave, nor is it looked for. It is all night—night forever."

29. Harriet Tubman was nicknamed Moses for her work on the Underground Railroad chiming with the spiritual "Go Down Moses," while Frederick Douglass working in the more sentimental tradition of the slave narrative/

expose cast himself as a Jesus figure reaching out to draw the symbolism of the cross in parallel with the slave strapped out to be lashed, and citing an unnamed and (unknown) "Judas" figure who betrayed his first escape attempt.

30. Frederick Douglass, *The Narrative of the Life of Frederick Douglass* (Oxford: Oxford University Press, 2009).

31. In Larry Neal's "The Ethos of the Blues" he quotes Clarence Simmons: "A blue mood—since prayers often seemed futile the words were made to fit present situations." Larry Neal, "The Ethos of the Blues," *The Black Scholar* 3, no. 10 (Summer 1972): 42–48.

32. The folk song "Run, Nigger, Run" is a folk song of 1851 that tells of a slave escaping the plantation and slave-owner patrols. With history coming back around it would be included in the 2013 film *12 Years a Slave*.

33. The *Original Seeds* compilations volume 1 and 2 reveal the depth and breadth of Cave's early influences, also suggesting tangential songs that seem connected to the early Bad Seeds musical universe.

34. So potent was the mythos of the bluesmen that alongside the tarnish of the blues as "the devil's music" they were not allowed to bring their guitars ("devil box") into church, or even its front yard.

35. In his autobiography, Barry Adamson remembers the band listening to Elvis during the recording of *Firstborn*. Finding himself addled by procaine he joins the backing vocals group, at once ashamed and admiring of Cave's ability to tap into a foreign energy of a musical inheritance that should have been his: "'Train Long Suffering' probes at my poor open wound of a soul with a blunt pen." Barry Adamson, *Up Above the City, Down Beneath the Stars* (London: Omnibus Press, 2021).

36. In hoodoo two roads crossing form an X, a reminder of the Central African Kongo cosmogram: "It is at the crossroads where many Africans believe one will witness the powers of God and emerge from the waters spiritually renewed."

37. Robert Johnson's masochistic "Preaching Blues (Up Jumped the Devil)" was no doubt a direct inspiration on Cave's own 1988 song, which nonetheless takes the tale further into the comical excess of debauched violence and damnation and away from the original trials from which blues music was born.

38. Cave actually knew very little of Blind Lemon's music. The song grew out from a brief fictional piece Cave wrote around the blues player, based upon a few biographical details he found.

39. On the road into Jericho Jesus sees Zacchaeus sitting up in a sycamore tree just to get a glimpse of Jesus. Zacchaeus, a former tax collector, gave away half his wealth to the poor as an example of faith. Perhaps Cave sees something of this generous spirit in Jefferson, or he is characterized as Jesus and the tree is the watching post of his passing, the rumor of money blown through its leaves.

40. Cave employs the cane as a visual symbol of blindness, another blues-man's burden to be overcome. It is the persistent sonic image in the song's tap-hop-bop rhythm. Long after Jefferson has faded from life his contribution to music still stands without him.

41. His few recordings were feted by contemporaries such as John Lee Hooker, Son House, and B. B. King, and their subsequent inheritors Carl Perkins and Elvis, unlike Buddy Bolden whose ghost notes only survive as memories and testimony of others.

42. His cause of death is variously noted as a heart attack in a snowstorm, poison from a jealous lover—Johnson—and an attack from a wild dog. Myth heaped upon myth.

Chapter 3

1. From the silent eyes of "Watching Alice" to the murderous lovers of "Deanna," however noble or misguided are the lovestruck characters of Cave's songs, they are all too often left clinging to a sensation of feeling they will never catch or hold as their own.

2. In Red Hand Files #196.

3. Roland Boer, "Love, Pain, and Redemption in the Music of Nick Cave," *Literature & Aesthetics* 19, no. 2 (December 2009).

4. Cave would say that some of the album's songs were written with his heart in his mouth, a situation of both emotional tension and intense honesty.

5. John Payne, "Improvisations with Nick Cave," *LA Times*, November 29, 2010.

6. Nick Cave lecture, "Secret Life of the Love Song," delivered at the Atelierhaus der Akademie der Bildenden Kunste, Vienna on September 25, 1999. *Saudade* is a word that reaches across the related dialects in the Portuguese and Brazilian character, though there are similar parallels in other language cultures including the German *sehnsucht* and Welsh *hiraeth*.

7. The song is inspired by Cohen's (unrequited) infatuation with Velvet Underground singer and solo artist Nico, who Cohen noted was pursued by an "army" of well-known musicians in New York during the late 1960s including Jackson Browne, Bob Dylan, and Lou Reed.

8. In tarot the Thief is often represented by seven swords, which translates to theft or someone "getting away with it." The Lovers card suggests relationships and choices; its appearance suggests a decision about an existing relationship, a temptation of the heart, or a choice of partner, where a lifestyle or relationship may be sacrificed.

9. In the second single from the *Tender Prey* album (1988), the cover art has Cave again gazing insouciantly at the camera with little red devil horns cutely

added to his shadow, the whole image tinted blood red—wings off flies—hearts on sleeves.

10. The film draws upon classic lover-murderer couples of *Bonnie and Clyde* (1967) and later repeated in the film *Natural Born Killers* (1994).

11. Jack Barron, "The Needle and the Damage Done," *NME*, May 1988.

12. The Red Hand Files #59, September 2019. Cave's close collaborator would later have a child by Cave's close collaborator Andrew Dominik.

13. In the Portuguese tradition the swallow represents loyalty and faithfulness; in the song they have turned against the lover.

14. This song overturns the high-flying escapades of rainbows and stars to come on "Brother My Cup Is Empty." They now become cursed omens of good times gone bad.

15. In the song's title Cave takes a postmodern stab on *From Here to Eternity*'s thwarted hopes for a better life set within the rank-and-file drudgery of a US military base. The authentic hero of Montgomery Clift is punished for his insubordination and dies in honorable service. Cave's antihero is tortured by an unconsummated love that goes nowhere but circles around the headspace of his lonely room; like the song's throbbing piano, its urgency is driven by compulsive repetition, unable to let go of something we can never have.

16. Inspiring another hymn to paranoia and self-loathing, Magazine's "Song From Under The Floorboards" driven by John McGeoch's hypnotic spiraling guitar riff.

17. Has he passed her in the street, been served by her in a café, nightclub, gas station, hospital (she wears a uniform, or is this just a cocktail dress); has he followed her home—does he even know her real name—or is she always the imaginary ideal woman divided by the brick and glass of their separate lives?

18. In Carson McCullers' 1967 novel *Reflections in a Golden Eye*, we observe a quartet of damaged people on an army base trapped in a tangled web of voyeuristic longing and loathing; she has it that through the eyes of love and desire we become most real, illuminated but also held captive in the gaze of the beholder.

19. Mark Mordue, *Boy on Fire: The Young Nick Cave* (New York: Atlantic Books, 2021).

20. Screamin' Jay Hawkins also has a black magic schtick. The lyrics read like standard blues, but on record they're akin to a voodoo incantation.

21. On "We Real Cool" Cave would present the image of miracles and wonder revealed to him when resting in his wife's black hair; replacing the tears and lost kisses of *The Boatman's Call*, he is safe there but also overwhelmed by his brushes with beauty.

22. With terrific insight, the songwriter Matt Malone noted the shared ambience with Charles Baudelaire's prose-poem "A Hemisphere in Your Hair"

NOTES

(published in 1862 in *Le Spleen de Paris*): "Long, long let me breathe the fragrance of your hair. Let me plunge my face into it like a thirsty man into the water of a spring, and let me wave it like a scented handkerchief to stir memories in the air." It ends: "Long, long, let me bite your black and heavy tresses. When I gnaw your elastic and rebellious hair I seem to be eating memories."

23. "Nick Cave—Portrait of a 21st-Century Genius." *Mojo*, March 2009.

24. Consider also Cave's cover of John Lee Hooker's "I'm Gonna Kill That Woman" (from *Kicking Against The Pricks*) – I love you to death.

25. Red Hand Files #167, September 2021. This would also be referenced in the *One More Time with Feeling* documentary 2017.

26. During interviews Cave would be protective, guarded even, about the inspiration from external influences: "My muse is not a horse, and I am not a horse in a race."

27. "If thine eye offends thee, pluck it out."

28. *Stranger in a Strange Land* (BBC Southbank Show, 2003).

29. Nick Cave lecture, "Secret Life of the Love Song," delivered at the Atelierhaus der Akademie der Bildenden Kunste, Vienna on September 25, 1999.

30. Reynolds, Simon. "Of Misogyny, Murder and Melancholy: Meeting Nick Cave," *National Student Magazine*, 1987.

31. "There is no such thing as a moral or an immoral book. Books are well written, or badly written. That is all." Oscar Wilde, *The Picture of Dorian Gray*.

32. Speaking to Mark Mordue, Cave acknowledged that in keeping with the aesthetic of the best rock music his songs brought bigger ideas into a more immediate creative form—the point at which religion, sex, and death converged.

33. Nick Cave in conversation with David Peace at The Southbank Centre, London. September 9, 2009.

34. Cave would mention the Grinderman song "Love Bomb" in a similar vein of the manipulative male, trying to get inside women's heads, just to get into their pants: "The character in the song isn't me, he's a sexual predator who listens to Woman's Hour to get tips on chat-up lines and the way women think."

35. Ellis is a fine writer, but aside from the formulaic *American Psycho*, a veiled portrayal of his father, aspects of which Ellis himself would grow into, he has since only succeeding in rewriting the same books, often set in the 1980s, and publishing a dour pro-Trump "memoir" as he slid beyond middle age and into conservatism; meant to agitate younger readers by advocating for the wonder years of the 1970s when everything was edgy, dangerous, free, and righteous—he is living there still. The first fifty pages of *Lunar Park* are great though.

36. Kate Mossman, "Nick Cave: 'I don't think art should be in the hands of the virtuous,'" *The New Statesman*, November 2022.

37. Like so many rock musicians, Cave often alludes to young women with ambiguity; they become little girls, sometimes bodies diminished by death as in

"Deep in the Woods," but it also works to make them vulnerable and innocent. The born victim in "Kindness of Strangers" and elsewhere is a pretty young thing.

38. This song also connects to Cave's "Do You Love Me Pt. 2" in its allusions to a pedophile, a crime Cave accepts as a terrible fact of life present in our world, but a controversial subject he does not shy away from.

39. Like Dennis "Des" Nilsenin's 1980s London, both men had latent homosexual impulses that they struggled to fully act upon. Seeking connection, Dahmer lying next to his victims and consuming their flesh, both men keeping body parts, Desmond watching television alongside the corpses months after they had killed them. A large part of their alienation stemmed from loneliness and the need for control to stop the young men from leaving them. Both serial killers were attracted to gay, vulnerable, young men.

40. Tom Engelshoven, "Nick Cave," *Oor Magazine*, January 2021.

41. This was Cave speaking in the year after the release of *The Boatman's Call*, an album both lovelorn and hostile to ex-partners. Cave was still feeling some stinging rebuke, though the album remains an elegiac, heartbroken, and bitter-sour-sweet attempt to show how love can bring out the worst and the best in us and remains one of our most honestly redemptive experiences. Barbara Ellen, "It's Hip to Be Hateful," *The Observer*, May 5, 1998.

42. Infamous as the woman who shot Andy Warhol, Solanas was angry after promises and encouragement from Warhol to help her stage her play in New York were suddenly forgotten and her calls ignored. As felicitous and wan Warhol would abandon many former collaborators as he would attract new hangers-on, shedding people as he went, other such victims including Edie Sedgewick. After being ignored for too long Solanas took her revenge against Warhol's greatest vulnerability, his body. Lucky to survive multiple gunshot wounds delivered at close range, he underwent horrific operations and was never physically or mentally the same. The open arts lab experiment of the Factory retreated into guarded quietude.

43. The violent fantasy text of SCUM would sometimes be made to seem all too real. On tour around the time of the *Kicking Against the Pricks* album (1986), producer Tony Cohen remembers a gig in Paris attended by angry feminists, which soon got out of hand: "Red was the color Jesus, blood everywhere! That was intense. I still remember how those women chased the band bus with broken bottles." Engelshoven, "Nick Cave."

44. After Brion Gysin Solanas was the real-life cut-up artist, she advocated razor blade attacks and castration in the name of equality to reduce male empowerment and sexual threat. Her visceral manifesto appealed to someone like Cave and his collaborator Lydia Lunch's postfeminism that invited equal opportunities for women to behave as badly as men. Cave makes a nod to Solanas in "More

News from Nowhere," where the loose love interest Betty X affirms her own identity free of the fatally flawed chromosome of Betty Y.

45. Joe Jackson, Nick Cave Interview, 1994.

46. The song's title alludes to the expression "hair of the dog." Short for "hair of the dog that bit you" is a colloquial expression in the English language predominantly used to refer to alcohol that is consumed as a hangover remedy (with the aim of lessening the effects of a hangover). The expression originally referred to a method of treatment for a rabid dog bite by placing hair from the dog in the bite wound.

47. Speaking in 1990 Cave pointed out the song's roots in relationships of the past revisiting the present: "I wrote the song because Anita and I would argue at a constant pace and I would always tell her to unleash the dogs and burn the bridges as a way of saying you can say what you feel but forget the past and let's move forward."

48. Lorca says, "I heard an old maestro of the guitar say: 'The duende is not in the throat: the duende surges up, inside, from the soles of the feet.' Meaning, it's not a question of skill, but of a style that's truly alive: meaning, it's in the veins: meaning, it's of the most ancient culture of immediate creation." Federico Garcia Lorca, *Theory and Play of the Duende: And, Imagination, Inspiration, Evasion*, Dallas, Texas: New Directions, 1981.

49. Jonathan Lethem speaks to Cave "addressing the love letter itself as an emissary: 'Go tell her/Go tell her.' Also worthy of Shakespeare is the verbal trick of using 'letter' (l-e-t) and 'tell her' (t-e-l). That has a power that any writer would die to harness." "Nick Cave's 30 Best Songs," *Uncut*, February 2015. The extreme literacy of Cave's approach is such that he has the lonely partner kiss his lover's name on the envelope in place of her.

50. The B side to "Into My Arms," "Little Empty Boat" would continue the album's mood with needling guitar, spare stabbed piano notes, and eerie strings. Cave seeks to avoid the drunken advances of a woman, excusing himself that his sad boat has no momentum and a damaged oar, like a bird's wing, suggesting perhaps his addiction or broken heart. The song twirls lost in a circle. For all its haughty sarcasm, Cave noted it as a "a gorgeous little jewel, a comic song."

51. For Mat Snow this was the album that made Nick Cave mainstream, distinctly more radio friendly, seeming ballad but also blues tales. In his foreword to a book of interviews with Cave Snow noted the renewed seriousness bestowed upon Cave in the wake of fatherhood, by broadsheet newspapers, invitations to the BBC, and academic lectures. The bastard child of postpunk turned prodigal son of alternative rock was now thrust into the big lights in the classic singersongwriter mold, again, a place many of his listeners never expected him to go.

52. The sonic range and depth of the piano makes it most versatile, switching from hellfire boogie into ambient escape; it is the instrument that unites

spit and sawdust rock and roll sin such as Jerry Lee Lewis and Little Richard to classical music of the church organ and the drawing room salon, while harking back still to the more austere tales of suffering and strife of the guitar bluesmen. For his part, Mick Harvey is no slouch on the piano; documentary clips from the *Your Funeral . . .* era show him walking through the stately, agonized chords of "Knocking on Joe."

53. Listen also to the beautiful guitar work of Mick Harvey that circles about the vocal melody "(Are You) The One That I've Been Waiting For?" as well as Blixa Bargeld's distorted cut and thrust guitar that rises and falls like a shark's fin rubbing up the wrong way through "Idiot Prayer," almost becoming an atonal "guitar solo" by the song's ending.

54. Harmon, Steph. "Nick Cave on PJ Harvey break-up: 'I was so surprised I almost dropped my syringe.'" *The Guardian*, August 2019.

55. A natural progression, *No More Shall We Part* displays some of the spark in Nina Simone's jazz-inflected piano, with her jumping run of notes tempered by her hook-savvy songcraft. In 2004's *Supernaturally* Cave pounds away at the keys with rhythmic force of her "Sinnerman." Cave described her final live performance as part of the 1999 Meltdown festival he curated "savage and transcendent." This event gave birth to Warren Ellis' spiritual journey of the new sacred relic of Simone's chewing gum stuck onto her Steinway piano, a story first recounted in *20,000 Days*, and in great depth in his 2022 book *Nina Simone's Gum*.

56. Elsewhere on *Grinderman*, Cave sings of climbing the ladders in his grandmother's tights. She was the woman who taught him his first stabs at the keys. He tries to reach to the heights of her adult playing, though he would complain that he learned only hard-hammering of chords and stiff-fingered notes. It was years before he arrived at the more fluid playing of his mid-career albums.

57. Drawing upon a traditional eighteenth-century Scottish folk song "Young Hunting," in Cave's version a jealous woman is the killer who murders her lover after he confesses he loves someone else. If she cannot have Henry, no one can, his dead body is thrown down a well, in the end he is lost to both women. The small bird that lands nearby, stalking his watery grave, stands like the eye of God, a marker of the crime he reminds the murderer of her guilt.

58. For her part Susie Cave would comment to her husband that while it was a beautiful video, seeing him move so intimately with a former lover was difficult for her to watch. For Cave also these songs must stand as old hurts blossomed back into blood reopening wounds of the past, never fully healed. Simon Hattenstone, "Old Nick," *The Guardian*, February 2008.

59. O'Neal, Lauren. PJ HARVEY TUESDAY #1: "HENRY LEE." *The Rumpus*, October 2013.

60. Red Hand Files #57, August 2019.

61. Though Cave would wrestle with the charges of misogyny, he would nonetheless be stitched up by headlines such as "It's Hip to Be Hateful" that played against his attempts to show the mutual longing and enmity of collapsed relationships on *The Boatman's Call*. Ellen, "It's Hip to Be Hateful."

62. PJ Harvey has remained more or less silent about the emergent relationship and its subsequent breakdown. In 1998 she completed one of her densest and most brilliant hard-left-turn albums *Is This Desire?* Paying almost zero attention to the split with Cave, it focuses more Harvey's continuing struggles with depression: "I wanted to write for myself, about myself. Like someone looking in on me." ("Cat Woman," *The Guardian*, January 1999.)

63. Listen to the KCRW live studio session recorded in 2015 loaded with even more venom. Cave alters his lyrics slightly but delivers them with urgency alongside Warren Ellis' more strident see-sawing violin. It is a great example of when The Bad Seeds play live, they elevate a song to a different dimension, reinvigorating the arrangement while drawing upon the core strengths of the original.

64. Interviewed on *The Boatman's Call* tour, Sala Kongresowa, Warsaw, Poland, May 22, 1997.

65. Cave notes that "Far from Me" took him four months to write, the same length as the relationship with PJ Harvey it describes. After some years of separation Cave's marriage to Viviane Carneiro would end in divorce by 1996.

66. Red Hand Files #132, January 2021.

67. It might also be Charon, the riverman of the Styx, who ferries the dead to hell. The album is Cave's own purgatory of love lost, and at its end he finds himself in exile.

68. I mishear a PJ Harvey lyric from her 1998 song "Angelene." Both the unkindness and joys of the world are laid out before her: "Legs open like a rose / road," echoing her confrontation of the limits between love and sex. Her lyric carries shades of Cave's earlier song "She Fell Away" (1986), where he laments the loss of a girl who lay open like a road, guiding him through some madness but falling from her own path, she sheds him like a skin and returns into shadow—another uncertain fate we are left to wonder upon.

69. Lifted direct from the J. D. Salinger short story "Pretty Mouth and Green My Eyes."

70. As described by Shakespeare in *A Midsummer Night's Dream*, "Love looks not with the eyes, but with the mind," where Shakespeare would cite Cupid's blindness. He points toward the metaphysical connections of love, beyond the physical world of surface and appearances.

71. The 2013 song "Mermaids" would speak to Cave having to attend a speed awareness course after crashing his Jaguar into a speed camera in 2010, an event that he joked made him a "local hero." The song's lyric transmutes

this into husband alertness training, recognizing the demands of marriage to be constantly present alongside one's partner, taking the wheel where necessary and also staying aware of what might lie ahead. This lyric might also be rooted in Cave's interest in psychotherapy, as in the filmed session with Darian Leader from *20,000 Days*.

72. The Red Hand Files #199, July 2022. Cave almost goes full Greek via the poet John Keats, where beauty becomes truth and goodness, one of the few certainties we can cling to.

73. The Red Hand Files #180, January 2022.

74. Red Hand Files #177, December 2021.

75. The Philip Larkin poem "Arundel Tomb" concludes with a final line like an epitaph: "what will survive of us is love." The tombstone shows a couple lying together, side by side, the woman's pelvis and leg subtly turned toward her husband, the folds of the alabaster stone show the curve of her hip, their bodies closing on one another, his hand resting against her thigh and her hand reaching to rest in his. It is a powerfully sensual image for Larkin, seen and evoked rather than a personal expression. Still, it shows how the remembrance of powerful feelings can outlast us.

Chapter 4

1. Cave believes the song has been played at almost every Bad Seeds show since it was written in 1988.

2. The "mercy seat" or "atonement cover" refers to the gold lid over the Ark of the Covenant. Often depicted as being made of gold and topped with two cherubim, more like avenging angels, it is typically translated as propitiation or sacrifice of atonement of Christ on the cross. It is believed that the Blood of Jesus dripped down from the cross through the earth onto the ark situated in a cave known as "the Holy of Holies." The splendor of the true mercy seat is contrasted with the wood and wires of the electric chair.

3. The song might be considered an inheritor of Denis Johnson's 1992 episodic novel *Jesus' Son*, with its main character, Fuckhead, a thwarted, haunted addict and petty criminal.

4. With clear echoes in Cave's script for *The Proposition*, Kelly's life ended in 1880 after being hunted down by the Australian police, his brothers burned to death in a final shootout. Kelly, in his home-fashioned armor looking like a cross between the Tin Man in *The Wizard of Oz* and a medieval knight, was wounded in the leg through a chink in his armor and sentenced to hang. Nonetheless, his letter determined he was to have the final word.

5. "The Wild Colonial Boy" is a traditional anonymously penned Irish-Australian folk ballad that tells the story of a bushranger in early colonial Australia who dies during a gunfight with local police. According to a report in *The*

NOTES

Argus in November 1880, Ann Jones, the innkeeper of the Glenrowan Hotel, had asked her son to sing the ballad when the Kelly gang were at her hotel in June of that year.

6. Patrick Donovan, Australian music industry expert, talks about the tone of Kelly's deathbed letter in the documentary *Do You Love Me Like I Love You*, with Cave using the tone of defiant murderer to add a harsh commanding presence to his voice.

7. Humbert is the villain of the novel, but as its wordy protagonist who tricks us with languid storytelling, we begin to root for him in his deluded "struggle" of love. Whereas the truly amoral Clare Quilty is the real nemesis who steals Lolita away from him, Humbert presents himself as the "lesser" evil—but this is pure self-deception. Nabokov makes a further point: "The twinkle in the author's eye as he notes the imbecile drooping of a murderer's underlip, or watches the stumpy forefinger of a professional tyrant exploring a profitable nostril in the solitude of his sumptuous bedroom, this twinkle is what punishes your man more surely than the pistol." Vladimir Nabokov, *Lectures on Literature*. London: Mariner Books, 2002: 376.

8. Reynolds, Simon. "Blissed Out: The Raptures of Rock." *Popular Music*, 1991.

9. From the original fall of Lucifer (Morning Star, bringer of the dawn, Isaiah 14:12, with Luke 10 ["I saw Satan fall like lightning from heaven"]) there follows under his dark shadow Adam and Eve cast out from the garden of Eden into the real world.

10. Like "The Good Son" many other Bad Seeds songs use the song's title as chanted "yeah, yeah, yeah" chorus, the very essence of pop music. When asked about The Bad Seeds' use of repetition Cave said it was a chance for the band to take a song higher, to go up one more notch to eleven. There is also a Dionysian frenzied element to this, hammering home a sound or an idea.

11. The lyric is thought to be inspired by American folk singer Odetta "Another Man Done Gone" (a song Cave would vaguely remember was made famous by Johnny Cash in 1963). On the surface the tale of a man deserting his lover, the song's roots are much deeper. As an African American spiritual it refers to a slave wearing a chain "done gone from the county farm." Perhaps he has run away or he has only escaped his chain through death. Repetition is the slowly clanking sound of the body coming to rest, as if the shackles' noise had outlived his death.

12. There are again echoes of The Bad Seeds' earlier album, *The Firstborn Is Dead*, and Cave's Tupelo, echoing the birth of Elvis alongside the death of his twin.

13. The "mark" itself is widely debated with a number of odd theories around caste and heritage and sexuality. It is often considered to be a spiritual

sign. It nonetheless dooms Cain to a kind of eternal life; lest anyone should harm him, the damage would be returned back upon them sevenfold.

14. In "Foi Na Cruz," the line chanted by the Brazilian choir, Cave had instructed them to follow his flattened lamenting voice, where the singers wanted to put a more lively, gospel voice into it. Kid Congo Powers remembers them throwing up their hands: "we will just pretend that we are dead, then." Cave sings of sleep, slumber, and folding of hands, a peaceful lullaby of death and passing. Viviane Carneiro remembers Cave's interest in Brazilian culture's relationship to religion and its passion for the imagery of Christ.

15. Tony Dushane, "NICK CAVE MONDAY #28: 'JACK THE RIP-PER,'" *The Rumpus*, March 25, 2013, https://therumpus.net/2013/03/25/nick-cave-monday-28-jack-the-ripper/.

16. "I was nervous about showing that to the group. I felt they would think it was too unreasonable, or too over the top, to produce an ode to a murdered woman, a severely murdered woman."

17. Cave would also recollect readings from Shakespeare's *Titus Andronicus*, one of his less remembered but bloodiest and physically cruel plays.

18. Anwen Crawford, "The Monarch of Middlebrow," *Overland*, no. 197 (Summer 2009), https://overland.org.au/previous-issues/issue-197/feature-anwyn-crawford/. The italics are Crawford's emphasis, with "shrew" a loaded Shake-spearean term that speaks to coquettish tension of love's favors invited and spurned, measure for measure, presumably in the (un)fair play of romance.

19. Red Hand Files #7, November 2018.

20. Conrad makes the striking association that in the final death that ends the story of Bunny Munro Cave rewrites his own narrative of being present at his father's passing. Beyond this, the traumatic event encourages the bloody flood-gates of Cave's songwriting to open up, as a form of control over-writing death.

21. Jennifer Nine, "From Her to Maturity," *Melody Maker*, May 1997.

22. Andrew Male, "The Bad & The Beautiful: 50 Greatest Songs of Nick Cave" / "Something Monstrous," *Mojo*, no. 319 (June 2020).

23. In his poem "Law of the Jungle," Rudyard Kipling sets out a series of rules in verse, allowing that animals should kill to eat and for the good of their pack and cubs. He commands: "But kill not for pleasure of killing."

24. Like a snake that will bite out of fear as it is misunderstood, this is the spurned child Euchrid Eucrow who lashes out against the community in-kind. How could he be anything but a permanently maligned misanthrope when unkind treatment is all he has ever known?

25. There is a contrast implied in Cave's songs between each animal fulfill-ing its nature, the wolf to the lamb, predator to prey, and the creatures who transgress their role in society, either reverting or deviating from their common path, reflected in a French phrase: when the dog turns into the wolf. In Red

Hand File #180, January 2022, Cave would mention that he had been reading the "devouring lion" passage from the Gospel of Thomas (the 'lost' gospel not present in the Bible). It states: "Jesus said, Blessed is the lion which becomes man when consumed by man; and cursed is the man whom the lion consumes, and the lion becomes man." Perhaps it suggests that man might make a better nature of the beast, but in consuming man the beast lowers itself to human level, or it simply advocates for the need to kill or be killed.

26. Cave claimed that the book *Collected Works of Billy the Kid* was a major influence for the writing of *And the Ass Saw the Angel*—in particular, the pit of decomposing animals. He remembers the scene of inbreeding forty wild dogs by a man named Livingstone who is later devoured by the beasts he created. Johnston, Ian. *Bad Seed: The Biography of Nick Cave*. London: Little, Brown Book Group, 1996.

27. See Cave and the band's slick pelvic thrusting throughout their live performance of the track on *Gotterdammerung* 1982.

28. The band name also seemed to encompass the shared attitude and style of the individual musicians who grew around it, a group of outcasts and rebels who could not be made to fit into a neat musical hole elsewhere. The rebel spirit feeds The Bad Seeds inimitable sense of "last gang in town" swagger.

29. In a suitably dark twist Rhoda's mother confronts her daughter, who confesses to several murders. After feeding her sleeping pills the mother, in guilt, shoots herself, but the girl survives and is free to kill again. The 1956 movie version flipped the script to a "happy" ending where Rhoda is suddenly killed by a lightning strike (of divine intervention?), while her mother, Christine, survives a suicide attempt, and so justice is seen to prevail.

30. The plot of *The Bad Seed* is more or less repeated in *Murder Ballads'* "The Curse of Millhaven," set against a thundering polka stomp, the serial killer Loretta (almost) getting away with it—she willingly surrenders to her fate.

31. In 2022 Cave would create a series of seventeen hand-made ceramic sculptures, *The Devil—A Life* drawing upon his art school education and inspired by his collection of Victorian Staffordshire "flatback" pottery figures. The work charts the twelve stations of the cross, marking Jesus' passage toward crucifixion; the pieces move from the devil's birth, through youth, age, and experience and into death.

32. Driven by a powerful forward momentum "Red Right Hand" borrows some of the swagger from Tom Waits' scuzzy grind "Way Down in The Hole," though it doesn't necessarily go anywhere, just deepens in its groove. Waits' track also provides the theme tune for TV crime series *The Wire*.

33. The song appears in the first three *Scream* movies and later featured in *The X-Files*.

NOTES

34. See also Billie Holiday and particularly Nina Simone's rendition of "Strange Fruit" depicting lynched black people swinging unnaturally in the breeze. It was later sampled for Kanye West's powerful but typically self-serving "Blood on the Leaves," which becomes an egotistical antiabortion anthem.

35. "Red Right Hand" is perhaps best known as the theme tune to Birmingham gangster epic *Peaky Blinders*. Speaking about the song, the show's writer Steven Knight said, "There is a swagger, poetry, fallibility, flawed masculinity to that song that we aspire to in the show. That song gives you that world in your belly." Peter Watts, "His Dark Materials," *Uncut*, Take 273, February 2020.

36. The hands capable of both violence and kindness, destruction, and creation, are perhaps inspired by Robert Mitchum's performance in *Night of the Hunter*, posing as a preacher whose tattooed fingers give away another side to his past; he remains a marked man.

37. Where the "White Elephant" of the title is the persistent memory of a decaying conservative ideology of the right to bear arms steadily losing ground to random acts of gun violence, the track carries some of the deep sarcasm of John Lennon's satirical psycho-sexual anthem "Happiness Is a Warm Gun," where the orgasm, opiate high, and death become embroiled as a corruptive and empowering force of domination over human beings—finding joy in misery.

38. Cash—the original man—in black claimed he wore his dark suit for the poor, the suffering, and the dying, not unlike a wayward preacher, a trend that Cave seemed to naturally take up in his own aesthetic.

39. In a 2023 interview with *Unherd*, Cave would claim the song as one of his most controversial: "For example, there's a particular song of mine called 'Stagger Lee.' This is a famous Bad Seeds song, and it's offensive on many, many levels." Though he found that in performance, everyone simply enjoyed the music. The author finds "Stagger Lee" quite benign. For me it is more the dark and violent tales of abusive relationships and sexual politics on the 1994 album *Let Love In* that keep me raising my eyebrows.

40. Perhaps Bargeld was intended as the inheritor of Rowland S. Howard's autodestructive guitar tone, which producer Tony Cohen remembers pushed ear-shredding high treble against Tracy Pew's subterranean bass thud, cutting through everything else. Johnston, Ian. *Bad Seed: The Biography of Nick Cave*. London: Little, Brown Book Group, 1996.

41. The ballad is apparently based on the killing of a man named Billy Lyon by an already notorious badman named Lee.

42. Cave would choose to subvert all this menace with the most 1990s music video imaginable. The Bad Seeds had a 'fun' single and consequently a hit album. Cave knowingly wears a skinny-fit pink Take That T-shirt; a mirrored allusion to the camp-queer love of Kylie Minogue. The Bad Seeds never looked more louche and furiously resigned, standing atop individual risers sentenced

to play laid-back, groove-driven rock and roll in primetime hell for the next thousand years, with two menswear model dancers gyrating and slinking on the spot, the shoot could have been a David LaChapelle video, overexposed vampiric skin, gloss and smoky shine like gun metal.

43. Cave drew heavily upon Olive Woolley Burt's 1953 book *American Murder Ballads and Their Stories* as source material for the origins of the twentieth-century murder ballad tradition, a form of oral history but also a warning against the dangers of life. From its bloody handprint cover it confirms all the great cliches of the genre from "wronged husbands, victims of unrequited love, reluctant suitors, thieves, oppressed union members, outlaws, and self-appointed administrators of justice."

44. This intense narcissism between wolf and the cattle of sheep fuels Jim Thompson's protagonist Lou Ford.

45. Tony Lanham, "Murder He Wrote, Nick Cave's Gruesome Balladry Is All In Good Fun" *Request,* March 1996

46. One elderly woman's statement to Peter Sutcliffe highlights the venom and contempt employed to 'other' him: "Who do you think you are? You damn well think you're God or something. God giveth life, god take it away, not you—I think you are the devil itself."

47. In Moore's semi-authoritative account, the royal physician Dr. William Gull was charged by Queen Victoria to silence a group of prostitutes with knowledge of an illegitimate royal heir, the first serial killer, before the word was created by the press of the period. An antihero alternative to the folk myth of figures such as Robin Hood, he captured popular imagination to become iconic, fueling the legend, dark tourism, and a wealth of media, books, movies, etc.

48. "An unholy racket"—Sebastian Horseley, wit, addict, dandy, self-crucified artist.

49. Like the erstwhile "Joe" who appears throughout many of Cave's 1980s and 1990s songs, "Jack" is also a recurring name, particularly across *Let Love In*, where Cave uses him to embody the jester or jack-in-the-box, as the horrific surprise, a continued danse macabre of sick-sad laughter in the face of death and tragedy.

50. The soundtrack is a haunting, cagey sound reflecting the unsettled mood of the prison, jokingly written off by Cave as tin whistle and female whispers. It leans on the sonics of early Bad Seeds and Bargeld's *Einstürzende Neubauten* before them. Heavy on foreboding there are dissonant clanging metals, heavy bass, and shrieking guitar tones, alongside a haunting flute like a tin whistle that manages the idea of a maudlin Australian tone. Bargeld noted the real theme of the film was the character of architecture versus humanity, the suggestion of imminent violence intercut with brief interview segments edging toward a

prison conspiracy for the murder of a guard in order to incite a riot and pull in more funding for the prison.

51. John Hillcoat originally intended to make a film adaptation of Abbott's book *In the Belly of the Beast*, (1981) but when this project failed to come together, he simply drew upon the book as source material to reflect its interest in high-security incarceration.

52. In Roman law, a person convicted of a crime where the punishment included loss of their legal rights as a person was civiliter mortuus—a person without civil rights.

53. Abbott, Jack Henry. *In the Belly of the Beast*. New York: Arrow Books, 1981.

54. "To illustrate: to walk ten miles in an enclosed space of ten feet is not really movement. There are not ten miles of space, only time." / "We are all so guilty at the way we have allowed the world around us to become more ugly and tasteless every year that we surrender to terror and steep ourselves in it." Abbott, Jack Henry. *In the Belly of the Beast*. New York: Arrow Books, 1981.

55. The films *The Green Mile* and *Monster* make that last walk toward death row the final steps, out of life into death. Considering the fate of Jesus, destined to die upon the cross, Connor Harrison noted the leap of time and into fate this carries, like "The Mercy Seat": "Jesus is burdened with a cruelty typically offered only to the terminally ill, to the suicidal and death row inmates. In the moment that death is given an ETA, it unfolds from the vague horizon of existence." The certainty of our finite existence is accelerated, if not to the present, then the idea of the future, endlessly deferred.

56. The horrors of (spiritual) self-mutilation are hinted at. Speaking to *NME* in 1987 Cave offers an explanation toward deeper spiritual abuse: "It is a metaphor in a lot of ways, which I'm very proud of as a song, could almost be saying something about the world . . . guards and prisoners and bars and loneliness, unfulfilled desires, it seems to have some sort of resonance. The prison situation seems to be a vehicle for just about everything I'm interested in writing about."

57. The song's insistent slow melody carries echoes of The Birthday Party's "Jennifer's Veil." The pregnant pauses from note to note carry their own slow-burning urgency.

58. In *The Proposition* we meet the oldest brother and leader of the outlaw gang Danny Burns. Versed in poetry he bandies about the term "misanthrope," reflecting the state of broken men existing in a brutal and broken world. Cave's script offers a Christlike parable for Guy Pearce's protagonist as the Judas caught between the fates of two brothers: ordered to trade the leader of the gang for the life of the innocent, dim-witted brother who has been captured by the authorities.

NOTES

59. In his more recent pronouncements, Cave would seem to align himself closer to Buddhist principles of ethics, where a sense by living well is achieved not in a continual struggle to alleviate or repair suffering but by not adding to it.

60. Cave finds these hollow men feckless and disinterested, much like a former government official who endured shame and disgrace when during a global pandemic that killed thousands he partied, drank wine, joked, and laughed in his offices as the world shrank into isolation and thousands died alone. And then he lied about it.

61. It's hard not to hear the song hark back to Shelley's "Ozymandias," a statue without legs, or legs without a statue, floating, sunk into its decline. These great edifices to man are doomed to fall apart—nothing is forever. Here the traveler begins his speech. He tells the speaker about a pair of stone legs that are somehow still standing in the middle of the desert. Those legs are huge ("vast") and "trunkless." "Trunkless" means "without a torso," a pair of legs that stand tall but stand for nothing beyond hubris.

62. Perhaps informed by his reading of Marx's *Das Kapital*, a doomed epic that nonetheless points toward a better world where people matter more than money.

63. When we think of the evils of exploitation, consider the slogan over the gates of Auschwitz concentration camp, *Arbeit Macht Frei*, "works makes us free," which had its mirror in the Russian gulags forced labor camps and more recently in the detainment of Uyghur populations in China.

64. On "Rings of Saturn" Cave offers a powerful resonance, lamenting the return of slavery, perhaps in its modern contexts, but with a twist on the word "gone" he suggests a double meaning that, along with racism, it never really went away.

65. Suggesting the removal of the ability to cry, it carries an echo of the pedophile character Mason Verger in Thomas Harris' Hannibal Lecter series who bears the juicy trait of using a tissue to soak up the tears of his child victims to add flavor to his martinis; the bitter salt becomes the taste of other's pain. We assume tears to be the expression of hurt or empathy, therefore someone who does not cry must be emotionally dead inside. This is a sentimental view chiming with banality of evil, echoing the innate normality and warped humanity of its perpetrators.

66. Maria Popova, "Nick Cave on Songwriting, the Mystery of the Unconscious, and the Sweet Severity of Truth," *Brainpickings*, August 5, 2022.

67. It is not simply the terror of Icarus' descent, it is the metaphorical horror of his undoing, witnessed by his father Daedalus who had warned him of the hubris of flying too close to the sun. The stripping away of his feathers as the wax melts, his form and brilliance is diminished, and his loss of flight is a human being undone; the beauty of life's myriad possibilities fall with him.

Icarus' disappearance beneath the water marks his crossing over from one realm to the next. I always felt that Jimi Hendrix's "Castles Made of Sand" made this same point with equal beauty, a passing ship meets the desolation of a suicide, and a surprise attack kills the young brave in his sleep, the ship sails on blindly—everything collapses—as it must, sand into sea.

68. While on the campaign trail Wallace was shot five times. Being hit in the spine and chest, he was paralyzed from the waist down for the rest of his life.

69. In his book *Rings of Saturn*, W. G. Sebald recounts reading a newspaper article about World War II atrocities committed by Croatian fascists said to far exceed the cruelty and barbarity of the German SS. It mentioned an Austrian lawyer Kurt Waldheim, who was believed to have been a member of the SS and helped to organize the deportation of Jewish people as acts of ethnic cleansing across Greece and Yugoslavia, including Serbian populations in Bosnia. He denied all knowledge of these atrocities and in 1972 he became elected Secretary General of the UN. In 1977 he was chosen to record a message of greetings and goodwill onto golden phonograph records, "The Sounds of Earth" transmitted into space by the Voyager II satellite that the signals might be picked up by extraterrestrial life-forms, as the two passed between Jupiter and Saturn in alignment. What might have been the scream of the persecuted and the dying was instead a friendly welcome on behalf of Earth, "seeking peace and friendship," an ironic step toward humility and hope nonetheless delivered by a man with blood on his hands.

70. Where "West Country Girl" shows the female character stroking her beloved fat cat, "As I Sat Sadly . . ." presents the kitten traded back and forth, the measure of innocence, but it remains an animal, true to its own nature, still carrying the threat to swipe with the strength of a bear's paw.

71. The "better angel" is a phrase drawn from Shakespeare, Dickens, and fully realized in Abraham Lincoln's first inaugural address of 1861.

72. Blixa Bargeld, real name Christian Emmerich, also Minister Emmerich of Wise Blood.

73. From Shakespeare's *Macbeth*.

74. Red Hand Files #149, May 2021.

75. To glance aside at John Donne, there is a deeper humanism shared in Cave's conception of the unkind world, where all human life is part of a shared whole. In his famous poem "No man is an island" written toward the end of his life, Donne hears the bells sounding prayers for a recent death and wonders if it is himself in the other's place: Each man's death diminishes me/For I am involved in mankind/Therefore, send not to know/For whom the bell tolls/It tolls for thee.

76. Red Hand Files #158, July 2021.

NOTES

Chapter 5

1. A Paris theater running from 1897 until 1962, the Grand Guignol became a specialized naturalistic horrorshow of graphic onstage performances of violence meant to delight and appall audiences, with semi-realistic, lo-fi gore—there is something of this in Cave's sincere excess onstage, rolling around screaming into the microphone.

2. Red Hand Files #138, March 2021.

3. Barry Adamson remembers Cave's landings were split evenly between solid and safe and physical injury—nonetheless, the show must go on.

4. As with Prometheus it is the reach for the forbidden glory, like the extended guitar solo or the scissor kick or knee drop, that leaves the musician dropping a bum note or falling flat on their face. It is the difference between those willing to try, and fail, to move beyond the safe space of their creative comfort zone.

5. The band's name seems to follow Mark E. Smith's line, naming The Fall after a lesser-known Albert Camus book. It is tempting to consider the eponymous Harold Pinter play where a loner in a seaside boarding house is forced into a mock birthday party by two strangers while he insists it is not his special day; other sources claim a reference to a scene in Dostoyevsky's *Crime and Punishment*. The band was the antithesis of its namesake; they were the party crashers, joy corrupted, banners torn down, and the towering cake destroyed—happiness isn't everything . . .

6. When The Birthday Party broke up Pew intended to study English literature at university but would sadly die young from a brain hemorrhage aged twenty-eight, caused by head injuries sustained during an epileptic seizure.

7. As noted by both Ian Johnston and Mark Mordue, Cave and Tracy Pew would find a hobby in casual acts of destruction—crashing on purpose became an exercise in letting go.

8. Barbara Ellen, "It's Hip to Be Hateful," *The Observer*, May 5, 1998.

9. *Freaks* depicts a group of circus entertainers, played by people with real-life deformities, disabilities, and gender differences. They are set against the "big people," humans with idealized attributes, such as Hercules the weightlifter and Cleopatra the great beauty; alongside this, it is their "normality" that sets them in a position of superiority above the freaks. The "big people" are the villains of the piece, figures of cruelty and exploitation against the freaks, the "decent circus folk"

10. Jack Barron, "The Needle and the Damage Done," *NME*, May 1988.

11. Cave does not perform these songs. The lyrical image is visually strong, but on a moral level it is too much crude junk, even for The Birthday Party.

12. On being inducted into ARIA Hall of Fame in 2007 Cave pointed out that only he was invited to receive the award. While The Bad Seeds had endured

many incarnations and were populated by international musicians, Cave argued that they played across the world making authentic Australian music, and listed members accordingly, as well as The Birthday Party for a defining influence across Australian music and across the rest of the world.

13. Bary Adamson, *Up Above the City, Down Beneath the Stars* (London: Omnibus Press, 2021).

14. Andrew Male, "The Bad & The Beautiful: 50 Greatest Songs of Nick Cave" / "Something Monstrous," *Mojo*, no. 319 (June 2020).

15. Adamson, *Up Above the City, Down Beneath the Stars*; Tom Engelshoven, "Nick Cave," *Oor* magazine, January 2021.

16. Bleddyn Butcher's best photograph: Nick Cave in Berlin, Ben Beaumont-Thomas, *The Guardian*, November 2016. Australian humor is hard to define, but it is fair to surmise that the desert-dry caustic wit is ultimately a self-effacing leveler for all concerned—not jokes that bear a grudge—though looking back on his past, Cave sometimes noticed that it was also used to bring people down from a position of confidence in the abilities or genuine achievement, making it hard to stand out in a town like Wangaratta.

17. Brian Orloff, "Nick Cave Sings the Blues," *Rolling Stone*, October 22, 2004.

18. A direct descendant of *The Boatman's Call*, the next Bad Seeds album, *No More Shall We Part*, often seems racked by spiritual crisis. In some respects, one of Cave's most explicitly religious albums, it is also cut through with a dark, dry heart of mockery. If life is a joke, then death is only the punchline.

19. In the song's final explosion of rage, we find Cave consumed with the vision of swinging a hammer after paparazzi who huddle like vultures awaiting the next downfall. He finds them figures of hate for what they have done to people he loved. Elsewhere on "Darker with the Day" Cave sings of the threat of exposure, being left in the cold exiled from fame, while also being overexposed by the camera flashes and zoom lenses the same way his friend Michael Hutchence was hounded for his extramarital affairs and drug use.

20. See Nick Cave and Seán O'Hagan, *Faith, Hope and Carnage* (Edinburgh: Canongate, 2022). Cave also reiterated this view in the live Q&A at London's Southbank Centre in winter 2022.

21. Swift was Irish but also borrowed the dry conservative tone of acerbic British wit, which brought sarcasm to wither and weary the opponent under a mask of insincerity.

22. Luke 17:27: They did eat, they drank, they married wives, they were given in marriage, until the day that Noah entered into the ark, and the flood came, and destroyed them all.

23. Cave offers further play of ideas where the statue, or rather the politicized elephant in the room, is a body of ice, weeping, melting; a decaying figure,

it is also verging on slapstick, the vision of a heavy symbol eroded by the lucidity of the sun's gaze.

24. Bleddyn Butcher's best photograph: Nick Cave in Berlin, Ben Beaumont-Thomas, *The Guardian*, November 2016.

25. The protection of statues . . . dead stone gods, deaf to the future.

26. Cave returns to the straight-up junk anthem of "Mutiny in Heaven," recycling the term "utopiate." This time it is Karl Marx's definition of religion as the opiate of the masses replaced by capitalist neoliberal bliss, the new drug of ultimate pleasure is the overbearing power of mutual consent and consensus politics. Also offering a line of Joycean verve in describing inebriated souls: "The tipsy, the reeling and the drop-down pissed."

27. Amusingly, a 1996 song of the same name recorded by Hillsong Worship Church of Sydney, Australia, would present the very straight opposite to Cave's split loyalties of "God Is in the House: "God is in the house, there is no doubt / God is in the house, can't keep Him out."

28. Mat Snow, *Nick Cave: Sinner Saint: The True Confessions*, ed. Mat Snow (London: Plexus, 2015).

29. Cave is influenced by the poems of Stevie Smith, adopting her cool, sardonic attitude to life, not unlike the melancholy writing of Dorothy Parker. Casually cruel the way that life just is sometimes, Cave's earlier songs take a backhand to our complacency, shattering the illusion of a comfort zone in wealth, status, and class that can never be maintained. As for Smith, as good as things get, the bittersweet edge of tragedy is always there in the shadows, and to that she cannot help but raise a lingering, knowing smile—nothing is for free.

30. Cave's great plays on goofiness emphasize the particular idea of fun in his songs. On "I Had a Dream Joe" Cave pins down the vacant man standing inside of his "ridiculous seersucker suit," all dressed up but with nothing to say—in contrast to his own labors. Cave would condemn empty-headed suit as a symptom of decadent, monied society.

31. He revisits the song with "Idiot Prayer." This time embittered love brings Cave to the point of mutual annihilation, determined that his lover should feel his pain, the death of a heart that will never love again.

32. In 2013's B side "Needle Boy" Cave would shout down the threat of the "money man" forcing coins down the throat of his guardian voodoo doll. Speaking in 2022 Cave would commonly declare himself a conservative loyal to traditional values but not party politics. In keeping with Cave's heroic reading of *Das Kapital*, his economic views no doubt remained divided. Proverbs 23: "Labour not to be rich: cease from thine own wisdom."

33. Cave expanded on this in a Red Hand Files question, rejecting Bukowski's poetry as unworthy of reality, even "cloyingly sentimental about his own place in a world he viewed with abject contempt," a feeling Cave identified in

his younger self. Cave takes issue with Bukowski's seeming inability to produce something authentically beautiful and not self-serving. Bukowski compared poetry to taking a shit, an affront to Cave's view of the sublime. He would refer to Bukowski as the "bukkake of poetry," a splurger of overwriting, noting different ends of the literary spectrum. Perhaps Bukowski was referring more to the cathartic and enervating process of easing words onto the page. Red Hand Files #154, June 2021.

34. The emasculating situation is an interesting shift for Cave. The pointed sexual threat of the men in his songs overcoming and often brutalizing women is flipped onto the male protagonist, who, as Cave alludes, cannot become erect himself, leaving him a blunted instrument. As ever, the recourse to violence is the first and final "male" option. See also the "love scene" of the film *Wake in Fright*.

35. For further discussion on the use of the terms "fag" and "faggot" in music, see my book on David Bowie, *Silhouettes and Shadows* (Backbeat, 2023).

36. Elsewhere, Cave is a fan of the paintings of cats by Edwardian artist Louis Wain, a schizophrenic increasingly given to overwhelming daytime visions. Cave said, "His art has a visionary intensity that is uniquely his own, and the book, quite simply, blew my mind. I fast became a Wain disciple."

37. In the music video for "Jubilee Street" we see Ray Winstone, a lonely and dejected man who keeps returning to a prostitute who takes his money but offers no love in return. He is stuck in a pattern of behavior he cannot break out of, echoing the song's lyric where Cave presents his dilemma as the deadweight of troubles like a shadow.

38. Cave revisits "Jubilee Street" on "Finishing Jubilee Street." Cave looks back on the process of writing songs, a distinctly autobiographical meta-narrative that is transmuted through a dream.

39. On "There She Goes My Beautiful World," when Cave joked about Gaugin, he was laughing at a part of himself. When a man gets older and lusts after younger creatures he runs away to the tropics where women are more scantily clad in the tropical heat. A self-satisfying vision of aging lust, the artist embraces lechery to find a new integrity as he surrounds himself with beautiful creatures.

40. A fan who was just turning eighteen asked the sixty-three-year-old Cave how he coped with the aging process, in response Cave quipped: "Grow a porn star mustache and learn the electric guitar—it worked for me." Red Hand Files #153, June 2021.

41. Red Hand Files #153, June 2021.

42. At the end of the book Cave cited all apologies to Lavigne and Minogue and perhaps admits to a deeper transgression that his writing was, quite literally, "darker and more invasive." When asked about the future of the film script that

the hybrid project was born out of, Cave hinted with a wry smile that perhaps Lavigne could play herself in the film.

43. The blackly comic irony behind the unlikeable and seedy character of Bunny is the esteem in which he is held by his son, none the wiser to his father's darker peccadillos, it is a cruel twist he lives in bliss ignorance of the painful truth.

44. Cave explained the shifting focus of pop culture icons to *The Guardian*'s Alexis Petidris in 2013: "The whole thing came about because I was in Madame Tussauds with my kids and they were hugging Miley Cyrus's waxwork. Elizabeth Taylor as Cleopatra was in the next room. They were groping Miley Cyrus, and I'm going, well, hang on a second, you've got Elizabeth Taylor here. 'Who?'"

45. On "Jesus Alone," the first track from *Skeleton Tree*, Cave buries the song's ideal of the romantic sea maiden, forcing his choked-out words half born out of grief down her throat, a protest against the possibility of wondrous strange creatures, a ghost song lost to the sea.

46. Cave's friend Frederic Wall would produce a reimagined version of this image, *The Painting of the Green Woman*, as seen in Cave's Berlin office room in the *Stranger in a Strange Land* documentary. See also *Stranger Than Kindness* (Edinburgh: Canongate, 2020).

47. See Alan Bennett, *The History Boys* (New York: Farrar, Straus and Giroux, 2006).

48. A similar sentiment is expressed in the Bukowski poem "Shower," about a former lover Linda King. He starts grossly erotic, washing of bodies, and then speaks of the love she brought into his life, how it leaves with her, after it has given so much feeling. its absence as a new pain, "when you take it away, do it slowly and easily / make it as if I were dying in my sleep." Bukowski speaks with much sentimentality, but nonetheless the shift from the descriptions of sexualized bodies into something deeper wrestles with the forces of love, and we hear his agony in the lover leaving behind something of themself.

49. Cave had done his research. Kennedy had a hernia and wore a special corset to correct his weak posture as well as suffering from the extremely rare Addison's disease, which gave him his healthy 'golden' glow and increased his sex drive. The upright stack of bones veiled in a sexy, shroud is at once a powerful image of vulnerability and erotic allure.

50. Still drawn to challenging material that other artists would not touch, Cave nods to the inexplicable contrasts of life, in one day working on the soundtrack for the *Dahmer* series then going on to do an audiobook recording for the children's book he had written as part of *Cave Things*. Working through these extremes we see the challenge between the dark character of the persona working on challenging material and the human individual wanting to make

something nice for kids. To admit to this duality is to reenforce both sides of the contradiction, to be more complex, more real than audiences might have you be.

51. Phil Sutcliffe, "King of Pain." *Mojo*, January 2005.

52. Cave and O'Hagan, *Faith, Hope and Carnage*.

53. Cave and Sean O'Hagan in live discussion, Southbank Centre, 2022.

54. Cullen Murphy, "Who Do Men Say That I Am?" *The Atlantic*, December 1986.

55. In a rundown of other artists' favorite Bad Seeds tracks, Mick Harvey, by then an ex–band member, noted Cave's provocative stance was guaranteed to force a reaction from his listeners: "It's the deeper, inner human workings that Nick repeatedly probes. They can be gut-wrenchingly confronting, heart-breakingly delicate, disturbingly violent, or just plain funny, and sometimes all of these at once. But they are always pushing at the boundaries of the listener's own emotional and moral positioning." "Nick Cave's 30 Best Songs," *Uncut*, February 2015.

56. Speaking to Rolling Stone in 1994, Cave would admit that he ad-libbed much of the song's lyrics. Having a core idea and a few key lines in mind, he riffed on the mystery wrapped in an enigma that would become an iconic nightmare.

57. "Why I Write" (essay originally published in the *New York Times Book Review* in 1976).

58. In 2021 Cave established his own line of merchandise and clothing, Cave Things, tagged as "Beyond merchandise, before art," a tongue-in-cheek exploration of Cave's creative world, drawing on lyrics and imagery from his songs to create modern artifacts.

59. It is uncomfortable to look at the Nick Cave we know now and to attach past quotes and misdeeds to him in the context of his records made at that time (1984). And while Cave does not seem to shy away from performing difficult material, there are still great songs that are not often performed live. Cave admits a vivid disdain for any art made safe, manifest by vox populi or censorship committee, though he would perform "Papa Won't Leave You, Henry" uncensored for the *Idiot Prayer* live film.

60. See Red Hand Files #155; also, David E. Sloane, "The N-Word in *Adventures of Huckleberry Finn* Reconsidered," *The Mark Twain Annual* 12, no. 1 (2014): 70–82.

61. Cave would state his unambiguous disappointment with the censorship: "Time and time again the integrity of this magnificent song is tested. The BBC, that gatekeeper of our brittle sensibilities, forever acting in our best interests, continue to mutilate an artifact of immense cultural value."

62. In 2021 The Rolling Stones would drop "Brown Sugar" from their live sets, not simply for its fetishization of sex with Black women as a sweet thing, a commodity to be consumed, but more for its framing of the sexual abuse of

slaves transported from Africa to America. Although the song still persists as the first track on The Stones' lascivious classic 1971 album *Sticky Fingers*, their decision to excise it from contemporary live setlists is only a thin line drawn perhaps decades too late.

63. The rampant violence of Stagger Lee in the roast tradition sees the barman and Stagger trading verses, or spitting bars, if you will, to outdo one another. The constant one-upmanship is the testing waters of extremity; see Method Man's long and profane litany of wild tortures featured on Wu-Tang Clan's extreme skit "Method Man." Instead of fluid freestyling he trips, hesitates and stutters to utter ever more extreme ways of physically punishing his good friend as an enemy. All in good fun, of course.

64. As a case in point: "That Stagger Lee does not shoot Billy Dilly with an actual gun at all, but that his being 'filled full of lead. Bang! Bang! Bang!' was simply a metaphor for the force of Stag's ejaculation, and Blixa's terrifying and inhuman screeching at the end orgasmic in nature. This made me wonder, chillingly at the time, what sleeping with Blixa must be like—something I am sadly unable to elaborate on." Red Hand Files #72, November 2019.

65. Red Hand Files #86, March 2020.

66. Cave's openness to the interpretation of the listener over the singer, where the song becomes theirs, literally in the public domain, reminds of Roland Barthes' "Death of the Author." This new relativism makes songs new and change over time, as people do, though the words remain irredeemably the same. We remain the listener, a distant receiver each seeking our own kind of truth in the songs.

67. From the age of eighteen Israeli citizens are eligible to do national service in the IDF, with the average age of participants between nineteen and twenty-one. That is a lot of trigger-happy young adults without much real-life experience or responsibility under their belts, but with a live gun in their hands.

68. Speaking to *Rolling Stone* in 1994 Cave decried the musicians who would try to become the "voice of a generation," losing the power of personal expression and forsaking art in the name of politics.

69. In Red Hand Files #186, March 2022, Cave would be questioned about the split values of support for Ukraine but not for joining the Israeli boycott. Cave would point out his sympathy for all oppressed peoples and hesitantly mention that he had been involved with several charitable projects in support of Palestinian schools.

70. Leonard Cohen would take an opposing view, in a brutally acerbic poem, "Kanye West Is Not Picasso," published in 2015. He seems to scold West for the self-comparison.

71. Manchester's prodigal son, who celebrated the melancholy power of his home city, would desert it for sunny Los Angeles and limp from record label to

label, repeatedly "canceled" for his casual racism and poor songwriting, only to disappear up his own solipsistic black hole.

72. Though Kanye West is his own artist and mouthpiece, it should be noted that behind almost every hip-hop record stands a roster of musicians and producers shaping sound and making the record happen—albeit under creative direction—making the musical recordings both Kayne's and not-Kayne's.

73. West claimed to be immune from criticism because he was simply too bankable, his music too beloved. He was dropped by fashion labels he had accused of racism after trolling his audiences with White Lives Matter T-shirts, proclaiming "slavery was a choice," making anti-Semitic remarks, and vocalizing support for antiabortion laws, putting the horse before the cart by crying in self-pity that his mother had almost had him aborted.

74. In a 2023 interview with right-wing media platform *Unherd*, Cave would jest that he began his musical career just wanting to fuck people off, half-joking that he now found the greatest rebellion to be found in conservatism and going to church.

75. Red Hand Files #197, June 2022.

76. Once asked if he would rather have dinner with Jesus or the Devil, Cave answers without hesitation: "For me, Jesus Christ is one of the most enigmatic and exciting characters around. It would be more than a privilege to spend a day with him," explaining by way of contrast, "I wouldn't have a clue what to do with the devil."

77. But this stands less so for the failed artists whose designs are reduced to hard-minded concrete arguments of eugenics, tax exile and pseudo-intellectuals; see self-proclaimed guru and false prophet of young men Jordan Peterson, a man who became addicted to benzodiazepine and went into a coma after going on a meat-free diet while arguing humanity should borrow from the neurology and social patterns of the lobster, after writing a series of self-help-for-idiots books.

78. Looking back to The Birthday Party's own version of the primal scream, eating out John Lennon's bleeding heart from the *Plastic Ono Band* album, Cave admitted to his divebombing sense of angst that seemed overflowing in those early days. It was the necessary path of destruction toward creation, the continual revolution of rock and roll that later sees the king executed by his former subjects, the audience call for blood. Ellen, "It's Hip to Be Hateful."

79. Rowland S. Howard would express dismay at the internalized frustration between band and audience, both trying to force an authentic expression or reaction but falling into their prescribed roles of entertainment and spectators.

80. The sharply fractured syntax of Cave's lyrics, more barking dog than considered songsmith, already point to the future abstraction he would realize more fluidly on albums like *Push the Sky Away* and *Skeleton Tree*.

NOTES

Chapter 6

1. Where Cave begins one of his earliest chanted chorus lyrics Simon Critchley, writing about David Bowie, referred to poetry and art as creating an amalgam with words delivered through another medium. Here the power of the rock song becomes the poem setting itself on fire. Simon Critchley, *On Bowie* (London: Serpent's Tail, 2006).

2. Barbara Ellen, "It's Hip to Be Hateful," *The Observer*, May 5, 1998.

3. Red Hand Files #190.

4. In his 2009 article for *The Monthly* Peter Conrad notes an echo of a line from Coleridge's "Rime of the Ancient Mariner," "I pass like night from land to land," suggesting a roving killer who brings death in his shadow.

5. In Milton's original lines, fear of God becomes reverence:

> *What if the breath that kindled those grim fires,*
> *Awaked, should blow them into sevenfold rage,*
> *And plunge us in the flames; or from above*
> *Should intermitted vengeance arm again*
> *His red right hand to plague us?*

6. For more on Manson and the blood graffiti see my book *Into the Never: Nine Inch Nails and the Creation of* The Downward Spiral (Essex, Connecticut: Backbeat, 2020).

7. On the extended version of "O'Malley's Bar" Cave goes into Agatha Christie overdrive with a beating from an ashtray big as a brick, multiple shootings—into various body parts—he reels off so many unusually specific deaths they start to become freakishly banal, but he does it with such zeal and relish it's hard to ignore.

8. PJ Harvey and Anita Lane would contribute some backing vocals and some crying, respectively.

9. Steve Janes, "Nick Cave Murder Ballads Interview," *With Guitars*, 2011.

10. Embracing surrealist Antonin Artaud's idea of the theater of cruelty, in 1981/1982 Nick Cave and Lydia Lunch would write their own theater of revenge, a series of fifty one-act plays, almost doggerel, which the authors describe as running the gambit of "nature's supermen." Their graphic titles sound like a crossover point between The Birthday Party tracklisting and a Bad Seeds album ("Hells Wheels Called Elvis," "Fresh Cunt in the Can," "Deep in the Woods," "Hard on for Love"), while the plays themselves suggest two addicts in a dark place, each trying to out-write their partner, but in the other's hand.

11. Robert Sandall, "Nick Cave: Renaissance Man," *The Word*, March 2003.

12. A B side to *The Boatman's Call*, "Come into My Sleep" would offer a fuzzy R&B bass riff and gospel leanings where sleep suggests the possibility of happy dreaming, not morbidity.

13. The stark contrast of Cave's hair, dyed black since his teens, and alabaster white skin subverted the sunshine tan-happy image of Australia. There would be little variation in Cave's appearance over the years, his hair veering from the "jelly black" Elvis quiff, mad spiked bangs, and the move toward an extended 1980s shoulder-length mullet, his only concession to that decade. The pitch darkness of his hair frames and threatens to overcome the sharp aquiline lines of his chin and cheekbones, the skull peering through the face. In 2020 British men's style magazine *GQ* would run a guide to copying Cave's hairstyle, demanding daily blow-drying and root boosting.

14. Contrary to what was often seen as a threatening stance, Pew is best remembered by his bandmates as caring, bookish, and wickedly funny, particularly in the accounts gathered by Mark Mordue. Rowland S. Howard would find himself absorbed into Pew's mixed metaphor as he sat around in his apartment surrounded by *Playboy* magazines, drinking a beer and reading Plato's *Republic*, where everything was a private joke, but only Pew knew the punchline. Johnston, Ian. *Bad Seed: The Biography of Nick Cave*. London: Little, Brown Book Group, 1996.

15. Mark Mordue would point out that Cave's bands were formed at a relatively young age by people who of course had little experience of death or attending funerals. Though several members were raised in antisocial, broken homes, it was Cave who would be most disturbed by the loss of his father at the still young age of twenty-one.

16. Gothic scholar Nick Groom notes that while Lord Byron's physician in Switzerland Polidori birthed the original vampire story, Cave seemed to live it—at least through his songs. From the same evening in which the gathered houseguests were charged to write a short horror story, Mary Shelley, wife of the liberal poet Percy Byshee Shelley, would write *Frankenstein*, the birth of a monster made from dead body parts by the eponymous doctor.

17. Johnston, Ian. *Bad Seed: The Biography of Nick Cave*. London: Little, Brown Book Group, 1996.

18. The short-lived Nick Cave and the Cave Men would become The Bad Seeds, a formidable band unit with a somewhat domineering singer-songwriter at its heart.

19. In his suit Cave dodged the punk uniform of the leather jacket. He would be stopped in the street, accused of being a city boy stockbroker. Responding with a curt "fuck off," Cave's sharp practicality echoes the wisdom of artist duo Gilbert & George, who pointed out that a suit, with its pockets, removable jacket, and rolled up sleeves was infinitely useful for dressing up or getting down and dirty.

20. *Larrikin* is an Australian English term meaning "a mischievous young person, an uncultivated, rowdy but good-hearted person," or "a person who acts

with apparent disregard for social or political conventions." In UK English, "a bit of a lad."

21. This early track carries a preeminent echo of 2001's "As I Sat Sadly By Her Side." The crumbs of love are poor comfort where emotional distance grows between the lovers as they stand within reach of physical intimacy.

22. The idea that we somehow conceal something of ourselves by the armor of our scar tissue as mental or physical alienation, echoes the idea of the Anima Christi prayer: "Within your wounds hide me." That we should lose ourselves in the suffering of a martyr, "By his wounds we are healed." Not unlike St. Teresa struck by the arrow of God as spiritual awakening, Yukio Mishima vividly describes his first (homosexual) sexual encounter masturbating over the icon of Saint Sebastian, bound and pierced by arrows. This is masochistic holy sacrifice made sacrilege.

23. If the cover of "Avalanche" was an act of carnage, The Bad Seeds' genre-blurring of Cohen's "Tower of Song" is an abortion of style, veering from Cave's own interpretation of the "Madchester" style, voodoo to rockabilly. The band refused to settle on a definitive mood and made a riotous carve up of a classic that only they could.

24. To read more, see my book *Silhouettes and Shadows: The Secret History of David Bowie's Scary Monsters (and Super Creeps)* (Essex, Connecticut: Backbeat, 2023).

25. This is Tom Jones "Sleeping Annaleah" sonic evisceration.

26. Noah and Moses appear in the lyrics, recast as dwarves. As noted by critic Nick Stone they are biblical giants reduced to handmaidens for the endless parade of the circus that keeps on rolling from town to town, trailing death behind it.

27. Drugs began as a helping hand for The Birthday Party to escape their current squalor. Cave noted that with the proximity of the Eastern heroin trade, the scene back in Melbourne was culturally more accepting of hard drugs, with people regularly "chipping away," compared to the shock of the British underground who saw heroin as the last rung of a long and slippery ladder toward the bottom of a society still riddled with the plague of class distinctions.

28. The final chorus closes with some choice departing words, broken "Latin" standing in with florid junkie outbursts. "Ars infectio porcio Dio," "The craft of the infected Pig God," "Hypuss Dermio," and "vita rex" play on "the life of a Hypodermic King," and finally "scabo murem per sanctum dio" becomes "scabbed mouse / rat scratched by the holy god."

29. The cup in hand lyric chimes with the empty cup rattled against the bars of a jail cell; the good times can make you high and happy but also keep you stuck inside your addiction.

30. The B side "Rye Whisky" carries more of the drunken dirge and slurred vision compared to the furious acoustic guitar rhythms that drive "Brother My Cup Is Empty."

31. Despite moving on from drugs on a personal level Cave often returns to heroin references in his songs. It remained a recurring motif across songs such as "Fifteen Feet of Pure White Snow" and "Opium Tea."

32. Speaking in 1994 Cave declared himself more or less clean, speaking about sustained speed and heroin use in Berlin making him an object of self-isolation. Even after being busted for drug offenses in London several times in one year Cave was spared jail time, but only if he underwent forced drug rehabilitation.

33. Famous for the dash as splintered, connective tissue between the lines, her poems were often untitled aside from first lines and are numbered accordingly 479. She throws up the tension between the irrepressible spirit of life against the nihilistic death drive:

> *Because I could not stop for Death—*
> *He kindly stopped for me—*

34. Cave would allude to the vague emotional numbness immediately following his father's death, remembering nothing of the funeral or the days after it. Ginny Dougary, "The New Romantic," *The Times Magazine*, March 27, 1999.

35. "Nick Cave," The Talks, 2015.

36. For his part, Warren Ellis often skips any questions about his own former drug use, referring to it as the least interesting part of his life.

37. *The Boatman's Call* is uniquely informed by these repeat visits to rehab. "(Are You) The One I've Been Waiting For?" reflects upon the sterile atmosphere of sitting on benches, drinking tea, and reciting The Serenity Prayer.

38. Red Hand Files #120, October 2020.

39. Janes, "Nick Cave Murder Ballads Interview."

40. Huckleberry Finn is a young man, a child really, preoccupied with death. The distant ache of mortality makes him feel that death is never far away: "I felt so lonesome I most wished I was dead." This extreme fatalism finds its way into Cave's earliest music, jousting with death the way a cat continues to play with a half-dead mouse, as if the outcome might be different.

41. From the title track "Abattoir Blues" Cave manages to balance funny lines of waking up, clean and sober, with the plastic pleasure of a chain store Frappuccino coffee, faux luxury instead of being on the wrong end of a syringe or with a stranger in his bed—nonetheless he remains riddled with anxiety for the future and with self-doubt of his place within it.

42. Cave would mention this point earlier: "When I read the quote from a younger nick cave saying he needs catastrophes in his life to create, these words

sound somewhat like the indulgent posturing of a man yet to discover the devastating effect true suffering can have on our ability to function, let alone to create." Red Hand Files #121, October 2020.

43. Professor Nick Groom sees "We Real Cool" as "a heart-rending meditation on memory, the past, and children, the lyric reaches out more widely to wonder whether the child is father to the man, and the mystery of the Trinity: how God the Father comprehends God the Son."

44. The album cover of *Skeleton Tree* would perform a stark expression of minimalist design. In its digitized green font set against darkness, we see a crepuscular glimpse of a pulse expressed in the suggestion of a blinking cursor as a sign of life. It echoes the faint glow screen Cave speaks to on the closing title track—a jittery television becomes the revolving image of static as white fire, like its title, showing the ghost expression of life. Ina Harrison nails down the gentle symbolism of the track: "fallen leaves and a candle in the window articulate loss and non-loss."

45. Cave would reflect that the film perhaps began something of an emotional thaw for him and his wife: "It gave Arthur's absence, his silence, a voice. This shifted something hugely in me. I mean, Susie and I were like birds trapped in an oil slick. We were incapable of moving. And this film had a freeing sort of effect on us." Chris Heath, "The Love and Terror of Nick Cave," *GQ Magazine*, April 27, 2017.

46. Cave would reference one of his favorite poets, W. H. Auden. In his lecture on the love song, he talks about children growing up in expectation of the great traumatic experience, always waiting for it to happen, and when it does their young fears seem to be confirmed as life presents itself as a more "serious matter."

47. Mark Mordue is quick to point out that Cave often states the incorrect age, his father having passed when he was twenty-one, a few short years that actually make all of the difference.

48. Speaking on *The South Bank Show* in 2003.

49. The author Sarah Perry points to the Bible and the Tower of Siloam's collapse as a tragedy that yields a test of faith. The story highlights that bad things can, and will, happen in our lives—tragedies without purpose or reason—but in knowing this, how then should we live our lives? Embracing the existential hinge, we live in defiance of tragedy. As Cave sings on The Bad Seeds' B side "Accidents Will Happen," "an accident is just an accident," meaningless in itself—but sometimes with devastating repercussions—marked by the terror of coincidence.

50. Red Hand Files #6, October 2018. A response that would later become known as Cave's "Letter to Cynthia."

51. An emotional state of melancholic or profoundly nostalgic longing for a beloved yet absent something or someone.

52. Even though the video that shows Cave and Blixa wrecked on drink aboard their little rowboat is drenched in Rimbaldian irony, the song marks a turning point at which the band would shift away from detachment toward more directly intimate songs.

53. Andrew Male, "The Bad & The Beautiful: 50 Greatest Songs of Nick Cave" / "Something Monstrous," *Mojo*, no. 319 (June 2020).

54. Michael Dwyer, "Album by Album with Nick Cave," *Rolling Stone Australia*, July 1998.

55. Mat Snow, Nick Cave: *Sinner Saint: The True Confessions*, ed. Mat Snow (London: Plexus, 2015).

56. Speaking in 1997 Cave would note the need for "infinite patience" with children. He would also sing a more sedate lullaby about lambs to his newborn son, as a possible Bad Seeds song. Blixa encouraged him to put it away, to keep it for his family. It would later become the B side "Sheep May Safely Graze." As in William Blake's "Little Lamb Lost" the lamb of God is the figure of pure innocence, new life cast onto earth with the anthropomorphism of Jesus turned back against the human.

57. *Saturday Times Magazine*, March 27, 1999.

58. A man would write to Cave in Red Hand Files #23 having lost his wife and finding himself left alone to care for his daughter. He would return to respond to Cave later in #187, having reread McCarthy's novel *The Road* and seen the film, tracing a parallel between the hazards of the COVID-19 pandemic and the metaphor of the desolate earth in *The Road*. Again, the duty of caring for others becomes an act of survival set against the horrors of loss. This echoes the struggle of the book in which the narrator raises the child up to an expression of God's grace and wonder: "The child is my warrant, and if he is not the word of God, then God never spoke."

59. Indeed, Cave continues to confront the taboo of trying to speak about death and our fear of loss (and being lost). The consequences of this are a great sadness that moors us to life: "In the hysterical technocracy of modern music, sorrow is sent to the back of the class where it sits, pissing its pants in mortal terror." —Nick Cave, *The Secret Life of the Love Song & The Flesh Made Word: Two Lectures by Nick Cave* (1996)

60. Mark Mordue, "Nick Cave: 'Being forced to grieve openly basically saved us,'" *Irish Times*, May 8, 2017.

61. Sam Leith, "'Loss is a thing that we become': Nick Cave on Grief, Faith and Why He's a Conservative," *The Spectator*, December 2022. Elsewhere Warren Ellis remembers Cave hearing the music for "Magneto" and having an idea that seemed to intuit the rest of the song: "What you're hearing is Nick actually

singing along to a piece where he doesn't even know how it's gonna go. There is something extraordinary about being in that moment." Ryan Leas, "Warren Ellis on the Past, Present, & Future of Nick Cave & The Bad Seeds," *Stereogum*, November 17, 2021.

62. On the album's closing title track "Skeleton Tree" Cave offers soothing reassurance that things are "alright," reassuring himself as much as the listener. It was the only song written after Arthur's death.

63. Seven years after the death of his fifteen-year-old son Arthur, Cave's son Jethro Lazenby died at age 30. https://www.today.com/parents/dads/nick-cave-son-jethro-died-rcna27967.

64. Leith, "'Loss is a thing that we become.'"

65. Accordingly, the songs that span the loose trilogy of recent Bad Seeds albums would seem to speak to one another suggesting a continuous phase of compressed time.

66. Cormac McCarthy's *The Road* presents a condensed and intimately raw expression of family connection that would draw upon several road trips taken with his eleven-year-old son, John, who he suggested was in many ways coauthor of the book. The writer would include verbatim lines in the book's dialogue: "John said, 'Papa, what would you do if I died?' I said, 'I'd want to die, too,' and he said, 'So you could be with me?' I said, 'Yes, so I could be with you.' Just a conversation that two guys would have." John Jurgensen, "Hollywood' Favorite Cowboy," *Wall Street Journal*, November 2009.

67. Red Hand Files #151, June 2021. In *Faith, Hope and Carnage* Cave would compare the great reveal of Jesus' return that follows the period of mourning as a powerful analogy for the origination of a creative idea, gradually unfurling itself to the artist. This is not a transaction of sacrifice; it is the opportunity of rebirth for the survivor, those who are left behind to grieve.

68. Mordue, "Nick Cave."

69. Cave would explain that as parents and as people he and Susie were forced either to fight and resist against their situation of deep grief or to be overwhelmed by it, like a tide, from which some people never wholly return.

Chapter 7

1. Of course, to one side there would be a much larger room with a desk at which Cave could sit and type, with stairs leading up to his live-in landlord's spacious apartment, but this was not the postcard-sized image that was needed.

2. In the fictional meta-documentary *20,000 Days on Earth* (2014) we see Cave in 2012 typing at a desk, one of the few musical artists with his own songwriting office and regular nine-to-five working hours. Cave inhabits this workspace like the mental interior lined by bookshelves, not just to furnish a

room but to expand the imagination: buildings blocks of new worlds. We are presented with the image of the artist living within and alongside his archive.

3. As The Bad Seeds themselves made a point of transition in their songwriting in 1990's *The Good Son*, the producer Flood remembered the album sessions ended at a studio in Kreuzberg at the very moment the first section of the Berlin Wall came down. A symbolic new phase where for a band like The Bad Seeds, a more mainstream turn was actually quite radical.

4. For example, the chorus lines of Greek drama would spotlight the moral lessons behind the acts of the players, Nietzsche's *Birth of Tragedy* would highlight the twinned gods of Apollo and Dionysus as the poles of drama. They are often assumed to be polarized as gods of reason and virtue, chaos, and rebellion, respectively, but they are overlapping figures, both betraying their own flaws.

5. Although Cave would admit to the power of music over the flattened words of books like the primal immediacy of the duende there is something immediate about music that other art forms cannot do: "I can't get from Shakespeare what I can get from The Ramones."

6. Cave's references across Lyre of Orpheus and Abattoir Blues respectively would converge Greek myth of loss and doomed romance (Orpheus) alongside creationist legend met with real-world evolution in "Fable of the Brown Ape," creating a wild new ahistorical truth that subverts both traditions. Flannery O'Connor's short story "Enoch and the Gorilla" (1952), adapted into her novel *Wise Blood*, takes a sarcastic stab at the man who tries to reconnect with his humanity dressed in a monkey suit—also evoking the irony of the civilized man in a business suit—who is only ever an evolved ape.

7. Like all good stories and quotes, the attribution of this line shifts, having been restated and reimagined over time. For Didion it appears in her 1979 book of essays, *The White Album*.

8. Cave would admit to the power of songwriting: "It allows me the freedom to move beyond the declared world and into the uncanny and unfamiliar world. As a songwriter I have made a commitment to uncertainty and to embrace that which I do not know."

9. "Nick Cave: The Last Rock Star." *Spin Magazine*, February 1989.

10. The exhibition presents a living archive reaching across the past toward the future, a "shattered history" that Cave saw as a comment on "the fragile and vulnerable nature of identity."

11. Will Self would wisely quip that the literary biography was basically porn for writers, sitting at their desk reading about how other famous writers sat at their desk seeming to reel off continual pages of genius prose with little or no effort. Then, after they have spent all day reading about other writers, they are left to wonder 'Why can't I do that?'

12. It's interesting to note that Cave's booklists rarely include books about musicians or cultural criticism or even the history of music. Where Bowie was almost immediately postmodern, Cave began fascinated by gospel and blues music, admitting to the compromise of rock and roll overturned by postpunk, moving beyond genre.

13. As with his interest in hip-hop Cave is also interested in many African and African American authors who loom large; he also mentions seminal anthologies that bring together international writers some writing in English others in translation—*Technicians of the Sacred: A Range of Poetries from Africa, America, Asia, Europe and Oceania, and Barbaric Vast & Wild: A Gathering of Outside & Subterranean Poetry from Origins to Present*

14. First published in 1860 and compiled by Francis James Child.

15. In Inverness, a man named Charlie would give Ellis a songbook of Scottish and Irish folk tunes, sparking another mutual interest in the songwriting duo.

16. "Nick Cave's 30 Best Songs," *Uncut*, February 2015.

17. Adamson noted that his last record with the group Kicking Against the Pricks was "extraordinary" and that Cave's cover of The Seekers' "The Carnival Is Over" helped to define his sound going forward: "the art of saying goodbye." Andrew Male, "The Bad & The Beautiful: 50 Greatest Songs of Nick Cave"/"Something Monstrous," *Mojo*, no. 319 (June 2020).

18. Red Hand Files #25, February 2019.

19. The connection that comes when thoughts transition into lines that seem to reach out and grab you is expressed in Alan Bennett's play *The History Boys*. The boys' wayward teacher Hector talks about the joy of reading with the particular resonance of poetry, how a seemingly minor and personal expression can grow into something universal: "a thought, a feeling, a way of looking at things—which you had thought special and particular to you. Now here it is, set down by someone else, a person you have never met, someone even who is long dead. And it is as if a hand has come out and taken yours."

20. Donne bears an interesting parallel with Cave. A brilliant and performative preacher, he managed the celestial metaphysical concerns, with love poetry that used mind and body, was bound to carnal desire. He made sex verge on holiness but tempered it with a healthy fear of God—his work seems to anticipate Cave's intimations on *The Boatman's Call*.

21. Red Hand Files #198, July 2022.

22. Alexis Petridis, "Nick Cave's Greatest Feat," *The Guardian*, 2013.

23. The tree's indifference to the "little bird" could be Twitter, the "discourse" squawking away, feeding into Cave's mistrust of the mob mentality that can encourage blind-eyed groupthink from which "there is nowhere to hide."

The song carries the threat "we know where you live," though for many keyboard warriors, their life exists predominantly online.

24. From the French *enjamber*, to "stride over." cummings, for example, made sharp cuts mid-sentence, so the reader must follow the split thought down to the next line break. Without rhyme to blindly follow the reader is led along more by the sensation of disjunction.

25. An interesting thought via the musician Jehnny Beth.

26. A loose definition of poetry: a thought or feeling recollected in a moment of tranquility.

27. Nabokov, ever the natural perfectionist, claimed he never put ink to paper without first having each page mapped out in his head, so that writing became a pure mission of getting his inner vision down on paper, for the reader. He once critiqued the idea of passing around rough drafts of one's writing, comparing it to handing around a petri dish of the writer's "sputum"; of course, not deigning to use the more basic terms "phlegm" or "snot."

28. "I love the terror of nothing. Then you find a little idea and you grab it." Ellis shares Cave's forthright praise of his right-hand collaborator: "Nick will look at me, or I'll look at him and there's this incredible energy." The sharing of these moments is the driving force behind many bands, where music expresses what cannot be spoken. Male, "The Bad & The Beautiful."

29. Petridis, "Nick Cave's Greatest Feat."

30. Amanda Petrusich, "Nick Cave on the Fragility of Life," *The New Yorker*, March 23, 2023.

31. Warren Ellis would note with some surprise how "Jubilee Street" began as a series of chords while he and Cave were doing the *West of Memphis* soundtrack that would become a centerpiece of current live shows. Interviewer Ryan Leas pointed out how it seemed to mark a sonic and spiritual turning point for The Bad Seeds. Ryan Leas, "Warren Ellis on the Past, Present, & Future of Nick Cave & The Bad Seeds," *Stereogum*, November 17, 2021.

32. Male, "The Bad & The Beautiful."

33. Johnston, Ian. *Bad Seed: The Biography of Nick Cave*. London: Little, Brown Book Group, 1996.

34. Cave's earlier vocal style snapped and leapt with the tongue as a whip lashing about the words borrowing, Jim Morrison's leery swoon and Shane MacGowan's slurry snarl, later settled into a smoky croon, the dark side of Sinatra's moon and Elvis after hours.

35. Red Hand Files #202, July 2022.

36. Again, a seeming forthrightness can be delivered as a high-minded "fuck you" to the reader. Take T. S. Eliot's mass of footnotes appended to *The Wasteland*, a ghost trail of half-absorbed influences and his explanation when

questioned what he *meant* in one line of the poem: "Lady, three white leopards sat under a juniper tree." Eliot defiantly restated the line.

37. Like so many other musicians (Bowie!) Cave would draw upon the influence of his forebears by osmosis. He later realized that he had inserted the line "the elms and the poplars were turning their backs" into the song "Loom of the Land," having lifted it from *Lolita* and forgotten to amend it later. Kruger, Debbie "Nick Cave: The Songwriter Speaks." *Weekend Australian*, July 30, 2005.

38. To dig a little further into this, Martin Amis made the case for letting the reader make up their own mind about a character by presenting them with an illuminated and fleshed-out portrait, rather than the author instructing them what to think or feel: "The novelist retains his instinct to correct the erring puppets he creates. How will he do this? Not by trite punishment or improbable conversion, not by candid censure, not by any process of penitence and redemption; and not, finally by any displacement of the cautionary tale. Nabokov does it by rendering, as open-endedly and as perilously as he can, and by letting his style prompt our choice." Amis, Martin. *The Sublime and the Ridiculous: Nabokov's Black Farces*. New York: William Morrow, 1980.

39. It should be noted that Cave's mother Dawn was a librarian, so while he did not emerge from a house of established artists with wealth, connections, and pushing intent, he was raised in a supportive space where there was access to books and the encouragement to read them broadly and deeply.

40. In much the same way the recurring name Joe (of "I Had A Dream . . .") appears on several other Cave songs, such as "Knockin on Joe" and The Bad Seeds' cover of "Hey Joe."

41. Henry is the "average" white male, who also sometimes performs in blackface. This is not Berryman writing a Black character but playing a white man knowingly playing up to a cliché, satirizing the "White Negro" hipster of Norman Mailer, performative Blackness, problematic, almost certainly wrong, but the wearer of multiple masks would layer his fictions embedded beyond artifice. Though given the tacit approval of his friend Ralph Ellison; Berryman's portrayal is nonetheless controversial.

42. Kid Congo Powers remembers first meeting Cave, their twinned shadows of wild hair and holding a copy of the Malcolm Lowry novel *Under the Volcano*, a day in the life of a ruined, alcoholic ex-consul in Mexico, he teeters toward connection and feeling with others but inevitably sways back toward self-destruction and shows how addiction can deaden the spirit even as the person tries to escape from themselves.

43. Berryman's preoccupation with death is the persistent shadow through the *Dream Songs*: "We hafta die. / That is our 'pointed task. Love & die. / —Yes; that makes sense. But what makes sense between, then?"

44. Berryman offered the insight that art could be produced on a knife edge, and that making something great was a demanding balancing act: "The artist is extremely lucky who is presented with the worst possible ordeal which will not actually kill him. At that point, he's in business." Though with Berryman's disastrous personal life of continued alcoholism, neurosis, and broken relationships his path led to a seemingly inevitable suicide ending a tragic life of great creative brilliance and insight but not enough to save himself from himself.

45. Moving from reality to the necessary mimesis of art, Cave's title seems to bounce off from Louis Armstrong's rendition of "What a Wonderful World." Again, assuming a darker logic Cave claims that for all the song's praising of the earth and everything in it, it becomes the springboard to reflect upon how much we have to lose: "from the dark sacred night to the bright blessed day." Kruger, Debbie "Nick Cave: The Songwriter Speaks." *Weekend Australian*, July 30, 2005.

46. In "Dream Song 3, a Stimulant for an Old Beast," Berryman finds his own nemesis: "Rilke was a *jerk*."

47. Mark Mordue, "Nick Cave: 'Being forced to grieve openly basically saved us,'" *Irish Times*, May 8, 2017.

48. In poetry a full stop (or period) is called the caesura, the point at which the line ends and you cease speaking to let a thought settle and the mind catch its breath.

49. Cave's scattered rhyme meets with the maudlin repetitions of Edgar Allen Poe's poem "The Raven " and the persistent chiming phrases of "Eleanor" and "Nevermore." *Lolita*'s Humbert Humbert vainly and with a well-meaning love of literature tries to impress on Lolita the cadence of Poe's lines in the poem *Ulalume*: "It was night in the lonesome October / Of my most immemorial year." She moves closer, eager to hear more. Humbert's subtle performance is as much genuine love of language as it is the desperate need to impress. It is this habit that Lolita adopts from him and returns, with ardor.

50. See Cave's brilliant account of writing the song in Red Hand Files #85, February 2020.

51. Cave speaks of this time in the *Carnage* book.

52. For the song's title Cave was no doubt inspired by W. G. Sebald's 1995 book *Rings of Saturn*, an account of a long walk around Suffolk/Sussex that merges fact and fiction as to become indivisible. The book describes Sebald's own "arc" as both a narrative curving back on itself and the shape of his route going full circle. What sounds like a sedate exercise is measured by the trajectory of internal pressure, like a tightened screw. Sebald's stride is wound down by glancing visions of twentieth-century violence and atrocity, the endeavor of artistic lives and the muted landscapes of the disappearing coastline.

NOTES

53. From *Skeleton Tree* a neutralized emotional ground zero searching for something that is not "there" where on *Ghosteen*'s "Galleon Ship" Cave becomes alive to the idea of renewed presence seen everywhere he looks.

54. "Shattered Ground" from *Carnage* uses similarly dense lyricism. Wreathed around the listener Cave reels off the lines like they had just blown through his mind. Darting words pin down the vision of a scarf abandoned by a woman who goes running off into the tall grass, he races after trying to catch it, and with it the dream of her. As she goes a few feet ahead, it streams and winds like a snake through the reeds, immediately slipping its bonds, he is still running.

55. Where the canon and the accumulated biography threatens to swallow up the artist.

56. For his part Cave was torn between the idea of revisiting old works and letting them what they are. In a 2009 interview he explained that he would go back revise *And the Ass Saw the Angel*: the book when first released was largely unedited, "we just put in the good bits" and as a consequence he was never entirely satisfied. It brings back the idea that the work of art is never entirely finished, merely abandoned; it lives again through the reader and the performer where the art finds a life of its own beyond the artist.

Chapter 8

1. This is Dylan Thomas' "Time ticked around the stars." Our circadian rhythm shapes the idea of progress toward some end, when the clock simply "ticks over" into a new day.

2. Alternative names Lucifer, Hesperus after a Greek God, William Rimmer's ink drawing *Evening (Fall of Day)* from 1869 of a winged man/angel upside down as if night brought descent from grace.

3. In certain mythologies the eastern door (where the sun rises) is thought of as the passage of the living, the western door (where the sun sets) is for the dead, making their final exit with the dying sun.

4. In his poem *The Hour of Twilight*, George William Russell recounts that at the sinking of the sun each day life is remade new, tomorrow presents the future of new possibilities, while the stars remain fixed and certain, seeming to withhold the promise of change.

5. William Blake's "Auguries of Innocence": "To see a World in a Grain of Sand and a Heaven in a Wild Flower, hold Infinity in the palm of your hand and Eternity in an hour."

6. As Rilke said, "Beauty is but the beginning of terror. We can barely endure it and are awed when it declines to destroy us."

7. On "As I Sat Sadly By Her Side" as a man and a woman contemplate the true nature of the universe, populated by stars and the tenor of dark light

"forever falling," it draws behind it a kind of terror that also manages to be both lovely and amazing. She acknowledges the natural gravity of life, and to her this tragedy is a source of beauty that comes alongside the happenstance of wonder, where the collapse of moral boundaries is talked to death, the potential power of space can seem both vital and meaningless.

8. Cave sings of the measurement of a man, questioning how he might fit into God's scheme of things, in Isiah 40: "Who hath measured the waters in the hollow of his hand, and meted out heaven with the span, and comprehended the dust of the earth in a measure, and weighed the mountains in scales, and the hills in a balance?"

9. Sirius, in Greek mythology, was the dog of the hunter, Orion. The constellation includes the star Sirius, the "dog star." It used to be thought that Venus was the brightest object in the sky, but this is not correct.

10. The change of day always holds the wild night over us, where in the uneasy nocturnal calm of "Anthrocene" we can only see a few feet in front of us, pitched toward our own meridian line at the edge of the world's turning, until dawn the world becomes a place of renewed mystery.

11. In his "Canticle of the Sun," a song written in 1224 months before his death when he was already blind, St. Francis of Assisi speaks to "brother fire" and "sister water," from sun to moon as elemental forces leavened into weightless metaphor. "Brother Sun, who brings the day; and you give light through him. And he is beautiful and radiant in all his splendor!"

12. The workaday mop leaning against the wall casts its own shadow. Its tendrils creep toward us like the wandering roots of a tree in Sartre's novel *La Nausee*. It seems to be both crawling about and immovably still, a bland phantasm become shocking and surreal. This could be a bad trip or a blinding flash of panic at suddenly seeing things as they really are, perhaps for the first time, overwhelmed with sensation, the prisoner finds it too real to bear.

13. By "inscape" Hopkins means the unified complex of characteristics that give each thing its uniqueness and that differentiate it from other things

14. It is the subtle creaking noises, achingly familiar like the tap tap echo of the finger against the syringe in Ondaatje's *The English Patient*, sound persists as the last lethal bubbles of air squeezed out of the needle, a ghost breath before meeting and mingling into blood to form a stormy sky contained within glass.

15. In David Bowie's redemptive "Ashes to Ashes" these are "little green wheels" scraping after him, threatening to carry his overdosed corpse away, seeing his death foreshadowed. Bowie claimed to have been inspired for this image by the shaky scrape of the tea trolley at the BBC, from the prosaic to the threatening and terrifying force of the sublime.

16. We look to Jack Kerouac's explosive friends who, like the fireworks, are never dull, they continue to burn, pop, and fascinate—a pretty image—but

unsuited for a world that contains so much chaotic and uncertain shifting, and where so many bright things fade out.

17. The flipside to Cave's cover of Elvis' "In the Ghetto." Cave declares himself the king of the blues, his shoes caked with mud from the delta rivers that now meet the effluence of the city streets, like "Saint Huck," the moon brought low is the dream tarnished by the stain of reality.

18. The traditional dance of the whirling dervish presents the universe in miniature, orbiting dancers cycling around the imaginary sun. The dancers maintain balance and avoid dizziness by snapping their heads the opposite way with each rotation, realigning their inner head balance, so they continue onward but are always looking backward.

19. "We Real Cool" also lays on the repetition following on the trail of high-flying heeled shoes.

20. In the "Shattered Histories" section that opens the *Stranger Than Kindness* book (2020) Cave presents a vision of matter tied to the momentum of space, its symbology carrying fatalistic tones: "the pieces of you spin apart, a million little histories, propelling themselves away at a tremendous rate. they become like the hurtling stars, points of retreating light, separated only by your roaring need and the distant sky itself."

21. The hanging star or rings of Saturn's rings offer something to hold onto, the child's dream depends upon it. Later on, Cave coins the vision of the child leaving the bucket and space on the beach and going up to the sun.

22. A fan would ask Cave about the meaning of his lyric from the song "Hollywood," "the kid drops his bucket and spade / and climbs into the sun," which Cave refers to as "two short lines that draw to an abrupt and brutal halt the main body of the epic song" as the moment of the child's death, the passage from this world to a place beyond. Red Hand Files #202, July 2022.

23. Across *Ghosteen* Cave focuses on elemental feelings and metaphysical states to describe visions taking place beyond time. Shedding concrete details, he reaches for fantastical symbolism. Imagery of horses, ships, and trees, and forces of fire, space, and stars all become vehicles for meaning under the aegis of life, God, and death.

24. Cave would reveal this lyric in the first issue of the Red Hand Files in September 2018, leaving us to wonder about the mark left by the spear of destiny that remains a wound that weeps for Christ as to drink the tears of his blood.

25. Mark Mordue, "Nick Cave: 'Being forced to grieve openly basically saved us,'" *Irish Times*, May 8, 2017.

26. Bowie makes good use of this on the title track of his *Station to Station* album.

27. Cave entertains the unreal but very true hope of return that people in grief often feel, that the longed-for person will walk back through the door. We

hear their voice, weighted by pained expectation and moving through the spaces they once passed through, surrounded objects still wreathed by their touch.

28. The Little Prince stands awaiting return of the strange visitor to whom he unpacks and explains his life, performing the same actions and expecting them to yield a different result: they have gone, they shall return—science does not accommodate the beautiful irrationality of hope against all other evidence to the contrary.

29. Like Bowie's circular "Rebel Rebel" glam stomp riff slowed to a death march crawl moving toward ecstatic revelation in the song's close.

30. Ellis is often self-effacing of his native musical intuition and ability. Like the toy Casio keyboard Cave used to compose many songs for *The Boatman's Call*, Ellis shows how the right take and a willful openness masquerading as *naivete* can produce music as forceful and involving as the most highly trained classical musician, evoking John Lennon's famous quote that as an artist he could take any instrument and get some kind of tune out of it.

31. The "real" lyre of the song was created by Warren Ellis butchering instruments: "It did spring from my dear friend and co-Bad Seed Warren Ellis buying a mandolin and sticking it through an amp and a distortion pedal and playing this music that did make the stones weep in agony. And he created this really excruciating sound, this really beautiful sound. And I guess I embellished it a little and turned it into 'The Lyre of Orpheus.'" Brian Orloff, "Nick Cave Sings the Blues," *Rolling Stone*, October 22, 2004.

32. Cave would mention the book *Late Victorian Holocausts* as recounting the famine caused by repeated drought and imperialist policies of food hoarding and mismanagement of native populations at the end of the nineteenth century. As Victoria's empire entered its peak decline it turned its back on the welfare of its colonial territories. Extracting resources turning it into wealth at the cost of human lives.

33. Wikipedia promises free information, crowd sourced and increasingly unbound by license and authorship, the machine of ideas becomes self-regulating, floating, and indistinct from humankind.

34. The poem, like Cave's song, suggests humankind as truant from God. On Genius.com the user "Rusholmeruffian" nails the friction of the juveniles in the poem as "all youthful swagger, streaked with a profound nihilism." The poem would later be banned perhaps for its defiant antiauthoritarian stance or imagined allusions to premarital underage sex.

35. Oxford Dictionaries declared "posttruth" as its 2016 international word of the year, reflecting what it called a "highly charged" political twelve months. It is defined as an adjective relating to circumstances in which objective facts are less influential in shaping public opinion than emotional appeals, a slow surrender to sensual impressions that "We Real Cool" seems to warn against.

36. Owen, Antony. *The Dreamer of Samuel Vale House* (Brighton: Pighog Press, 2012).

37. Every tech revelation is a false dawn. The philosopher Martin Heidegger argues that technology is noninstrumental, not simply a means to an end, and not just a human activity; it is a way of viewing the world that exists independently of humans. It does not work toward truth but "enframes" our worldview, limiting us to a tech-centered way of thinking. Beyond the verb "to Google" the brand is no longer just a web search engine but a systemic monopoly of thought as a way of seeing. In a 2008 *Guardian* interview Cave would brush off questions about his past with the command to "Google it."

38. Formulated by the German physicist and Nobel laureate Werner Heisenberg in 1927, the uncertainty principle states that we cannot know both the position and speed of a particle, such as a photon or electron, with perfect accuracy; the more we nail down the particle's position, the less we know about its speed and vice versa. Equally, this can become the overexamined life.

39. Cave's title and refrain is most likely borrowed from Flannery O'Connor's short story "Everything That Rises Must Converge." O'Connor's title is likely borrowed from Teilhard de Chardin.

Chapter 9

1. This image echoes the forlorn state of Adam and Eve suddenly feeling themselves cold and naked outside of God and the paradise Garden of Eden, when before they had been happy and free without shame.

2. Cave's spare piano echoes the dynamic force of Nina Simone's rolling notes of "Plain Gold Ring," an underrated influence on his piano style.

3. Most apocalyptic scenarios deal either with too much water or the lack of it, the fulcrum of environmental disaster, where films like *The Road* present a vision of the slow death of the planet, becoming a vacuum devoid of life.

4. Examining different classical paintings of Christ on the cross at Calvary point and the Mount of Olives, Connor Harrison finds a spiritual resonance beyond the representational image: "It's in that silence where art finds us out, within which it is impossible to lie." Connor Harrison, "My Own Personal Jesus," *The New Critique*, 2021, https://newcritique.co.uk/2021/04/05/essay-my-own-personal-jesus-connor-harrison/.

5. 1 Kings 19:12, King James Version (KJV 1900).

6. As shown by the Red Hand Files, Cave is not averse to the constructive possibilities offered by technology in its potential to connect with other people in a real and meaningful way. Cave would mention that he remains curious, anxious, and interested in what people think of his work. When *Ghosteen* was launched online via a series of connected YouTube videos that expanded the album artwork into a series of spectral and ethereal visuals Cave felt he had done

justice to the universe in which the album existed. But he was not prepared for the openly hostile comments from people who simply didn't like the record. As open as he was to criticism, no doubt he was unprepared for the number of cowardly keyboard warriors spilling vomit emojis all over his new music. But we cannot blame the technology entirely, rather it is the humans working behind the machines that drive misuse and abuse.

7. On the issue of climate change, the philosopher Peter Singer points out that the industrialized nations have a moral obligation to curb the decline and should always be doing more than they are to make a change.

Chapter 10

1. Shot by Bleddyn Butcher in Stepney in 1985 it is a surreal image, given Cave's gentle alienation from American culture filtered through his own lens. Cave naturally felt more at ease behind the piano but side from Little Richard and Jerry Lee Lewis he still knew it was the guitar that was the true symbol of rock and roll and beyond that the blues.

2. Fittingly Cave would call The Stooges' *Raw Power* "the album that changed my life," claiming he bought it sometime in 1975 on the basis of its cover image of a uniformly shirtless Iggy's silver hair and mascaraed eyes staring beyond the infinite. The protopunk force would also be present on earlier Bad Seeds track "Deanna."

3. Cave came to Dylan late, noticing his later more meditative albums, *Slow Train Coming* above the earlier 1960s hipster rebellion of the suits, speed, and shades era, just when he broke away from socially conscious folk to beat poet hipster skat of surreal escapism and broken grammar.

4. Though Cave was never ashamed of appearing to be somehow out of fashion or gauche, as evidenced in the odd balladry present on album cover *Kicking Against the Pricks*. Note Cave's decision to cover the Tom Jones song "Sleeping Annaleah."

5. Incidentally it would seem to confirm the postmodern car crash that was the rise of punk alongside Elvis' seemingly inevitable decline as the twin bookends for the beginning of the end of the twentieth century, as confirmed by the writings of Greil Marcus. Bleddyn Butcher recalls that by 1985 Elvis was already seven years dead, a time when it seemed, for everyone but Cave, that Elvis was something of a joke figure where bands such as The Clash rejected him as the old order well past it at his death and the opposite of what punk's short fuse intended to be.

6. Johnston, Ian. *Bad Seed: The Biography of Nick Cave*. London: Little, Brown Book Group, 1996.

7. Cave himself seems to have bristled where The Birthday Party were caught between the definitions of punk and goth, feeling no real affinity with any genre

but "good music." Postpunk is more about demarcating an era in which The Birthday Party was swept up. In much the same way that The Bad Seeds had to be shelved as "alternative," the band was certainly never indie in sound or outlook. Postpunk is nonetheless a gathering together of ever more disparate and highly original bands—after punk—the brilliant deluge.

8. On *Ghosteen*'s opening track "Spinning Song" the Elvis origin story of "Tupelo" becomes the passage of the original rock god whose saintly place can only be undertaken alongside his queen and later enshrined in death. This is also Cave, his own thick, black back-combed hair once menacingly struck into vicious spikes, more recently smoothed out, flattened. He has abdicated from the position of outrage he once felt compelled to uphold.

9. Greil Marcus sees both the joy and tragedy of 'The King' in the Elvis impersonator; the stand in for his own persona became so iconic that he could only watch from the side of the stage as others cavorted in rhinestone jumpsuits, wraparound pensioner shades, and a giant black quaff borrowed from a backcombed feral Alsatian. Alongside the iconic vision of Jesus, white skinned (!) wearing a loincloth and long hair, he is trapped in the popular imagination.

10. When asked about his own funeral, Cave mentioned that he would be happy enough with Elvis songs: "to be ushered into the next world by the voice of the greatest rock 'n' roll singer of them all. Kentucky Rain, that's what I'd like, Kentucky Rain and How Great Thou Art—Elvis singing gospel, with heaven and all its angels listening."

11. In "Mutiny in Heaven" Cave feels a rat creep over his soul, declaring "as thought as wassa back down in the ghetto!" the proto "voice" of Euchrid rearing his mute statue head into view.

12. Elsewhere Elvis sings the field spiritual turned gospel "Nobody Knows." The song sings of the troubles on the far side of slavery that cannot be understood unless one has lived through them. But where the song and Elvis' performance succeeds, like all great music, is for each singer to express their own struggle and strife through a song, hearing something of themselves in it.

13. Andrew Male, "The Bad & The Beautiful: 50 Greatest Songs of Nick Cave"/"Something Monstrous," *Mojo*, no. 319 (June 2020).

14. Male, "The Bad & The Beautiful."

15. Tom Engelshoven, "Nick Cave," *Oor Magazine*, January 2021.

16. Interview with the author 2020.

17. Joe Jackson. *"Nick Cave and Joe Jackson 1994. Two Elvis 'nuts' discuss the King in all his glory."* youtube.com/watch?v=YXwyPDXeIMM.

18. Greil Marcus, *Mystery Train: Images of America in Rock 'N' Roll Music* (New York: Plume, 1975 [2015 edition]).

19. The ghost of "Tupelo" would be revisited in disaster-hit cities such as New Orleans' hurricane Katrina in 2005, bringing flood in its wake, or the

lifeless vistas of abandoned Detroit. Such real-life sites of devastation and decline would later become shoot locations for the 2009 film *The Road*. These scenes might have had an influence on Cave's vision for "Anthrocene" and setting of emotional desolation and environmental self-destruction.

20. On "Red Right Hand" Cave further transposes his hometown into the exotic-seeming American terms of the wrong sides of the tracks, trading ghettos, the barrio, the Bowery, and slums for small-town rural Australia.

21. Bushfires would ravage plains and mountaintops, only for the eucalyptus trees to return from ashes, one of the hardiest and most resilient plants to first emerge after a fire, n their shedding of bark they are also one the most flammable.

22. Sam Leith, "'Loss is a thing that we become': Nick Cave on Grief, Faith and Why He's a Conservative," *The Spectator*, December 2022. Cave's work prefigured the Australian apocalyptic wasteland movie witnessed from *Mad Max* (1979) to *The Rover* (2014), the new spaghetti Western taken to fresh extremes of hopelessness and violence.

23. The phrase "he went on down the road" is repeated throughout Cormac McCarthy's novel *Child of God* (1968) in which the jilted misanthrope Lester Ballard keeps walking through worsening situations toward the center of his seeming inevitable downward spiral.

24. First published in 1959 as *The Children*, it was repackaged for modern publication in 1971 to tie in with the movie produced by director by Nicolas Roeg. It takes a controversial tack from the source material and deals more explicitly with the loss of innocence of the children removed from white Western civilization alongside the nascent sexuality of the teenage girl character and her difficult relationship with the aboriginal boy.

25. Another echo from *Child of God*, where McCarthy defines his protagonist with the line, "A malign star kept him," suggesting the image of stars are bad omens and signs of misguided people such as the haunted character of "The Good Son."

26. Cave makes a further allusion to "Red Right Hand" with an invisible stain of blood that he feels others can see casts him into guilt.

27. Cave speaks about Dalton's "perfect" version of "Something on My Mind" playing in the car, where days turn into night. He was forced to pull over in tears noting that The Bad Seeds had always been trying to capture something of that song's essence in their music.

28. *Pod Like a Hole* podcast, Nick Cave and the Bad Seeds: Henry's Dream, Thursday Feb 18, 2021.

29. Roddick, Nick. "Ballad of the Wild Boys." *Sight And Sound*, February 2012.

NOTES

30. There is parallel history of colonial violence between Australia and the United States, with imperial powers seeking to overcome indigenous populations of the land who were moved on, murdered, imprisoned, enslaved, ghettoized, displaced onto reservations, pushed to the bad side of the tracks, the line in the earth that demarcated an outer zone of wilderness, very literally beyond the pale. The biographer and music journalist Mark Mordue acknowledged this as a factor in the birth of the Australian nation but notes that for Cave America remained a dreamscape onto which he projected his own fantasies, making his adaptation of the blues distinctly apolitical.

31. "Saint Huck" becomes a parable of the rural-urban clash when the country boy wanders into the city. Perhaps there is a parallel here for Cave moving into the punk scene of Melbourne from Wangaratta. This blind idealism would later become the dream of shifting to the Californian dream and the permanent Teflon sheen of Hollywood. The New York end of this sucks up poor Larry (Lazarus). Like the madness of Genesis' *The Lamb Lies Down on Broadway*, the innocent is swallowed up in tides of shit and swill, the inner city swill of temptation and exploitation.

32. Testament to this, the film was retitled for the global market as *Outback*. Like *Walkabout* before, the film was somewhat misrepresented as the total rural Australian experience, fulfilling cliches and giving the audiences what they wanted to see of Australia.

33. "I wanted to recreate what I felt and saw—the heat, the sweat, the dust, the flies," the film's director Ted Kotcheff said, pushing his audience to be "unconsciously sweating." Using harsh lighting and stripping all "cool" colors out of the set to emphasize an oppressive palette of red, orange, and brown heat, it was as manipulative/exploitative as it was explorative. Such was the overriding power of the landscape's image that the film was rebranded *Outback* in the United States.

34. Placing himself as an Australian first and foremost and forever, Cave would spend significantly more time in the old country of ancient Europe and in the upside down urban dreamscape of London and Brighton, both mythic and humdrum, set beneath the intemperate English weather. Though the sharper edges of Cave's accent still cut through his most anglophone phrasing.

35. Cave was offered to rewrite a script for the film owned by Ridley Scott but he found the task of converting the book's relentless force into a movie narrative overwhelming: "And it wasn't working, the rewrite, so I just sent it back and said, 'I don't want to be the guy who fucked it up. You can be the director who fucks up *Blood Meridian*, but I don't want to be the writer.'"

36. The Judge alludes to the fact that man is the natural predator of humanity. Everything built will inevitably return to ruin, one generation after another.

37. Nick Cave's work would resonate alongside the writing of Cormac McCarthy. The two seem to walk almost hand in hand, one artist reflecting the other. Where McCarthy would exploit death as the true nature of life, his bleak projections still allow for the struggle around moral codes, Cave would continue to affirm a spiritual conviction both because and in spite of the evil found throughout the world.

38. "I tried to get the rights to Billy the Kid," says John Hillcoat. "I met Ondaatje in London when he was up for the Booker Prize for The English Patient. But because The English Patient suddenly became enormous, someone bought up all his books." He would turn toward the Cave-scripted *The Proposition* instead. Roddick, Nick. "Ballad of the Wild Boys." Sight And Sound February 2012.

39. These tensions are echoed in the colonization of Australia and the use and abuse of indigenous aboriginal people as slaves.

40. Historian Fredrick Jackson Turner put forward the "Frontier Thesis," arguing that the frontier was the lifeblood of American democracy, settling and surviving on the bleeding edge of America's western progress, cultivating a sense of egalitarianism that pitted every man for himself in harsh individualism.

41. Professor Aaron Gwyn, Episode VIII: The Fire Which God Has Put There The Meaning of Blood Meridian's Epilogue, 28 Jan 28, 2023.

42. Speaking at the Southbank Centre in 2022 Cave casually dropped in that Morrissey happened to be one of the greatest ever songwriters we have. It is hard not to think of his line, "The songs that saved your life," from that knowingly comparing his own discography with the brevity of The Smiths, both worked within their powerful niche.

43. In a *Guardian* interview Warren Ellis would praise the celestial music of Alice Coltrane, his all-time hero, contrasting making music with meditation, art without objective, allowing a song to become what it needs to be.

44. In religious concerns there is liminality in sacred spaces between heaven and earth. With their own sense of time it can also be said that in liturgical acts we can transcend earthly shapes to another place, in much the same way that Cave talks about the intensely physical but spiritual elevation of the rock concert where both band and audience, preacher and congregation are as one body and mind, sharing a mutual experience.

Chapter 11

1. Cave would refer to certain passage that he struggled to do justice in trying to explain or reword them: "a scene of Christ walking through a crowd, and a young girl, who has had an issue of blood for 13 years, walks through the throng and takes hold of the end of Christ's robe. He stops the crowd and says, 'Why did you touch my robe?' She shrinks back, 'I touched it because I've had

this issue of blood.' And Christ heals her. I found this to be very powerful." Lindzee Smith, Nick Cave Interview, *BOMB*, April 1, 1990.

2. BBC Radio 6, Nick Cave interview with Jarvis Cocker, September 2010.

3. Nick Cave, *And the Ass Saw the Angel* (London: Black Spring Press, 1988).

4. O'Connor would spend much of her adult life using crutches before succumbing to her illness aged just thirty-nine.

5. As Butler points out, the saints, like Jesus, were all too human. The example of their lives mirror our common struggles: "They were once what we are now, travelers on earth. They had the same weaknesses we have. We have difficulties; so had the saints."

6. Cave, a distinctly unorthodox Christian, often mocks dogma while revering aspiration of religion and spirituality without demanding the fulfillment of strict principles.

7. Cave makes much use of the more archaic term "issue" to describe the flow of blood or other bodily fluids. Again he is rooted in the language of the Holy Bible.

8. French: the *little death*.

9. Full name: Church of the Immaculate Heart of Mary.

10. In this passage Christ has returned back to life where the rock is rolled away from Jesus' tomb but it is found empty. Then two of his disciples travel on the road to Emmaus and a stranger walks beside them, recounting scripture. They eventually realize it is Jesus. Feeling that they have seen a ghost, they come to understand that even when he had died, he never left them.

11. The song is infused with the spirit of John Donne's metaphysical poetry, using allusions to sex against the metaphor of the cold, hard stone body of the church, then bringing them together to realize the weightless spirituality the physical world represents. Cave sees the undying statues of the apostles and wishes himself in their place: silent, immovable, no longer vulnerable to pain.

12. While the latent eroticism of Christianity liturgy, expressed in the continuance of life and death, would be an inspiration for Cave, he would move away from the murky relationship of lovely creatures as performative bodies and find a new sincerity in his later love songs. Echoing the nobler sentiments of "Song of Songs," a hymn to love and sex within the church of marriage, Cave brings lust back around to a duty-bound act toward procreation and the continued lifeblood of the family.

13. Known for the phrase, "Let nothing perturb you, nothing frighten you. All things pass. God does not change. Patience achieves everything." The expression "This Too Shall Pass" / "All Things Pass" is sometimes attributed to her. This is an adage thought to occur from Persia; often thought to appear directly in the Bible, the phrase is altered somewhat in meaning and language: "And ye

shall hear of wars and rumors of wars: see that ye be not troubled: for all these things must come to pass, but the end is not yet." Implying a further fatalism that bad things must happen in the world, the original expression is more of the Buddhist leaning: all things good or ill will come to an end, and yet others will also take their place (Matthew 24:6).

14. Cave would express admiration for deeply traditional German gothic painters, such as Stefan Lockner, and would later reflect how in art school he was scolded for the "sleazy" erotic paintings he produced, pushing the boundaries of "art."

15. From The Bad Seeds' first album, *From Her to Eternity*.

16. Young man's quest, etc.

17. Aussie phrase: "you little ripper" Cave having fun with a cultural cliché at his own expense in England "go on my son" or "you beauty"—a shout at the races.

18. *Stranger in a Strange Land*, BBC Southbank Show, 2003.

19. Hugo Race: "For Nick, From Her To Eternity was an important record. He had to make a break with the past, as well as do something that didn't reflect The Birthday Party but had the same energy." "Nick Cave's 30 Best Songs," *Uncut*, February 2015, https://www.uncut.co.uk/features/nick-cave-s-30-greatest-songs -chosen-by-the-bad-seeds-his-famous-fans-and-cave-himself-37741/4/.

20. As in the song "Ol' Man River," it keeps on rolling, relentlessly. In Cave's song it is a wave of life in flux met with unending tears.

21. When asked about the Hieronymus Bosch–style density of the text, Cave referred instead to Cameron's imagery plastered across his walls: "Rather than Bosch, I'd prefer to say that if there were certain images that I used when I was writing the book, they would be Julia Margaret Cameron's photographs—I put one on the cover of the book." Smith, Nick Cave interview.

22. Already in 1865 the rough-worn sepia tone of her photographs' false nostalgia was criticized by the *Photographic Times* as being "smudged, torn, dirty, undefined, and in some cases almost unreadable." Her aesthetic shares some of Cave and The Bad Seeds' scratchy and scuffed aesthetic of their earliest music, brilliantly performed but in the recording/capturing there is a brittle friction to spite surface perfection.

23. One of the most interesting commentaries on the Bible points out that that there might certainly have been real people bearing the same names, such as the apostles Mark et al., but that details of real events, a crucifixion, someone being baptized, for example, are elevated to miracle status. One on reading the Bible is full of wonderful stories that give us something to believe in beyond the everyday.

24. It's a neat thing that Cameron also photographed Alice Liddell and her sisters, the love interest and inspiration for Lewis Carroll's *Alice in Wonderland*.

Carroll was in love with the girl and often photographed her in various states of undress, as well as proposing marriage to her father. He was later disinvited from visiting the family again.

25. Venus is the mother of Cupid, god of love in a number of cultures. He shoots arrows fatalistically, making people fall in love.

26. Peter Sierksma, "Sometimes I think, this is God's voice speaking to me." Nick Cave. Trouw, 18th June 1997 (Dutch)

27. See also the solipsistic view of Judge Holden in *Blood Meridian*, an ubermensch who paints himself into a corner as both the first and the last man, a god on earth.

28. Jesus' own uncertainty about whether or not he was a conduit for God, a shadow cast by the holy ghost, or simply a man like any other who has been raised up to the position of messiah or false prophet. This plays into the heart of the fundamental Christian crisis of faith and shows the existential humility of Jesus. I was always struck by the metaphor of God as water, ice, steam. What John Donne refers to as the "three-person'd God," in his wild mutability God is never entirely one thing. This makes him unknowable.

29. David Brown and Gavin Hopps, *The Extravagance of Music* (New York: Springer Publishing, 2018).

30. In "The Mercy Seat" the left and right hands trade blows of "good" and "evil" bearing invisible stains. We have to allow for individual responsibility, albeit under God's eye.

31. William Blake shows Job as a man now in fear of life, in fear of loving in case his affection should wreak misfortune upon those he loves dearest, but still a step below the sour turn of Midas with wealth and sudden power, driven to bitterness to pay for his greed with forced humility.

32. Continuing the meta-contrivance of "I Am the Walrus" and "Glass Onion," he states, "I was the walrus," a reference to Lewis Carroll's poem from *Alice Through the Looking Glass*—each character is thought to represent Eastern and Western modes of spiritual faith. Both express suffering and the cruelty of kindness in the way they lead the oysters as gathered believers on a merry walk to be eaten by their maker and keeper.

33. A possible allusion to the threat posed by Islamic extremist suicide bombers as the next bringers of doom, with a reward for their services commonly noted as one of the promises of paradise listed in the Qur'an being a string of virgins ripe for sex.

34. From pain and struggle we should be led (in order to lead ourselves) toward a better life. Romans 8:18, KJV: "For I reckon that the sufferings of this present time are not worthy to be compared with the glory which shall be revealed in us." As if self-fulfillment might please God but also act as confirmation of following a holy and just path, true to ourselves and to others.

35. "Push The Sky Away" - Compare the initial chord sequence of from "Vincent de Maio" on the *West Of Memphis* documentary soundtrack they have very similar progression, about one year apart, the soundtrack can be seen as a dry run –a test run for emergent sounds–from a flood to a song about resurgence and regeneration.

36. Red Hand Files #197, June 2022.

37. For me one of the best songs Cave has recorded, it is more an outtake from the Dirty Three, Warren Ellis' former band. It manages to be crushingly bleak in its outlook for the hopes of mankind (after Jesus) but also deeply moving and uplifting as Ellis' soaring violin tears a hole in the sky, insanely beautiful but laden with doom to look upon.

38. Jack Barron, "The Needle and the Damage Done," *NME*, May 1988.

39. The joke of "Lazarus" is whether he should in fact dig upward, out from death and into life, not down toward hell and his continued suffering. Cave makes a casual nod "upstairs" to heaven but acknowledges that we can never truly know what is going on in God's kingdom.

40. Nick Cave, *The Flesh Made Word* (London: Ellipsis Press, 1996).

41. An odd similarity to Lou Reed's "Perfect Day" ("There Is a Kingdom"), the rousing chorus brings in the widescreen voice, an act of conviction, but also a hopeful calling, as if singing up to God himself.

42. The death row inmate of "The Mercy Seat" mired in psychosis is struck by objects become animate and alive with God's glory with a defining image of the face of Jesus in his bowl of soup, a welcome unto death or a banishment from life. J. D. Salinger's character Zooey Glass is remembered by her brother drinking a glass of milk expressing an incredible oneness with life (in its finitude) and the eternal (in the reach of dreams, emotions, and ideas).

43. Father Brown stories allow someone to wander the earth in sin, only to be pulled back by God with a single twitch upon the thread. The image of religious bondage is as powerful as the supposed self-enlightenment that spirituality should offer us. See the Evelyn Waugh novel *Brideshead Revisited*.

44. The 1966 novel *Silence* by Shūsaku Endō tells the story of two Portuguese Jesuit priest missionaries who venture to feudal Japan to find their mentor who has gone missing and to spread the word of God to an underground network of Japanese. The priests are visited by religious doubts discovering that their former mentor has apostatized, a rejection of faith performed by stepping on the *fumi-e*, a carved icon of Christ. The priests struggle with the spiritual silence of God; he neither speaks nor answers. The novel resolves that true faith is its own reward.

45. Barbara Ellen, "It's Hip to Be Hateful," *The Observer*, May 5, 1998.

46. Andrew Male, "The Bad & The Beautiful: 50 Greatest Songs of Nick Cave"/"Something Monstrous," *Mojo*, no. 319 (June 2020).

NOTES

Chapter 12

1. Pier Paolo Pasolini would make a film based on St. Francis' influence, spreading the word of God and mediating between the poor and powerful: *Uccellacci e Uccellini (The Hawks and the Sparrows)* (1966). The more literal translation of the film's title reflects the true state of nature: "Birds of Prey and Little Birds."

2. Later on 2008's "Moonland" Cave apes the groove and lazy summer guitar tone from The Isley Brothers' "Summer Breeze," Cave adopting lounge lizard bongos for a lover lost in the city unable to find the girl he wants, hoping that she needs him as much as he needs her.

3. On the track "Black Crow King" Cave presents the leader of the birds watching "his subjects" slaughtered and maimed by man. In his observations on death he begins to see all life with the wan killer's eye.

4. On so many songs the melancholy of death would be embodied into a deeper sadness: a black dog rubbing its muzzle to the window pane clouding the view with its eager breath or the cawing dark bird tap-tapping at the glass. The collective murder of crows stake out the dirt grave of Sorrow the horse, waiting to feast on his still staring eyes. In Max Porter's *Grief Is the Thing with Feathers* the crow leaves emblematic feathers on the pillow, a stalking shadow. The people left behind are as much haunted by memory as by the domineering presence of negative feeling.

5. Perhaps a nod to St. Francis of Assisi and his "Sermon to Birds," where all animals are both loving and beloved without doubt or question.

6. In "The Death of Bunny Munro," Cave perhaps hints at his own struggle with the seagulls of Brighton and how much he (Bunny) hates them.

7. The bird is so named for the way it feeds, hanging a worm or insect from a tree branch and gradually picking parts of its flesh away. Not all birds are so innocent or gentle as we might have them be.

8. An easy comparison here would be the anatomically evocative flower paintings of Georgia O'Keeffe, equally familiar, wild, and exotic, but also unknowable. They are straightforward images beautifully wrought that nonetheless manage to intimate a desire to be unfurled and admired.

9. Kruger, Debbie "Nick Cave: The Songwriter Speaks." *Weekend Australian*, July 30, 2005.

10. Red Hand Files #19, January 2019.

11. A distant echo from the body of the fly plucked apart in a game of she-loves-me-not, 1984's "Wings Off Flies."

12. Cave would mention in his list of beloved books Macgregor Skene's *A Flower Book for the Pocket*, a compact guide to flora and fauna. If not a book that Cave might carry about with him in nature, in search of beautiful things, then at least a point of reference.

13. "Gates to the Garden" is set in Bury-St-Edmonds where Cave walks past St. Edmundsbury Cathedral and makes a goth-like visit to the site. Where the church rises up the graveyard sinks downwards.

14. On a one-page note jotted on a letter-headed page from the Sir Stamford Hotel in Sydney titled THINGS TO REMEMBER Cave would record a list of influences and cultural touchstones, noting several kinds of flowers and creatures including hyenas, baboons, penguins, robins, sparrows, dandelions, camelias "any really, except lilies, don't like lilies much—stain clothes."

15. Gentle, fair and fleeting; the prettiness of flowers is their own curse, and ours to watch them die.

16. Cave would base the song on an eighteenth-century traditional Appalachian murder ballad made famous by The Everly Brothers, "Down in the Willow Garden," also known as "Rose Connelly." In the original a girl is presumed pregnant and murdered at the behest of the male lover's father, with the promise of money. Instead he hangs for his crime. As if in tribute Cave and The Bad Seeds would cover the song as the B side to "Wild Rose" with Conway Savage on vocals.

17. The poet Gabriel Garcia Lorca cites a Spanish duende lyrical song, perhaps an influence on Cave's use of the rose, a device of death and doom. Lorca speaks to the rose garden as a place of death, the cutting of flowers allows their bloom to flourish but all too briefly.

18. Ophelia is spurned by Hamlet as he pretends to be mad to uncover the plot of his father's murder, though he secretly cares for her. She chooses to drown herself rather than to live without love. As a tragedy the play is preoccupied by death, loss, and grief, overshadowed by the loss of Shakespeare's son Hamnet, after whom it is named in dark tribute.

19. It is unclear if Cave is being super literal here and talking about the genus of the Flame Tree. Peter Conrad notes Cave seeing the transmutation of holy metaphors into the raw hinterland of home, trading one extreme landscape for another. Australian artist Tony Clark painted a specially commissioned triptych, *Sections from Clark's Myriorama*, showing a row of stark burning trees, for the cover of The Bad Seeds' best-of album (1998). Cave wrote in the journal Art and Australia, "it looks like the Garden of Gethsemane seen through the conflagrating prism of the Australian outback." Peter Conrad, "The Good Son," *The Monthly*, August 2009.

20. In *The Road* trees persist only as deadwood, petrified into bone. Joel Mayward notes that alongside the route of purgatory the man follows with the boy, trees are mirrored in the silenced telegraph poles reaching tall as giant crucifixes. With all other plant and animal life long gone, they stand as totemic symbols for the extinction of humanity as the end of all life.

NOTES

21. Cave is perhaps drawing on American history of trees used for lynching, or even further back to Scottish medieval times where the "Dule Tree" would be a favored hanging site or used as a "gibbet," from which a dying criminal or their body would be displayed as a warning to others. Sometimes these sites might also become "trees of lamentation or grief" where family would gather to mourn a loss.

22. This resonance is continued on "Sad Waters," which features a line from a 1965 country song covered by Tom Jones, Elvis, and Johnny Cash, "Green Green Grass of Home." As a man wakes from a dream to face his execution, he remembers his dear Mary, "Hair of gold and lips like cherries." Actually about a man due to be executed, he longs to touch the grass of his homeland again and will later be buried beneath it under the shade of a tree.

23. "Strange Fruit" is a song written and composed by Abel Meeropol (under his pseudonym Lewis Allan) and recorded by Billie Holiday in 1939. The lyrics were drawn from a poem by Meeropol published in 1937.

24. The singer Odetta would record her own version of the 1920 traditional ballad "The Maid Freed from the Gallows" as "Gallows Pole" (1957) in which a woman about to be hung awaits members of her family to deliver gold or silver in order to pay off the hangman and let her go. Finally her sweetheart arrives with money and she is freed.

25. Straub's novel *The Throat* presents the image of the tree as restorative: "Once the pieces of the murdered man buried beneath the juniper tree called out and caused the children to bring them together; once a dead man was wrongly accused of terrible crimes. And once, when the parts of the dismembered man were brought together at the foot of the tree, the whole man rose and spoke, alive again, restored."

26. Peter Straub. *The Juniper Tree and Other Blue Rose Stories* New York: Subterranean Press, 2010

27. The passive-aggressive tone of instruction with the abuser planting their voice within the mind of the victim, as if speaking for them, is present in "Loverman" where Cave has the woman he desires be raped and murdered by the narrator, ending with the belief that they are the answer to one another's prayers.

28. Interview with Bill Sheehan, Peter Straub. Straub, Peter. *The Juniper Tree and Other Blue Rose Stories* (New York: Subterranean Press, 2010).

29. On "Papa Won't Leave You, Henry" the song struggles under the weight of rainfall—water ruins everything—so heavy he swipes at it and nearly misses, like the mad drinker. It threatens to wash the soul away as it wears the world thin.

30. *Today's Lesson* podcast highlighted that the Mary of the song "Sad Waters" could refer to the saint, both chosen child and virgin mother. In parts of France she is called "the lady of the willow." The tale of the blaspheming man

cuts a willow on the way to Mass that gushes blood as a sign of his sin, for which he is encouraged to repent.

31. Huck's nod to the "everchanging neverchanging" river (via the River Elbe in Hamburg, Germany) is a reference to the Liffey of James Joyce's *Ulysses*, his modernist take of the original Odyssey that Cave combines into vision of the Deep South dissipation, full with its own trials and temptations.

32. Mark Mordue, *Boy on Fire: The Young Nick Cave* (New York: Atlantic Books, 2021).

33. The small town of Cave's birthplace Warracknabeal bears the aboriginal translation: "the place of big gums shading the water hole," a preecho of another place and time overshadowed by a memory.

34. Michael Odell. Nick Cave interview, *Q Magazine*, March 2005.

35. On "Breathless" Tom Doyle sees Cave separated from his beloved, so he looks for their spirit in the consolations of nature, the Proustian reflex bringing him back to Susie Bick. The song speaks to the echo of "Nature Boy" in the recurring halcyon image of her, a future ghost from a (then) unknown life together resurrected and brought back to life, forever revisiting the moment of falling in love at first sight as it continues to endure.

36. Red Hand Files #157, July 2021.

Chapter 13

1. In the 2001 film *The Devil's Backbone*, a character asks, "What is a ghost? A tragedy condemned to repeat itself time and again? An instant of pain, perhaps. Something dead which still seems to be alive. An emotion suspended in time."

2. Peter Watts, "His Dark Materials," *Uncut*, Take 273, February 2020.

3. Ben Foster who worked with Cave and Ellis on the string arrangements for the album noted *Ghosteen*'s immersive atmosphere: "to be taken into a world and seduced and comforted and challenged by it." Watts, "His Dark Materials."

4. This sonorous reflection is also there in Cave and Ellis' "Three Seasons in Wyoming" from the *North Wind* soundtrack, where a theremin synth sound edges out into feedback.

5. "A type of music composition that utilizes recorded sounds as raw material. Sounds are often modified through the application of audio signal processing and tape music techniques, and may be assembled into a form of sound collage." Wikipedia. Such approaches were already in common use, particularly by The Bad Seeds' German contemporaries Die Haut (The Skin) and Einstürzende Neubauten (Collapsing New Buildings).

6. No doubt inspired by Blixa Bargeld's Einstürzende Neubauten—the band who recorded inside the superstructure of a concrete flyover in Berlin—when Cave and the band discovered that The Jam had left behind some sheets

of corrugated metal in order to build a drum house trying to capture a more garage rock sound. The band used this as a tool of percussion beating it with mic stands. "The Mercy Seat" was built around hitting the strings of the bass guitar with drumsticks, which Cave noted became more of a dense chordal hum counterpointed by the slower half-paced hymn of the lyric.

7. Across *DIG!* scraped and scratched guitar and violin feedback hiss through the bared teeth of the mix, a continuation of Grinderman with Warren Ellis' hack and slash fuzzed mini guitar that suits his playing as a noise or groove instrument.

8. Andrew Male, "The Bad & The Beautiful: 50 Greatest Songs of Nick Cave"/"Something Monstrous," *Mojo*, no. 319 (June 2020).

9. Ryan Leas, "Warren Ellis on the Past, Present, & Future of Nick Cave & The Bad Seeds," *Stereogum*, November 17, 2021.

10. "Galleon Ship" and the song "Wind River," from the eponymous soundtrack (2017), share a long synth whistle, a tune blown across a great expanse through chill ribs of the scenery. The foreshadowing of these sounds shows how deeply a tune can be ingrained in the back of the mind, a quiet pulse Cave was waiting to become louder, instinctual, and intuitive, that he could move upon.

11. Susie Cave would post a comment on the Vampire's Wife "Stuff" blog, noting a "dark haunted presence" within the track. She would reveal it to be a recording of Marianne Faithfull reciting a May Sarton poem "Prayer Before Work." Susie notes that after much production work Warren Ellis "sunk it deep into the song to create the strange, grave subterranean force that lies beneath."

12. In a world that has grown tired of millionaire "rock stars" bored and stiff in their legend, always promising a return to the past, Cave has grown more eager to experiment and evolve, rather than be forced to change as a matter of style or cultural relevance. This establishes *Ghosteen* as an act of genuine self-expression.

13. On the track "Hollywood" Cave would allude to a cougar that possessed "a terrible engine of wrath for a heart." Loosely based on "P-22," a mountain lion who roamed Los Angeles and was famously filmed prowling under the Hollywood sign, it presented a creature at once fearsome, wounded, and afraid. He found the spirit of this image jotted down in some of his first lyrical notes toward Ghosteen. Red Hand Files #221, February 2023.

14. With its bucolic imagery of nature, "Breath of Life" shows a diverse abundance of color and shape, similar to the flowers of earlier Bad Seeds albums.

15. DuBois would make his name producing artwork for numerous Konami videogames, particularly the Castlevania series, switching from vampires to scenes of Christian revelation.

16. In one of the earliest Red Hand Files, he offers gentle consolation to a grieving woman: "Dread grief trails bright phantoms in its wake," he continued.

"These spirits are ideas, essentially. They are our stunned imaginations reawakening after the calamity. Like ideas, these spirits speak of possibility." Red Hand Files #6, October 2018.

17. The album's title is a combination of the word "ghost" and the Irish-language suffix "ín" (anglicized as "een"), which translates to English as "little," "small," or "benevolent." However, the title has often been misinterpreted solely as a portmanteau of "ghost" and "teen."

18.

> *THE PEOPLE YOU LOVE*
> *BECOME GHOSTS INSIDE*
> *OF YOU AND LIKE THIS*
> *YOU KEEP THEM ALIVE*

The poet and artist Robert Montgomery produced these lines in 2010 as one of his visual text-based artworks "People You Love," in memory of his late friend, Sean Watson, who was hit and killed by a car in 2004. Well known for his work appearing as billboard posters, flaming words, and in this case illuminated in a series of light bulbs, Montgomery suggests light to embody the spirit of a memory. It's the notion of a life eclipsed by memory to become purely metaphysical, also harking back to an e. e. cummings love poem that suggests, "I carry your heart / here with me / I carry it in my heart."

19. Nick Cave and Seán O'Hagan, *Faith, Hope and Carnage* (Edinburgh: Canongate, 2022).

20. Though Cave doesn't use the term "ghost," the notion of presence and absence recurs throughout his songs. On 1992's "Papa Won't Leave You, Henry" the ghost of a woman persists long after she has gone, left or dead, and on 1994's "Nobody's Baby Now" Cave tries to put another ghost memory to rest, but she endures; on both tracks these spirits move *through* him, tangled around his soul in a mystical way he cannot explain or divine.

21. *Stranger in a Strange Land*, BBC Southbank Show, 2003.

22. A spiritual sense beyond denomination. This calls upon Tennyson's plea to his dead wife *In Memoriam*: "be near me / when my light is low." The ebbing of a life-force fading, this call has its presence in the act of lighting a candle in prayer.

23. It has the leavened air of prayer, a lightness of touch that is at once vital and fading, never settling in Cave's words. It is the sensation we feel but cannot see is wreathed around the song, like the promise of smoke.

24. We can see this transaction in the image of Orpheus and Eurydice. She is returned from the dead and allowed to leave the underworld, but Orpheus cannot help but turn back, or perhaps Eurydice calls his name. She will say her final goodbye, knowing that he cannot accept the fate of her true death, where

there is no hand in his, he clings only to blind hope. Orpheus loves and loses, twice, he himself is returned to a kind of living death as the damaged survivor, his life a testament to his pain.

25. Leonard Cohen wrote a well-known email to a dying friend, Marianne Ihlen, who was also facing a terminal illness: "Know that I am so close behind you that if you stretch out your hand, I think you can reach mine." He was soon to pass on himself.

26. There is something of Cave's imagery of ascendance of children on *Ghosteen* that echoes the work of the reclusive Chicago artist Henry Darger, who spent much of his life working on a 15,145-page epic illustrated book about Christian children in a holy war called *The Story of the Vivian Girls, in What Is Known as the Realms of the Unreal, of the Glandeco-Angelinian War Storm, Caused by the Child Slave Rebellion*. Cave admired what he called the "terrible beauty" of Darger's imagery. Ginny Dougary, "The New Romantic," *The Times Magazine*, March 27, 1999. For more on Darger, see Olivia Laing's *The Lonely City* (London: Picador 2016).

27. Carl Jung argues that where the sea might represent the subconscious, and the beach the conscious mind, the artist's job is to walk the tide line, distilling the essence of the moment and drawing upon the recent past. "Cat Woman," *Guardian*, January 1999.

28. Keith Cameron, "The Kindness of Strangers," *Mojo*, July 2017.

29. A fan of David Lynch, Cave too has become an avid practitioner of meditation: less a place in which to conceive of nothing but to clear all conscious thought so that something else might emerge from a place of unknowing.

30. Peter Watts, "His Dark Materials," *Uncut*, Take 273, February 2020.

31. Sean O'Hagan. "Warren Ellis," *The Guardian*, August 2021.

32. Male, "The Bad & The Beautiful."

33. Leas, "Warren Ellis on the Past, Present, & Future of Nick Cave & The Bad Seeds."

34. Warren Ellis tried to buy Alice Coltrane's ashram in California but could not raise the funds in time. It too was swallowed up in the wildfires of 2019.

35. Male, "The Bad & The Beautiful."

36. On her "Stuff" blog on the Vampire's Wife website Susie Cave continues an occasional playlist, Songs of Devastation. Cave reads her an email sent to his Red Hand Files blog asking for new songs to be added to the list. She chooses "Shattered Ground." Cave agrees the song is "pretty fucking devastating." Susie argues that the song also worries her: "Because your songs predict the future." https://thevampireswife.com/blogs/stuff/warning-listen-at-own-risk-no-20.

37. Cave has said he found himself plagued with dreams that spilled over into daytime visions. At one point he was surprised to discover that the horses

with manes of burning fire were suddenly extinguished; like him, they are simply living earthen creatures of soul and spirit, but nonetheless grounded.

38. A title lifted from a line in W. B. Yeats' poem *The Second Coming*.

39. Speaking in 2008 Cave would note the intense sentimentality of *The Road*'s closing speech from the dying father to his son, but argued that it offset the fierce pessimism that dominates the film. This allowed for more emotional flexibility in the soundtrack, the two extremes counterbalancing one another.

40. Joel Mayward observes that in *The Road* the fire is sometimes expressed in the book as the presence of the child as the forebearer of the future, bringing innocence and wonder to the overarching experience and authority of the parent figure, expressed as a force of better things yet to come. Mayward, Joel. "Carrying the Fire." *Bright Wall/Dark Room*, August 2016.

41. This line carries a great span from Cave's early memory of his father telling him that beauty will save the world, mentioned in "Nature Boy" (2004), carried forward into the present of "Bright Horses" (2020).

42. Cave would present buildings or spiritual sites infused with reverence as places of deeper meaning. On "(Are You) The One That I've Been Waiting For?" he shows these great works created by love, sorrow, and willpower can equally be destroyed by those same forces to become tombstones and ruins, absent places haunted by the ghost of decay.

43. It is important to note that this show found The Bad Seeds near the end of a whole summer of touring, playing large-scale venues and headlining almost every major festival across Europe.

44. Chris Heath, "The Love and Terror of Nick Cave," *GQ Magazine*, April 27, 2017.

45. The one constant Cave finds to deliver us from ourselves is our capacity for the resilience of hope. As if to paraphrase Philip Larkin's poem "Days," in the extreme earnestness of "Love Letter" Cave's argument seems to highlight that hope is where we live, even if it is only to survive.

46. Leas, "Warren Ellis on the Past, Present, & Future of Nick Cave & The Bad Seeds."

BIBLIOGRAPHY

Books

Abbott, Jack Henry. *In the Belly of the Beast*. New York: Arrow Books, 1981.

Adamson, Barry. *Up Above the City, Down Beneath the Stars*. London: Omnibus Press, 2021.

Brown, David, and Gavin Hopps. *The Extravagance of Music*. New York: Springer Publishing, 2018.

Cave, Nick. *And the Ass Saw the Angel*. London: Black Spring Press, 1988.

Cave, Nick. *The Death of Bunny Munro*. Edinburgh: Canongate, 2009.

Cave, Nick. *Stranger Than Kindness*. Edinburgh: Canongate, 2020.

Cave, Nick, and Seán O'Hagan. *Faith, Hope and Carnage*. Edinburgh: Canongate, 2022.

Chrostowska, S. D. "A Passing Glance: Encounters with Deadness and Dying." In *Beauty and the Abject: Interdisciplinary Perspectives*, edited by L. Boldt-Irons, C. Federici, and E. Virgulti, 59–81. New York: Peter Lang, 2007.

Critchley, Simon. *On Bowie*. London: Serpent's Tail, 2006.

Davis, Mike. *Late Victorian Holocausts: El Niño Famines and the Making of the Third World*. London: Verso, 2000.

Douglass, Frederick. *The Narrative of the Life of Frederick Douglass*. Oxford: Oxford University Press, 2009.

Ellis, Waren. *Nina Simone's Gum*. London: Faber and Faber, 2021.

Gambotto-Burke, Antonella. *Apple: Sex, Drugs, Motherhood and the Recovery of the Feminine*. London: Pinter & Martin, 2022.

Hochschild, Adam. *King Leopold's Ghost: A Story of Greed, Terror and Heroism in Colonial Africa*. New York: Pan, 1998.

Holley, Santi Elijah. *Nick Cave and the Bad Seeds' Murder Ballads (33 1/3)*. New York: Bloomsbury, 2021.

Johnston, Ian. *Bad Seed: The Biography of Nick Cave*. London: Little, Brown Book Group, 1996.

Kinchin-Smith, Sam, ed. *Read Write [Hand]: A Multi-Disciplinary Nick Cave Reader*. New York: Silkworms Ink Press, 2011.

Kleist, Reinhard. *Mercy on Me*. New York: SelfMadeHero, 2017.

Marcus, Greil. *Dead Elvis: A Chronicle of a Cultural Obsession*. Cambridge, MA: Harvard University Press, 1991.

Marcus, Greil. *Mystery Train: Images of America in Rock 'N' Roll Music*. New York: Plume, 1975 (2015 edition).

Mordue, Mark. *Boy on Fire: The Young Nick Cave*. New York: Atlantic Books, 2021.

Nabokov, Vladimir. *Lectures on Literature*. London: Mariner Books, 2002.

Ondaatje, Michael. *The Collected Works of Billy the Kid*. Toronto: House of Anansi Press, 1970.

Ondaatje, Michael. *Coming Through Slaughter*. London: Bloomsbury, 2004.

Snow, Mat. *Nick Cave: Sinner Saint: The True Confessions*. Edited by Mat Snow. London: Plexus, 2015.

Steiner, Adam. *Into the Never: Nine Inch Nails and the Creation of* The Downward Spiral. Essex, Connecticut: Backbeat Books, 2020.

Steiner, Adam. *Silhouettes and Shadows: The Secret History of David Bowie's Scary Monsters (and Super Creeps)*. Essex, Connecticut: Backbeat Books, 2023.

Straub, Peter. *The Juniper Tree and Other Blue Rose Stories*. New York: Subterranean Press, 2010.

Taylor, Leila. *Darkly: Black History and America's Gothic Soul*. London: Repeater Books, 2019.

Articles

Anderson, Ryan. "A Peculiarly Australian Kind of Hell—Revisiting 'Wake in Fright.'" Quillette, September 28, 2021. https://quillette.com/2021/09/28/a-peculiarly-australian-kind-of-hell-revisiting-wake-in-fright/?fbclid=IwAR2qEeadOgFDcr-TvcxP3ToZeQ2gP7S_JjiAOIE7DI6bY3U_-vvzbw8Hqrs.

Baker, Jeff. "Interview: Literate Rocker Nick Cave." Oregon Live, September 24, 2008. https://www.oregonlive.com/books/2008/09/interview_literate_rocker_nick.html.

Barron, Jack. "The Needle and the Damage Done." *NME*, May 1988.

Cameron, Keith. "The Kindness of Strangers." *Mojo*, July 2017.

Cangioli, Andrea. "Killer Instinct." Berlin, 1988.

"Cat Woman," The *Guardian*, January 1999. https://www.theguardian.com/the observer/1999/jan/17/life1.lifemagazine.

Conrad, Peter. "The Good Son." *The Monthly*, August 2009. https://www.the monthly.com.au/issue/2009/august/1329283055/peter-conrad/good-son.

Crawford, Anwen. "The Monarch of Middlebrow." *Overland*, no. 197 (Summer 2009). https://overland.org.au/previous-issues/issue-197/feature-anwyn-crawford/.

Dougary, Ginny. "The New Romantic." *The Times Magazine*, March 27, 1999.

Dunn, Jancee. "Q&A: Nick Cave." *Rolling Stone*, August 25, 1994. https://www.rollingstone.com/music/music-news/qa-nick-cave-50111/.

Dushane, Tony. "NICK CAVE MONDAY #28: 'JACK THE RIPPER.'" *The Rumpus*, March 25, 2013. https://therumpus.net/2013/03/25/nick-cave-monday-28-jack-the-ripper/.

Ellen, Barbara. "It's Hip to Be Hateful." *The Observer*, May 5, 1998.

Engelshoven, Tom. "Nick Cave." *Oor Magazine*, January 2021.

Fearon, Faye. "Nick Cave's Hair." *GQ Magazine*, February 2020. https://www.gq-magazine.co.uk/grooming/article/nick-cave-hair.

Groom, Professor Nick. "Ten Best Nick Cave Lyrics." *The Line of Best Fit*, 2013. https://www.thelineofbestfit.com/features/lists/the-ten-best-nick-cave-lyrics-137079/2.

Gwyn, Professor Aaron. *Blood Meridian Substack*, 2023. https://bloodmeridian.substack.com/.

Harmon, Steph. "Nick Cave on PJ Harvey break-up: 'I was so surprised I almost dropped my syringe.'" *The Guardian*, August 2019. https://www.theguardian.com/music/2019/aug/28/nick-cave-on-pj-harvey-break-up-i-was-so-surprised-i-almost-dropped-my-syringe.

Harrison, Connor. "My Own Personal Jesus." *The New Critique*, 2021. https://newcritique.co.uk/2021/04/05/essay-my-own-personal-jesus-connor-harrison/.

Hattenstone, Simon. "Old Nick." *The Guardian*, February 2008.

Heath, Chris. "The Love and Terror of Nick Cave." *GQ Magazine*, April 27, 2017.

Hunt, Drew. "Nick Cave: 'The best and most terrifying Australian movie in existence.'" *Chicago Reader*, October 30, 2012. https://chicagoreader.com/film/nick-cave-the-best-and-most-terrifying-australian-movie-in-existence/.

Janes, Steve. "Nick Cave Murder Ballads Interview." *With Guitars*, 2011. https://www.withguitars.com/nick-cave-the-murder-ballads-interview/.

Jurgensen, John. "Hollywood's Favorite Cowboy." *Wall Street Journal*, November 2009. https://www.wsj.com/articles/SB10001424052748704576204574529703577274572.

Kruger, Debbie "Nick Cave: The Songwriter Speaks." *Weekend Australian*, July 30, 2005.

Leas, Ryan. "Warren Ellis on the Past, Present, & Future of Nick Cave & The Bad Seeds." *Stereogum*, November 17, 2021.

Leith, Sam. "'Loss is a thing that we become': Nick Cave on Grief, Faith and Why He's a Conservative." *The Spectator*, December 2022. https://www

.spectator.co.uk/article/loss-is-a-thing-that-we-become-nick-cave-on-grief
-faith-and-why-hes-a-conservative/.

Lorca, Federico Garcia. *Theory and Play of the Duende: And, Imagination, Inspiration, Evasion*. Dallas, Texas: New Directions, 1981.

Mahmood, Fazal. "The Transverberation of Tracy Pew." *Rolling Stone*, April 6,
2021. https://au.rollingstone.com/music/music-features/the-transverberation
-of-tracy-pew-25685/.

Male, Andrew. "The Bad & The Beautiful: 50 Greatest Songs of Nick
Cave"/"Something Monstrous." *Mojo*, no. 319 (June 2020).

Manjoo, Farhad. "Snap Makes a Bet on the Cultural Supremacy of the Camera."
New York Times, March 8, 2017. https://www.nytimes.com/2017/03/08/
technology/snap-makes-a-bet-on-the-cultural-supremacy-of-the-camera
.html.

Maume, Chris. "Nick Cave: Devil's Advocate." *The Independent*, March 2006.
https://www.independent.co.uk/news/people/profiles/nick-cave-devil-s
-advocate-350562.html.

Mayward, Joel. "Carrying the Fire." *Bright Wall/Dark Room*, August 2016.
https://www.brightwalldarkroom.com/2016/08/08/carrying-the-fire/.

McMurchy, Myles. "The Red Cross Is Not All Right: Herbert Hoover's Concentration Camp Cover-Up in the 1927 Mississippi Flood." *Race, Ethnicity, and
Immigration in U.S. History*. 2004.

Mordue, Mark. "I have turned a corner and wandered on to a vast landscape."
The Guardian, May 5, 2017.

Mordue, Mark. "Nick Cave: 'Being forced to grieve openly basically saved
us.'" *Irish Times*, May 8, 2017. https://www.irishtimes.com/culture/music/
nick-cave-being-forced-to-grieve-openly-basically-saved-us-1.3075334.

Mordue, Mark. "Premonitions of Love." *Neighbourhood Paper*, 2017. https://
neighbourhoodpaper.com/features/nick-cave-premonitions-of-love/
?fbclid=IwAR232GrejoruC1n587jVvU4_Gk93z2f9mmQFzkBa
_WqC-Z9N1Zl2cQ9VheM.

Mossman, Kate. "Nick Cave: 'I don't think art should be in the hands of the
virtuous.'" *The New Statesman*, November 2022. https://www.newstatesman
.com/katemossmaninterview/2022/11/nick-cave-interview-art-virtuous
-music-grief.

Murphy, Cullen. "Who Do Men Say That I Am?" *The Atlantic*, December 1986.

"Nick Cave." The Talks, 2015. https://the-talks.com/interview/nick-cave/?fbcli
d=IwAR3RW9gRzRwyN7rcM6cKpfOUiwpAuffC7vqadLZZiYG7TthffVu
6NOjSBsc.

"Nick Cave—Portrait of a 21st-Century Genius." *Mojo*, March 2009.

"Nick Cave: The Last Rock Star." *Spin Magazine*, February 1989.

BIBLIOGRAPHY

"Nick Cave's 30 Best Songs." *Uncut*, February 2015. https://www.uncut.co.uk/features/nick-cave-s-30-greatest-songs-chosen-by-the-bad-seeds-his-famous-fans-and-cave-himself-37741/4/.

Nine, Jennifer. "From Her to Maturity." *Melody Maker*, May 1997.

Payne, John. "Improvisations with Nick Cave." *LA Times*, November 29, 2010.

Petridis, Alexis. "Nick Cave's Greatest Feat." *The Guardian*, 2013. https://www.theguardian.com/music/2013/feb/15/nick-cave-greatest-feat-artistic-honesty-retire.

Petrusich, Amanda. "Nick Cave on the Fragility of Life." *The New Yorker*, March 23, 2023.

Popova, Maria. "Let This Darkness Be a Bell Tower: Rilke's Timeless Spell for Living Through Difficult Times." *The Marginalian*, November 1, 2023. https://www.themarginalian.org/2023/01/11/let-this-darkness-be-a-bell-tower-rilke/.

Popova, Maria. "Nick Cave on Songwriting, the Mystery of the Unconscious, and the Sweet Severity of Truth." *Brainpickings*, August 5, 2022. https://www.themarginalian.org/2022/08/05/nick-cave-songwriting/.

"Professor Annelise Orleck." Edited by Simon Horn, Emma Fallone, and Graham Ambrose. *Yale Historical Review*, 2016.

Reynolds, Simon. "Of Misogyny, Murder and Melancholy: Meeting Nick Cave," *National Student Magazine*, 1987.

Roddick, Nick. "Ballad of the Wild Boys." *BFI*, 2012.

Sandall, Robert. "Nick Cave: Renaissance Man." *The Word*, March 2003.

Sierksma, Peter. "Nick Cave." *Trouw*. June 18, 1997 (Dutch).

Smith, Lindzee. "Nick Cave" *BOMB*. April 1, 1990. https://bombmagazine.org/articles/nick-cave/.

Sutcliffe, Phil. "King Of Pain." *Mojo*, January 2005.

Reynolds, Simon. "Blissed Out: The Raptures of Rock." *Popular Music*, 1991.

O'Hagan, Sean. "'I love the perversity of it': Bad Seed Warren Ellis on How Nina Simone's Gum Inspired a Book." *The Observer*, August 15, 2021. https://www.theguardian.com/books/2021/aug/15/warren-ellis-on-how-nina-simones-gum-book-interview.

O'Neal, Lauren. "PJ HARVEY TUESDAY #1: 'HENRY LEE.'" *The Rumpus*, October 2013.

Orloff, Brian. "Nick Cave Sings the Blues." *Rolling Stone*, October 22, 2004. https://www.rollingstone.com/music/music-news/nick-cave-sings-the-blues-120708/.

Watts, Peter. "His Dark Materials." *Uncut*, Take 273, February 2020.

Documentaries

20,000 Days on Earth. Iain Forsyth and Jane Pollard, 2014.

Nick Cave & The Bad Seeds. "Do You Love Me Like I Love You." https://youtu
.be/G01YzoQ3Kv8.

Stranger in a Strange Land. BBC Southbank Show, 2003.

Journals

Boer, Roland. "Love, Pain, and Redemption in the Music of Nick Cave." *Literature & Aesthetics* 19, no. 2 (December 2009).

Neal, Larry. "The Ethos of the Blues." *The Black Scholar* 3, no. 10 (Summer 1972): 42–48. https://www.jstor.org/stable/41206840.

Radio/Podcasts

BBC Radio 6. Nick Cave interview with Jarvis Cocker. September 2010.

Babicka, Joanna. "Genre and Language in Nick Cave's 'And the Ass Saw the Angel.'" 2011.

Diplomarbeit, University of Vienna. Philologisch-Kulturwissenschaftliche Fakultät BetreuerIn: Huber, Werner.

Pod Like a Hole podcast, Nick Cave and the Bad Seeds: Henry's Dream, Thursday Feb 18, 2021.

Video

"Bukowski Reads a Poem About Linda King." September 2010. https://www
.youtube.com/watch?v=Td678VDxYWk&ab_channel=doorsfan4ourever.

Jackson, Joe. *"Nick Cave and Joe Jackson 1994. Two Elvis 'nuts' discuss the King in all his glory."* youtube.com/watch?v=YXwyPDXeIMM

INDEX

Abattoir Blues / The Lyre of Orpheus (2004), 48, 78, 84, 122, 140, 222

Adamson, Barry, 5, 10, 16, 38, 84, 182

Amis, Martin, 97, 143

Australia, 35, 56, 71, 84, 88, 115, 118, 132, 183–190, 242

Bargeld, Blixa, 5, 7, 36, 67, 79, 116–117, 126

Bolden, Buddy, 24

Bond, Deanna, 30

Calvert, Phill, 82

Casey, Martyn, 5–6, 32

Cave, Arthur, 123, 129, 232–236, 249

Cave, Colin, 124–125, 142

Cave, Luke, 46, 126–127

Cave, Nick: Berlin, 18–20, 33, 38, 117–119, 132–133, 205–207; Brighton, 4, 11, 93, 96, 224, 238, 245; Christianity, 89–90, 136, 199–202, 212, 216–217; Drugs,

8, 20, 36, 38–42, 49–50, 82–83, 111, 118–120, 125–126, 132; Hair, 49, 113–115, 131; London, 40, 83, 114, 118, 149, 204, 212, 230, 244–245; Melbourne, 29, 68, 82–83; Suit, 49, 115, 145, 198; Warracknabeal, 185; Wangaratta, 64, 122, 183, 185, 188, 197, 228

Cave, Susie (*See* Nick): 221–222, 230–232, 237–238, 245, 249

Christ, Jesus, 14, 17–19, 59, 64, 89, 101, 106, 122–123, 129, 160, 168, 181, 191, 197, 204–205, 213–217

Crawford, Anwen, 61

Dahmer, Jeffrey, 44

Dig, Lazarus, Dig!!! (2008), 7, 193, 214

Dominik, Andrew, 124, 191, 232, 242

Douglass, Frederick, 22

Ellis, Warren, 17, 22, 115, 138, 140, 150, 162, 187, 195, 245

Elvis (The King), 14, 17–20, 179–185, 207, 210

Flood (producer), 38, 117
From Her to Eternity (1984), 68, 115, 141

Gambotto-Burke, Antonella (*nee* Black), 40
Ghosteen (2019), 76, 124, 146, 149, 159–161, 169, 172, 213, 217, 230–236, 238–239, 242–244, 250
Grinderman (band), 6–7, 94–95, 99, 104, 115, 125, 145, 233
Groom, Nick Professor, 162–164, 214
Gwyn, Aaron Professor, 192

Hamburg, 207
Henry's Dream (1992), 31, 70, 133, 143, 185–186
Hillcoat, John, 71, 186–187, 190

Jefferrson, Blind Lemon, 25–26, 37

Kicking Against the Pricks (1986), 137

Larkin, Philip, 79, 138, 144
Launay, Nick, 114, 140
Let Love In (1994), 7, 31–32, 45, 64, 70, 223

Marcus, Greil, 17–18, 67, 180–181
Mordue, Mark, 6, 120–122, 129, 142, 157, 162, 182, 228
Murder Ballads (1996), 47, 67, 112–113, 127, 223

Nabokov, Vladimir, 43, 106, 143–144

Nocturama (2003), 144
No More Shall We Part (2001), 48, 222

Ondaatje, Michael, 24, 190

Push the Sky Away (2013), 3–5, 8–10, 39, 52, 96, 124, 128, 139–140, 145, 154, 161–163, 174, 224, 233–234, 239

Race, Hugo, 10, 207

Saint Teresa of Avila, 65, 97, 204–205
Savage, Conway, 5–7, 48
Sclavunos, Jim, 5–6, 85
Skeleton Tree (2016), 47–48, 87, 123–124, 128, 146, 149–150, 160–161, 167–169, 194, 213, 235–238, 244–246
Steinke, Darcey
St Kilda (Beach), 82, 125, 134
Sutcliffe, Peter   , 61, 68–70

Tender Prey (1988), 29, 38, 59, 119, 132
The Birthday Party (band), 5–6, 17, 33–36, 59, 62, 81–84, 94, 106, 111–115, 118, 141, 224, 229
The Boatman's Call (1997), 28, 31, 46–48, 50–51, 75, 125, 128, 198, 223
The Firstborn Is Dead (1985), 13, 20, 25, 73, 183
The Good Son (1990), 23, 57–59, 63, 125–126
Tupelo (Mississipi), 14–17, 20, 181
Twain, Mark, 102, 205

Vjestica, George, 5

INDEX

Viviane Carneiro, 46, 49, 71, 126, 237

Your Funeral . . . My Trial (1986), 7, 37–38, 117

Wydler, Thomas, 5, 38, 85, 132, 169

ABOUT THE AUTHOR

Adam Steiner is the author of *Into the Never: Nine Inch Nails and the Creation of* The Downward Spiral and *Silhouettes and Shadows: The Secret History of David Bowie's Scary Monsters* and the novel *Politics of the Asylum*. He writes about music, street art culture, architecture, poetry, and transgressive fiction and lives in London, England.

www.adamsteiner.uk

www.ingramcontent.com/pod-product-compliance
Lightning Source LLC
Chambersburg PA
CBHW070402100426
42812CB00005B/1608